Drug Development from Natural Resources: Scope and Challenges

Drug Development from Natural Resources: Scope and Challenges

Edited by

SubbaRao V. Madhunapantula

Professor of Cellular and Molecular Biology, CEMR Laboratory
Department of Biochemistry, JSS Medical College
JSS Academy of Higher Education and Research
Mysore, Karnataka, India

A Publication from the Centre for Science & Technology of the Non-Aligned and Other Developing Countries (NAM S&T Centre)

ALLIED PUBLISHERS PVT. LTD.

New Delhi • Mumbai • Kolkata • Chennai • Bangalore • Hyderabad

ALLIED PUBLISHERS PRIVATE LIMITED

1/13-14 Asaf Ali Road, **New Delhi**–110002
Ph.: 011-23239001 • E-mail: delhi.books@alliedpublishers.com

17 Chittaranjan Avenue, **Kolkata**–700072
Ph.: 033-22129618 • E-mail: cal.books@alliedpublishers.com

15 J.N. Heredia Marg, Ballard Estate, **Mumbai**–400001
Ph.: 022-42126969 • E-mail: mumbai.books@alliedpublishers.com

No. 25/10, Commander-in-Chief Road, Ethiraj Lane (Next to Post Office)
Egmore, **Chennai**–600008
Ph.: 044-28223938 • E-mail: chennai.books@alliedpublishers.com

P.B. No. 9932, No. 15, 3rd Floor (Next to Vijaya Bank), 5th Cross, Gandhinagar, Karnataka, **Bangalore**–560009, Ph.: 080-41530285 / 22386239
• E-mail: bngl.journals@alliedpublishers.com / apsabng@airtelmail.in

Sri Jayalakshmi Nilayam, No. 3-4-510, 3rd Floor (Above More Super Market)
Barkatpura, **Hyderabad**–500027
Ph.: 040-27551811, 040-27551812 • E-mail: hyd.books@alliedpublishers.com

Website: www.alliedpublishers.com

A Publication from the Centre for Science & Technology of the Non-Aligned and Other Developing Countries

ISBN: 978-93-89934-15-1

Contributing Staff Editor: **Jasmeet Kaur**, *Programme Officer, NAM S&T Centre*

Published by Sunil Sachdev and printed by Ravi Sachdev at Allied Publishers Pvt. Ltd.,
1/13-14 Asaf Ali Road, New Delhi–110002

Foreword

Historically, natural products have been used since ancient times and in folklore for the treatment of many diseases and illnesses. Classical natural product chemistry methodologies have enabled the discovery of a vast array of secondary metabolites from terrestrial and marine resources. Many of these novel bio-active natural products have tremendous therapeutic and pharmaceutical potential which needs to be explored by the researchers, R&D agencies and other concerned institutions/industries alike.

In order to foster the great benefits of natural products, especially from terrestrial and marine natural resources, the *Centre for Science and Technology of the Non-Aligned and Other Developing Countries (NAM S&T Centre)* had organised an International Workshop on "**Drug Development from Herbs and Marine Medicinal Materials**" during 10-12 December, 2018 in Hai Phong, Vietnam in collaboration with the *Hai Phong University of Medicine and Pharmacy (HPMU).* The major objective of this Workshop was to provide a platform to update the existing knowledge on the subject and evolve new strategies and approaches for the utilization of terrestrial and marine natural resources for development of new drugs. The Workshop also focused on the research and development trends and best practices in drugs development from natural resources in non-aligned and other developing nations.

As a follow up, the NAM S&T Centre has brought out this book titled 'Drug Development from Natural Resources: Scope and Challenges' which comprises 13 papers contributed by the participants of the Hai Phong Workshop. The volume has been edited by Dr. SubbaRao V. Madhunapantula, Professor of Cellular and Molecular Biology, CEMR Laboratory, Department of Biochemistry, JSS Medical College, JSS Academy of Higher Education and Research, Mysore, Karnataka, India. The papers included in this book highlight the plans for developing drugs from terrestrial and marine natural products including medicinal plants research in the developing countries.

I congratulate the NAM S&T Centre for bringing out this valuable publication which will be of immense use to pharmacists, taxonomists, allied healthcare professionals, biochemists, biotechnologists, bioinformaticians, organic chemists, traditional healthcare professionals as well as pharmaceutical industries and others engaged in the field of drug discovery and development from natural resources.

I wish the very best for all the future endeavours of the *NAM S&T Centre* towards enhancing South-South S&T Cooperation amongst the NAM and other developing countries.

Prof. Dr. Pham Van Thuc

Former-Rector of HPMU and President of Hai Phong Clinical Immuno-Allergo-Asthamatic Association, Hai Phong, Vietnam

Introduction

Terrestrial and marine natural resources have been the most productive sources of leads for the development of drugs. A number of novel bio-active compounds derived from these natural resources are currently undergoing different stages of clinical and preclinical trials and testing particularly as, anti-inflammatory, cardiovascular, anti-diabetic, anti-malarial, anti-viral and anti-neoplastic agents.

Though the drugs from natural resources have been used since long for cure of a number of diseases but prophylactically, they have been neglected as far as the scientific records of their efficacy and safety are concerned due to their complex chemical structure.

A very few pharmaceutical companies are involved in drug discovery screening from natural resources. This is primarily due to the high cost involved in isolation and identification of pure compounds, difficulty in collection, complexity of structure of compounds and the absence of standard regulatory guidelines for natural products.

The newer approaches to drug development process from natural resources apply modern and advanced molecular biology techniques to screen and develop a large number of pure compounds having pharmaceutical properties, which may help facilitate the drug development process.

Considering the importance of the above subject, the *Centre for Science and Technology of the Non-Aligned and Other Developing Countries (NAM S&T Centre)* in partnership with the *Hai Phong University of Medicine and Pharmacy (HPMU)* organized an International Workshop on '**Drug Development from Herbs and Marine Medicinal Materials**' in Hai Phong, Vietnam during 10-12 December, 2018 which brought together 26 scientists, researchers and professionals from 16 countries including Bhutan, Egypt, India, Indonesia, Kenya, Malaysia, Mauritius, Myanmar, Nepal, Pakistan, Republic of Korea, South Africa, Sri Lanka, Turkey, Zimbabwe and the host country, Vietnam to evolve new strategies and approaches for the utilization of terrestrial and marine natural resources for new drug development including overcoming the possible limitations and challenges faced by the NAM and other developing countries.

As a follow up of the Hai Phong Workshop, the present book **'Drug Development from Natural Resources: Scope and Challenges'** is being published by the NAM S&T Centre which includes 13 scientific and technical papers contributed by the experts/participants from 8 developing countries namely: Egypt, India, Malaysia, Myanmar, Nepal, Nigeria, South Africa and Vietnam.

I appreciate the time and efforts put in place by the Editor of this book, Dr. SubbaRao V. Madhunapantula, Professor of Cellular and Molecular Biology, CEMR Laboratory, Department of Biochemistry, JSS Medical College, JSS Academy of Higher Education and Research, Mysore, Karnataka, India for the technical editing of the manuscripts. I also acknowledge the interest and valuable efforts of the entire team of the NAM S&T Centre and I am especially thankful to Mr. M. Bandyopadhyay, Senior Adviser for his guidance and supervision; Ms. Jasmeet Kaur, Programme Officer; and Mr. Pankaj Buttan, Data Processing Manager in compiling and proof reading of the manuscripts, liaising with authors of the papers, designing the cover page, formatting and taking all the necessary steps in giving a shape to this book.

I am sure this book will be of immense use to all those associated with issues related to drug development from terrestrial and marine natural resources.

(Amitava Bandopadhyay, *Ph.D.*)
Director General
NAM S&T Centre
New Delhi, India

Preface

Recent data from the market research report projected that the global herbal medicine market, which was valued at about 71 billion US dollars, will soon reach 100 billion US dollars mark by 2024. This rapid increase in the market value for herbal drugs is primarily due to (a) changing preference of consumers from allopathic drugs to traditional medicines such as Ayurveda, Unani, Chinese Medicines; (b) relatively lower toxicities associated with natural products; (c) feasibility to purify unique and difficult to synthesize pharmacological agents; (d) accumulating knowledge about the mechanisms of action of natural drugs leading to the development of better formulations; (e) feasibility to convert the identified molecules in to different dosage forms that include Tablets, Gels, Capsules, Syrups etc. Hence, research on herbal drugs is highly prioritized in the recent years.

The book "Drug Development from Natural Resources: Scope and Challenges" is a compilation of articles highlighting the richness of marine and land sources for various herbal medicines and their anti-microbial, anti-allergic and anti-cancer properties. Section-I is dedicated to the herbal drugs from sea, land and endophytes. It also covers the use of Ayurvedic formulations, essential oils, and other phytochemicals for managing allergic reactions and mosquito bites. The chapters in Section-II of this book describe the occurrence and usage of unique plants in minimally explored regions of the world such as Egypt, Nigeria, Nepal and Vietnam. Furthermore, various purification and analytical methods of analysis of natural products were also covered in this book.

I hope this book benefits the readers by providing key information about natural products and their health beneficial effects.

M.V.S.S.T. Subbarao

SubbaRao V. Madhunapantula

Professor
Department of Biochemistry
JSS Medical College
MYSURU.

Contents

SECTION 2: Medicinal Plants Research in Egypt, Vietnam, Nepal and Nigeria

Hai Phong Resolution

SECTION 1

Development of Health Beneficial Natural Products

Marine Natural Products for Drug Development: From the Bottom of the Sea to the Pharmacy

Jasmeet Kaur

Centre for Science & Technology of the Non-Aligned and Other Developing Countries (NAM S&T Centre), Core 6A, 2nd Floor, India Habitat Centre, Lodhi Road, New Delhi-110003, India

E-mail: jasmeetcaur19@gmail.com

ABSTRACT: More than 50% of the marketed drugs today are derived from natural resources. There are various emerging diseases which cannot be managed well with the currently available drugs in the market. Therefore, it is imperative to identify and explore the new sources of drug development. Marine environment, harboring a vast variety of organsims that are genetically and biochemically unique has become a top spot for the identification of new drug leads. However, research in pharmacology of marine resources is limited. Oceans contain more than 80% of diverse marine plant and animal species in the world. The enormous variety of marine species of plants and animals have the potential to screen for anti-bacterial, anti-fungal, anti-microbial, anti-inflammatory, anti-cancer, anti-malarial, analgesic, neuro-protective and immuno-modulator properties. Marine organisms such as sponges, diatoms, seaweeds, snails, worms, tunicates, fishes, soft corals, nudi-branchs, bryozoans, and marine micro-organisms have the tremendous potential to be exploited for the development of marine-derived drugs for commercial use. This review investigated and studied in detail the current global status of Marine Natural Products (MNPs) for drug discovery and development. The study has reviewed both the US-FDA approved marine natural products that are currently available in the market as well as the potential marine natural product candidates to examine and study pharmaceutical properties for therapeutic use. It concludes that the marine drug development is still in its nascent phase since there are various processes involved in the development of marine-derived drugs, right from the bioprospecting for identifiation of potential marine natural products, to their extraction and isolation, along with the evaluation of drug safety, efficacy and clinical testing and trials, before its actual introduction into the market. Looking at the massive potential offered by the marine environment for the development of drug, steps are currently being taken by medical pharmacologist to expedite the research.

Keywords: Natural Resources, Marine Environment, Marine Biodiversity, Bioactive, Marine Natural Products, Drug Development.

1. INTRODUCTION

1.1 Marine Environment as a Store-house of Biologically Active Natural Products (NPs)

Natural Products (NPs) are usually small molecules produced by a biological sources such as plants, animals and micro-organisms with a molecular weight below 3000 Da [Mann, Davidson, *et al.*, 1994]. They are often called '*secondary metabolites*' because, they have no primary function directly involved in the growth, development or reproduction. They are generally used by organisms to defend against predation, competition for space and food, inter-species communication for the purposes of mating etc. Natural products have long been used as traditional source of medicines. Historical examples of natural compounds isolated includes: (a) production of analgesic *morphine* from the plant Papaver somniferum (opium poppy) in 1803 and (b) the discovery of first antibiotic *penicillin* from the fungus *Penicillium notatum* by the bacteriologist Alexander Fleming in 1929 [Carter, 2011]. Since then, numerous other natural products have been isolated and identified with 60% of the drugs currently in market being of natural origin [Newman and Cragg, 2012].

Among the various suitable natural resources, the marine environment, harbouring a vast variety of organisms that are genetically and biochemically unique has become a top spot for the identification of new drug leads. 'Oceans' contain more than 80% of diverse marine plants and animals species in the world [Donia and Hamann, 2003]. Having enormous variety with great biodiversity and untouched areas of marine life, the prospects of yielding novel bio-active natural products from the oceans is tremendous. The marine species of plants and animals have the potential to screen for anti-bacterial, anti-fungal, anti-microbial, anti-inflammatory, anti-cancer, anti-malarial, analgesic and neuro-protective among the other pharmacological properties. Marine organisms such as *sponges, tunicates, fishes, coelenterates, echinoderms, soft corals, sea slugs, bryozoans, molluscs* and a variety of *marine micro-organisms* are the sources of bio-active natural products [Donia and Hamann, 2003]. Fish oils are one of the classic examples of marine-derived products used since ages. 'Marine pharmacology' is that branch of pharmaceutical sciences that focuses on substances with active pharmacological properties present in marine species of plants and animals. Marine biodiversity is very unique with structural and chemical features generally not found in terrestrial natural products.

Despite the fact that oceans cover more than 70% of the earth's surface, the exploration of marine ecosystem began in the mid 1970s [Dias *et al.,* 2012]. Due to technical limitations, exploitation of marine organisms started with the large creatures such as red algae, sponges and soft corals which produced a large variety of natural products with unquie chemical structures. Invertebrates alone comprise approximately 60% of all marine animals and were described as the source of more than 11,000 new natural products since 1990 [Blunt, Copp, *et al.* 2013, 2014]. With the continous exploitation of the marine environment, attention turned to micro-organisms such as marine cyanobacteria, marine fungi and several other groups of marine bacteria due to their biological uniqueness and habitat diversity, which resulted in their ability to produce novel bio-active natural products. It was even realised that many natural compounds isolated from marine macro-organisms such as sponges and tunicates, are in fact, the metabolic products of associated micro-organisms [Piel, 2009].

Due to the broad range of bio-activity, the marine natural products are exceptionally interesting and a source of high-value compounds for various application in the pharmaceutical industry.

In conclusion, marine environment constitute a potential research area with enormous economic and social revenues and increasingly involving the engagement of academia and industry in bringing more novel bio-active natural products into the market.

1.2 Sources of Marine Natural Products (MNPs)

Majority of the bio-active natural products have been isolated from following marine organisms:

- Sponges
- Coelenterates (sea whips, sea fans and soft corals)

- Tunicates
- Molluscs (nudibranchs, sea hares)
- Echinoderms (starfish, sea cucumbers)
- Bryozoans (moss animals)
- A variety of marine micro-organisms (including bacteria, fungi and cyanobacteria).

Sponges

Tunicates

Molluscs

Bryozoans

1.3 MARINE NATURAL PRODUCTS (MNPs): FROM BIOPROSPECTING TO CLINICAL TRAILS TO THE MARKET

There are various processes involved in the development of marine-derived drugs, right from the bioprospecting for the identification of potential marine natural product candidates, to their extraction and isolation, along with the evaluation and assessment of drug safety, efficacy and clinical testing and trials, before its actual introduction into the market. However, the process involves several challenges related to biodiversity access, sustainable supply and technical support and market access.

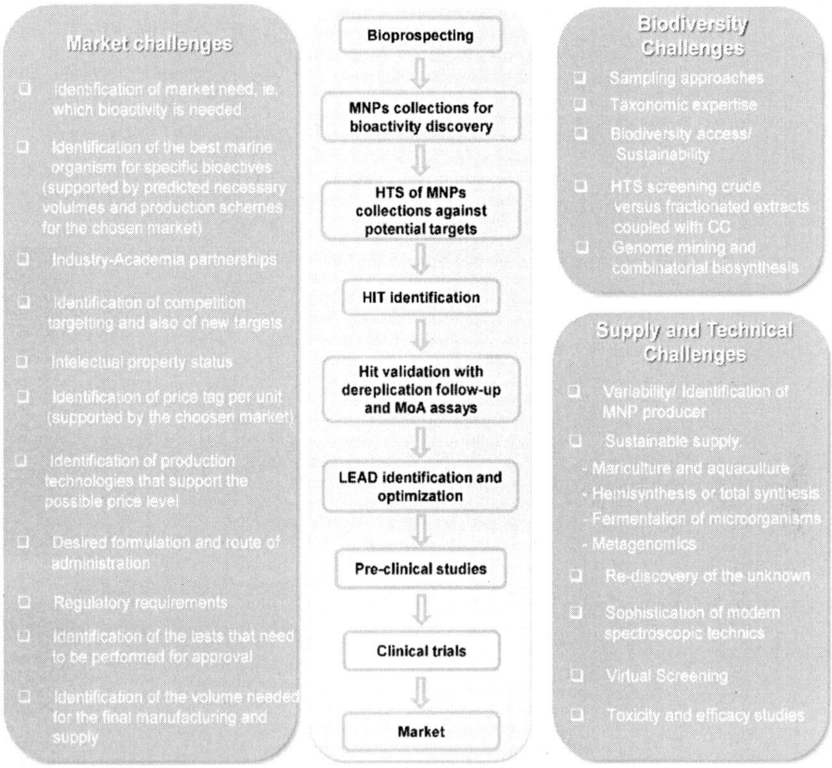

*MNPs – Marine Natural Products
*HTS – High Throughput Screening
*MoA – Mechanism of Action

Source: MDPI Open Access Journals.

1.4 CLASSIFICATION OF MARINE-DERIVED DRUGS

Marine-derived drugs can be broadly classified based on their potential as follows:

Analgesic Drugs

Ziconotide, an analgesic agent, was the first drug of marine-origin to obtain approval from the U.S. Food and Drug Administration (FDA) for treatment of chronic pain. Ziconotide has been extracted from the marine cone snail *Conus magus.*

Molecular Formula

$C_{102}H_{172}N_{36}O_{32}S_7$

Chemical Structure

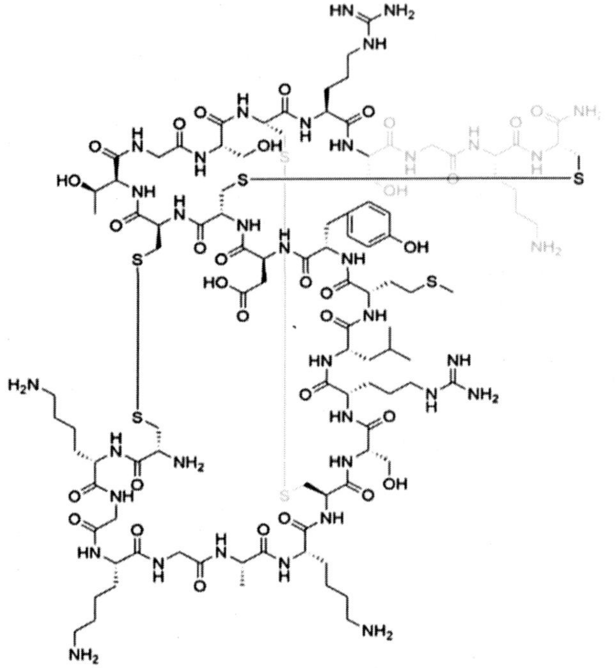

Anti-Bacterial Drugs

Eicosapentaenoic acid, a polyunsaturated fatty acid, isolated from diatom of marine origin *Phaeodactylum tricornutum* has found to be active against an array of gram-positive and gram-negative bacteria.

Molecular Formula

$C_{20}H_{30}O_2$

Chemical Structure

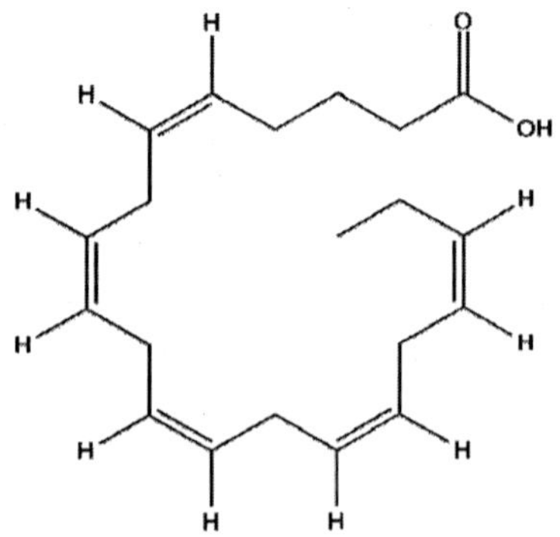

Anti-Cancer Drugs

Bryostatin, an anti-cancer drug, has primarily been obtained from the Bryozoan, *Bugula neritina,* although some forms have been extracted from sponges and tunicates. **Sorbicillin**-derived alkaloids Sorbicillactone-A and its analog Sorbicillactone-B has shown active against leukemia cells. Sorbicillactone-B has been derived from salt-water culture of bacterial strain *Penicillium chrysogenum* which has been isolated from a Mediterranean sponge, *Ircinia fasciculate.*

Molecular Formula

$C_{47}H_{68}O_{17}$ $C_{21}H_{23}NO_8$ $C_{21}H_{25}NO_8$

Chemical Structure

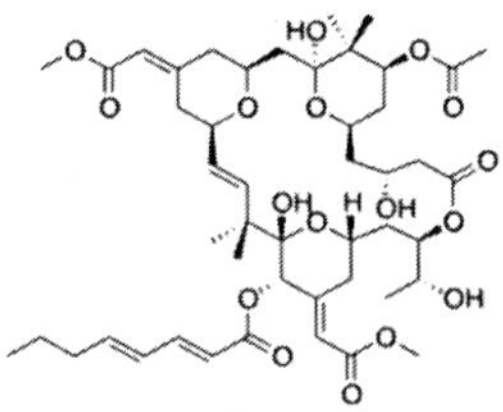

Bryostatin

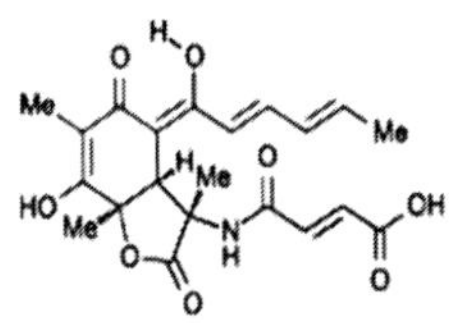

Sorbicillactone-A

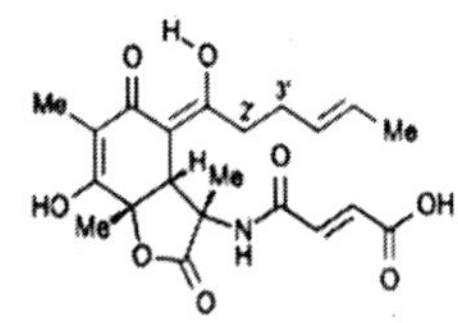

Sorbicillactone-B

Anti-Inflamatory Drugs

Methanolic extracts of Mediterranean sponge species *Spongia officinalis* has been found to have anti-inflammatory properties.

Anti-Microbial Drugs

Cephalosporins are well-known anti-microbial agents with a marine source of origin. Cephalosporin C has been extracted and purified from a marine fungus, *Cephalosporium acremonium.*

Molecular Formula

$C_{16}H_{21}N_3O_{8S}$

Chemical Structure

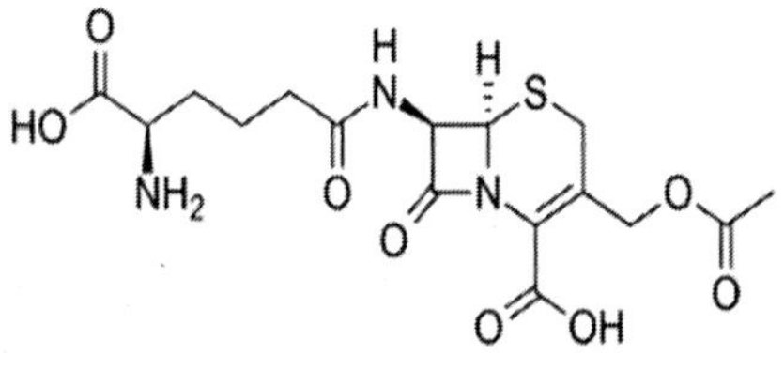

Anti-Malarial Drugs

Marine Isonitrile containing anti-malarial molecules have been extracted from a Japanese sponge Acanthella sp. The isolated molecules belong to kalihinene diterpeniods class, which also contains antifungal and anthelmintic compounds.

	R^1	R^2			R^1	R^2	
Ken1	NC	NC	kalihinene	**Ken5**	NC	NC	6-OH-kalihinene
Ken2	NC	NHCHO	15-form.-kalihinene	**Ken6**	NC	NHCHO	6-OH-15-form.-kalihinene
Ken3	NHCHO	NC	10-form.-kalihinene	**Ken7**	NHCHO	NC	6-OH-10-form.-kalihinene
Ken4	NHCHO	NHCHO	10,15-bisform.-kalihinene	**Ken8**	NHCHO	NCS	6-OH-10-form.-15-isothio.-kalihinene

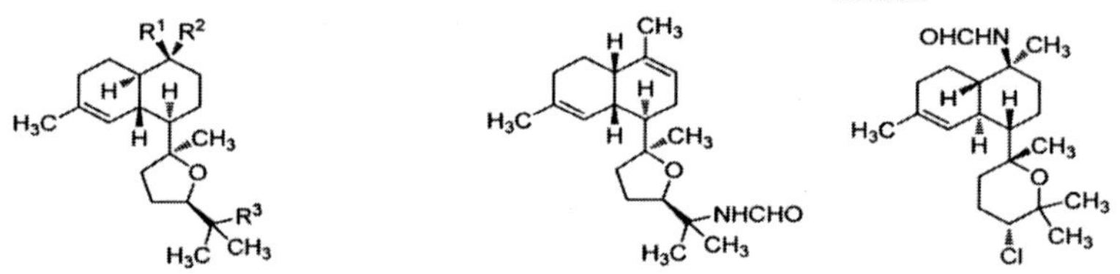

	R^1	R^2	R^3	
Ken9	NC	Me	NC	kalihinene A (di*epi*-kalihinene)
Ken10	Me	NC	NC	kalihinene B (1-*epi*-kalihinene)
Ken11	Me	NC	NCS	15-isothio.-1-*epi*-kalihinene

Ken12 F

Ken13 E

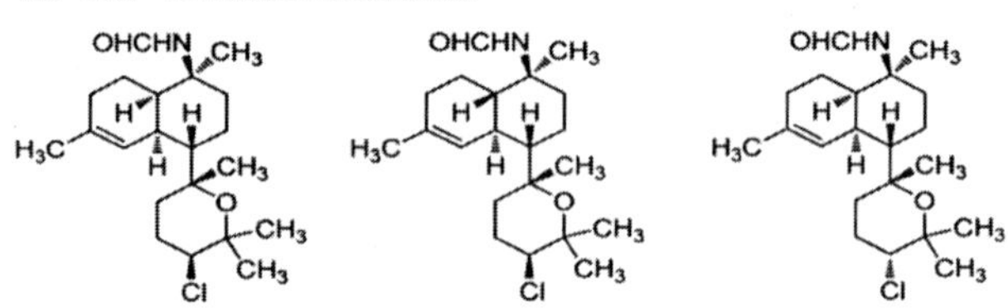

Ken14 X **Ken15** Y **Ken16** Z

Kalihinenes

Neuro-Protective Drugs

Methanol extracts of South Indian green seaweed *Ulva reticulata* has shown neuro-protection in Alzheimer's disease treatment.

Molecular Formula

CH_3OH

Chemical Structure

```
  H
  |
H-C-O-H
  |
  H
```

Anti-Viral Drugs

Exo-polysaccharides (EPS) extracted from the French marine sponge *Celtodoryx girardae* and its associated symbiotic bacteria found to have anti-herpes simplex virus-1 (HSV-1) activity.

Molecular Formula

$C_{23}H_{36}O_{18}$

Chemical Structure

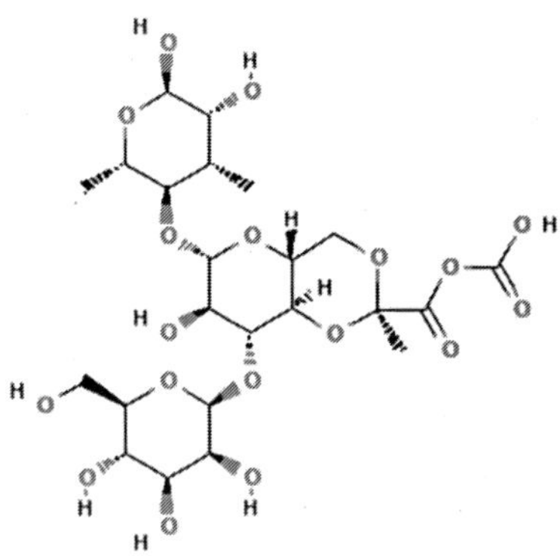

2. METHODOLOGY

Considering the massive potential of marine environment for discovery of drugs and development, this review investigated in detail the current global status of marine natural products. The study has reviewed both the FDA approved marine natural products that are currently available in the market as well as the potential natural product candidates that are in different phases of their clinical and pre-clinical trials and testing to examine and study its pharmaceutical properties for their therapeutic use.

Approach and Methodology of the Study

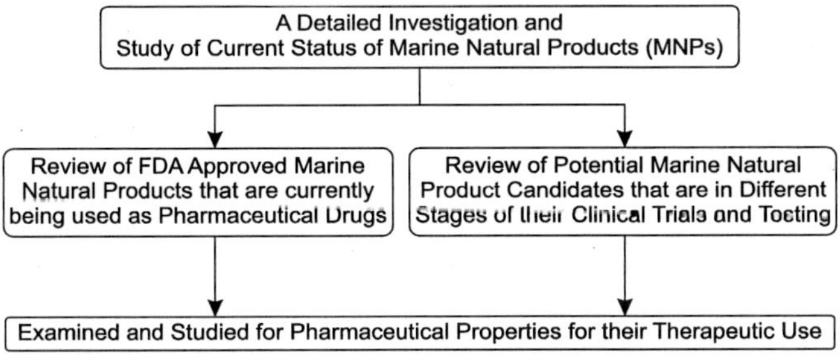

3. RESULTS

Clinical Status	*Natural Product (With Approval date)*	*Molecular Formula*	*Chemical Class*	*Marine Organism*	*Disease Area*	*Chemical Vendors*
US-FDA - Approved	Cytarabine (1969)	$C_9H_{13}N_3O_5$	Nucleoside	Caribbean Sponge *Tectitethya crypta*	Cancer, Leukemia	AbovChem LLC, NIH Clinical Collection, Aurum Pharmatech LLC, MolPort, BroadPharm
	Omega - 3 Acid Ethyl Esters (November 10, 2004)	$C_{22}H_{34}O_2$	Omega-3 Fatty Acids	Fish Mackerel and Salmon	Hyper - Triglyceridemia (elevated triglycerides)	VladaChem, Oakwood Products, AbovChem LLC, TCI (Tokyo Chemical Industry), MuseChem
	Ziconotide (December 28, 2004)	$C_{102}H_{172}N_{36}O_{32}S_7$	Peptide	Marine Cone Snail *Conus magus*	Chronic Pain	Aurora Fine Chemicals LLC, Sigma-Aldrich, Chemenu Inc., Biosynth, Glentham Life Sciences Ltd.
	Eribulin Mesylate (Halichondrin B) (November 15, 2010)	$C_{40}H_{59}NO_{11}$	Ketone Analogue	Marine Sponge *Halichondria okadai*	Metastatic Breast Cancer	MolPort, BioCrick, BLD Pharm, MedChem express MCE, AA BLOCKS

Clinical Status	*Natural Product (With Approval date)*	*Molecular Formula*	*Chemical Class*	*Marine Organism*	*Disease Area*	*Chemical Vendors*
	Brentuximab Vedotin (August 19, 2011)	$C_{6476}H_{9930}N_{1690}O_{2030}S_{40}$	Antibody Drug Conjugate	Mollusk/ Cyanobacteria	Hodgkin's Lymphoma	AbaChemScene, AK Scientific Inc. (AKSCI), AKos Consulting & Solutions, Aurum Pharmatech LLC, Hangzhou APIChem Technology
	Trabectedin (ET-743) (October 23, 2015)	$C_{39}H_{43}N_3O_{11}S$	Alkaloid	Tunicate Sp. *Ecteinascidia turbinata*	Soft-Tissue Sarcoma, Ovarian Cancer	BLD Pharm, MuseChem, MedChemexpress MCE, ZINC, AA BLOCKS

Clinical Status	*Natural Product*	*Molecular Formula*	*Chemical Class*	*Marine Organism*	*Disease Area*
PHASE – III	Tetrodotoxin 'Marine toxin'	$C_{11}H_{17}N_3O_8$	Guanidine Alkaloids	Fish Puffer fish, Globe fish, Toad fish	Chemotherapy Related Pain
	Soblidotin – Dolastatin derivative	$C_{39}H_{67}N_5O_6$	Peptide	Indian Ocean Sea Hare *Dollabellaa uricularia*	Types of Cancers - Sarcoma, Leukemia, Lymphoma, Liver and Kidney Cancer
	Plitidepsin (Aplidine)	$C_{57}H_{87}N_7O_{15}$	Depsipeptide	*Tunicates, Ascidian Aplidium albicans*	Cancer

Clinical Status	*Natural Product*	*Molecular Formula*	*Chemical Class*	*Marine Organism*	*Disease Area*
PHASE – II / III	Plinabulin – Halimide derivative	$C_{19}H_{20}N_4O_2$	Diketopiperazine	Marine Fungus *Aspergillus sp.*	Breast and Liver Cancers, Soild Tumors and Leukemia
	Pseudopterosin A	$C_{25}H_{36}O_6$	Diterpene glycosides	Caribbean Sea Whip *Pseudopterogorgia elisabethae*	Inflammation and Pain
	PM00104 (Zalypsis)	$C_{37}H_{38}F_3N_3O_8$	Alkaloid	Jorumycin/Sea slug *Jorunna funebris*	Lymphoma, Solid Tumors, Sarcoma, Endometrial and Uterine Cervical Cancer
	DMXBA (GTS-21) - Anabaseine derivative	$C_{19}H_{20}N_2O_2$	Alkaloid	Marine worms Nemertine	Schizophrenia, Central Nervous System
PHASE – I / II	Bryostatin 1	$C_{47}H_{68}O_{17}$	Polyketide	Bryozoan *Bugula neritina*	Cancer, Alzheimer's Disease and Dementia
	Hemiasterlin, E7974	$C_{24}H_{43}N_3O_4$	Tripeptide	Marine Sponge *Hemiastrella minor*	Cancer
	Marizomib Salinosporamide - A	$C_{15}H_{20}C_1NO_4$	Proteasome Inhibitor	Marine Actinomycete *Salinospora tropica*	Cancer, Melanoma, Lymphoma, Glioblastoma

Pre-Clinical Drug Pipeline - Supplying hundreds of Novel Marine Natural Products (MNPs) to the Clinical Pipeline.

4. CONCLUSION

Marine environment represents a relatively untapped source of biologically active natural products that can be used in pharmaceutical industries for new drug discovery and development. Having enormous variety with great diversity of marine organisms and virgin areas of marine life, the prospects of yielding novel bio-active natural products from the oceans is tremendous. The curiosity of science and pharmaceutical industries has established oceans as a prospective source of new potential drug leads. Presently, marine natural products that are being used as approved drugs by US-FDA for commercial use are mostly anti-cancer drugs, analgesic drugs and anti-lipemic drugs. Many other biologically active natural products are in different phases of their clinical trials to determine the benefits and risks of a new potential treatment. From drug discovery to FDA approval, developing a new drug takes at least 10 years on an average and costs around of $2.6 billion. Less than 12% of the candidate natural products that make entry into Phase-I clinical trials get approved by the FDA.

Drug development from marine natural products faces several challenges related to biodiversity access, sustainable supply and technical support and market access. It can be concluded that the drug development from the marine natural products is still in a nascent phase since there are various processes involved in the development of marine-derived drugs, right from the bioprospecting for identification of potential drug candidates from the marine organisms, to their extraction and isolation, along with the evaluation of drug safety, efficacy and clinical trials and testing, before its actual introduction into the market. The marine pharmacologists need to focus on research in this domain, looking at the massive potential offered by the marine ecosystem for new drug development.

REFERENCES

[1] Anand, T.P., Bhat, A.W., Shouche, Y.S., Roy, U., Siddharth, J. and Sarma, S.P. Antimicrobial activity of marine bacteria associated with sponges from the waters off the coast of South East India. *Microbiol Res.*, 2006; 161:252–62.

[2] Bhatnagar, I. and Kim, S.K. Marine antitumor drugs: Status, shortfalls and strategies. *Mar Drugs.* 2010; 8:2702–20.

[3] Blunt, J.W., Copp, B.R., Keyzers, R.A., Munro, M.H. and Prinsep, M.R. Marine natural products. *Nat. Prod. Rep.*, 2014; 31:160–258.

[4] Blunt, J.W., Copp, B.R., Keyzers, R.A., Munro, M.H. and Prinsep, M.R. Marine natural products. *Nat. Prod. Rep.,* 2013; 30:237–323.

[5] Carter, G.T. Natural products and Pharma 2011: Strategic changes spur new opportunities. *Nat. Prod. Rep.*, 2011; 28:1783–1789.

[6] Dias, D.A., Urban, S. and Roessner, U. A historical overview of natural products in drug discovery. *Metabolites.*, 2012; 2:303–336.

[7] Donia, M. and Hamann, M.T., Marine natural products and their potential applications as anti-infective agents. *Lancet Infect Dis.,* 2003; 3:338–48.

[8] Gerwick, W.H. and Moore, B.S. Lessons from the past and charting the future of marine natural products drug discovery and chemical biology. *Chem Biol.* 2012; 19:85–98.

[9] Imhoff, J.F., Labes, A. and Wiese, J. Bio-mining the microbial treasures of the ocean: New natural products. *Biotechnol Adv.* 2011; 29:468–82.

[10] Kijjoa, A. and Sawangwong, P. Drugs and cosmetics from the sea. *Mar Drugs.* 2004; 2:73–82.

[11] Mann, J., Davidson, R.S., Hobbs, J.B., Banthorpe, D.V. and Harbourne, J.B. (1994). Natural Products, their Chemistry and Biological Significance. 1st ed. Longman Scientific and Technical Longman Group; London, UK.

[12] Martins, A., Vieira, H., Gaspar, H. and Santos, S. Marketed marine natural products in the pharmaceutical and cosmeceutical industries: Tips for success. *Mar Drugs.* 2014; 12:1066–101.

[13] Mayer, A.M., Glaser, K.B., Cuevas, C., Jacobs, R.S., Kem, W., Little, R.D., *et al.* The odyssey of marine pharmaceuticals: A current pipeline perspective. *Trends Pharmacol Sci.* 2010; 31:255–65.

[14] Mayer, A.M., Rodríguez, A.D., Taglialatela-Scafati, O. and Fusetani, N. Marine pharmacology in 2009-2011: Marine compounds with antibacterial, antidiabetic, antifungal, anti-inflammatory, antiprotozoal, antituberculosis, and antiviral activities; affecting the immune and nervous systems, and other miscellaneous mechanisms of action. Mar Drugs, 2013; 11:2510–73.

[15] Meyer, C.A. The Global Marine Pharmaceuticals Pipeline. [Accessed on 8th May, 2019] Available online: http://marinepharmacology.midwestern.edu

[16] Mishra, B.B. and Tiwari, V.K. Natural products: An evolving role in future drug discovery. *Eur. J. Med. Chem.*, 2011; 46:4769–4807.

[17] Molecular Diversity Preservation International and Multidisciplinary Digital Publishing Institute [Accessed on 10th May, 2019] Available online: https://www.mdpi.com/1660-3397/12/2/1066.

[18] Murti, Y. and Agarwal, T., Marine derived pharmaceuticals-development of natural health products from marine biodiversity. *Int J. Chem Tech Res.* 2010; 2:2198.

[19] Newman, D.J. and Cragg, G.M. Natural products as sources of new drugs over the 30 years from 1981 to 2010. J. Nat. Prod., 2012; 75:311–335.

[20] Parker, C.N., Ottl, J., Gabriel, D. and Zhang, J.H. Natural Product Chemistry for Drug Discovery. Royal Society of Chemistry; Cambridge, UK: 2010. *Advances in Biological Screening for Lead Discovery.*

[21] Penesyan, A., Kjelleberg, S. and Egan, S. Development of novel drugs from marine surface associated microorganisms. *Mar. Drugs.* 2010; 8:438–459.

[22] Piel, J. Metabolites from symbiotic bacteria. *Nat. Prod. Rep.* 2009; 26: 338–362.

[23] Thakur, N.L., Thakur, A.N. and Muller, W.E.G. Marine natural products in drug discovery. *Natural Product Radiance.* 2005; 4:471–7.

[24] The Pharmaceutical Research and Manufactures of America (PhRMA). [Accessed on 15th May 2019] Available online: https://www.phrma.org/advocacy/research-development/clinical-trials.

[25] Vignesh, S., Raja, A. and James, R.A. Marine drugs: Implication and future studies. *Int J Pharmacol.* 2011; 7:22–30.

[26] https://www.mdpi.com/1660-3397/12/2/1066.

[27] https://pubchem.ncbi.nlm.nih.gov

[28] https://www.drugpatentwatch.com/p/bulk-api/eribulin+mesylate

Endosymbionts of Plants and Marine Organisms: A Search for Lung Cancer Drug

Vartika Mathur* and Garima Sharma

Animal-Plant Interactions Laboratory, Department of Zoology,
Sri Venkateswara College, University of Delhi,
Benito Juarez Marg, Dhaula Kuan, New Delhi-110021, India
*E-mail: vmathur@svc.ac.in

ABSTRACT: Lung cancer is one of the lethal forms of cancer world-wide, contributing 28% of the total cancer related deaths. In India, it is the most commonly occurring cancer form in males. Proactive research strategies for its treatment and management have led to major advancement in surgery, chemotherapy and radiotherapy. Chemotherapy, among these, is the most prevalent treatment. However, treatment complexities such as genetic and environmental factors, tumour heterogeneity, resistant tumour and secondary health problems are biggest hurdles in effective chemotherapy. Owing to these challenges, the need for novel, effective and safer therapeutic agents has led to evaluation of natural compounds from traditional medicinal plants especially bioactive compounds. However, production of bioactive compounds from host organism depends on specific stage, nutritional, stress and environmental conditions. Due to these limitations, exploring endosymbiotic micro-organisms from the host having medicinal properties provides a prospect of, inexhaustible and cost-effective source for bioactive compounds. Endophytes (plant's endosymbionts) produce similar metabolites as the host, as a result of their adaptation strategy. Compounds such as vinblastine, taxol, camptothecin, podophyllotoxin, topotecan and vincristine, are some of the examples of metabolites from endophyte origin used as anticancer agents. Another rich source of bioactive secondary metabolites is animals and plants of marine origin. Endosymbiotic microbes present in marine animals such as sponges, corals, starfish, bryozoans, sea urchins, fishes and prawns have recently emerged as rich sources of anti-cancer bioactive compounds. Since, marine biodiversity, are hardly explored, these sources may provide metabolites that may be used for therapeutic drugs against ailments, with minimum side effects. This review provides an insight to the symbiotic microbes with bioactive compounds with a potential in lung cancer therapy.

Keywords: Bioactive Compounds, Marine Endosymbionts, Chemotherapeutic Agents, Secondary Metabolites, Taxol, Host-Microbe Interactions.

1. INTRODUCTION

Cancer remains the second leading cause of deaths globally. Owing to its increased morbidity, cancer cases have been predicted to reach about 24 million in less than two decades (Are *et al.*, 2018). During recent decades, lung cancer has become one of the most lethal forms of cancers, contributing to about 28% of the total cancer mortality (Rawat *et al.* 2009; Iqbal *et al.*, 2017). Its common treatment therapies include surgical procedure, radiotherapy and chemotherapy. However, the treatment complexities can be further aggravated due to diverse nature of patients' genetic and environmental conditions, delay in diagnosis, patient age, drug side effects, tumour heterogeneity, concomitant diseases and resistant tumours (Wingo *et al.*, 1999; Behera and Balamugesh, 2004). Chemotherapeutic agents also cause secondary health problems such as hair loss, fatigue, diarrhoea, weakened eyesight, cardiomyopathy, ischemia, and dysrhythmias (Siegel *et al.*, 2012; Goyal *et al.*, 2017). Moreover, a major limitation in chemotherapy in India is the high dropout rates, leading to resistant cancers (Goyal *et al.*, 2017). Owing to these challenges, the need for novel, effective and safer therapeutic agents has led to evaluation of natural compounds from traditional medicinal plants.

Natural bioactive compounds are extra-nutritional or secondary metabolites produced by plants and animals (mostly lower vertebrates), that are increasingly being used for their antibacterial, antifungal, anticancerous and therapeutic properties (Cragg and Newman, 2004). Bioactive compounds from natural sources alone contribute to about 80% of the drugs available commercially for various therapeutic purposes (Singh and Dubey, 2015). With four of the thirty-five biodiversity hotspots in the world, India is rich in plants with therapeutic benefits and has about 2500 indigenous plant species being used in medicines (Samant *et al.*, 1998; Singh *et al.*, 2009; Singh *et al.*, 2019). However, production of bioactive compounds from these plants is dependent on various factors such as specific developmental stage of the plants, their nutritional availability, exposure to stress and environmental conditions (Chandra *et al.*, 2012; Dudeja and Giri,

2014). Under these specific conditions, the extraction of these metabolites becomes a tedious and challenging process. Extraction is further complicated due to isolation of the compound of interest from a plethora of secondary metabolites that are being produced by the plant, resulting in costly and time-consuming extraction process.

Another rich source of bioactive secondary metabolites is animals and plants of marine origin (Boopathy and Kathirsean, 2010). Endosymbiotic microbes present in marine animals such as sponges, corals, starfish, bryozoans, sea urchins, fishes and prawns have recently emerged as rich sources of anti-cancer bioactive compounds (Jin *et al.*, 2016). During recent years a significant number of metabolites have been reported from marine organisms. These metabolites range from various metabolites such as terpenoids, polyethers, macrolides, alkaloids, nucleosides and peptides (Dhinakaran *et al.*, 2012). Oceans, especially the Indian Ocean, is rich in marine biodiversity. However, extraction of these compounds from the organisms usually involves an invasive process that leads to removal of the host from the original habitat, thus resulting in loss of biodiversity, especially in cases of endangered organisms.

Attributed to these limitations, exploring endosymbiotic microorganisms from the host organism with medicinal properties provides a prospect of easily renewable, inexhaustible and cost-effective source for bioactive compounds. Endosymbiotic microbes not only adapt to the plant and animal systems but also play an integral role in their functioning and fitness. Owing to their adaptive capability these microbes are able to synchronize their metabolic profiles with the host but sometimes also produce unique and exclusive metabolites (Aly *et al.*, 2010; Kharwar *et al.*, 2011). Harnessing this property of host-microbe interaction may be beneficial from the view point of both economic as well as ecological environment. However, the association of these host-microbes is less intensively explored. This review article provides an overview to the possibilities of using endosymbiotic microbes as a source of novel and effective anti-cancerous compounds.

2. HOST-ENDOSYMBIONT INTERACTION

In plants, the endosymbiotic microorganisms that colonize intra and/or intercellular locations, without causing any pathogenicity are known as endophytes (Pimental *et al.*, 2011). While these endophytes themselves do not cause any pathogenicity to the plant, they do play an essential role in plant fitness. Microbe-plant association involves a bidirectional impact on physiology and metabolite production of the two partners (Bringel and Couee, 2015). Endophytes depend on the plant for nutrients such as carbon and nitrogen (Knief *et al.*, 2012, Kembela *et al.*, 2014). The host plant usually influences differential conditions that influence/inhibit the growth of various endophytes. On the other hand, endophytes are reported to produce various metabolites such as phytohormones, defence and volatile compounds that help the host in growth, improved stress resistance and anti-pathogenic effects (Farré-Armengol *et al.*, 2016). Often the endophyte protects the host from other phytopathogenic microbes by competing with them for the host resources. Plants experience constant fluctuations in temperature, relative humidity, sunlight exposure, drought and salinity conditions, which makes them a relatively hostile habitat for microbes. Accordingly, only selective microbial communities withstand such a habitat (Lindow and Brandl, 2003). Being present at the interface of plant surface and the atmosphere, endophytes are also known to affect the plant volatile emission, and in turn, these volatiles may have a significant role in determining the microbial composition in phyllosphere (aerial surface) and rhizosphere (roots) (Farré-Armengol *et al.*, 2016). All these factors together contribute the production of bioactive compounds that enable the endophytes to surviving the competitive plant host conditions. The atypical and specialized compounds thus produced by the endophytes enable microbes to adapt the host environment. The endophytes are also reported to produce similar metabolites as the host, due to their adaptation on the corresponding host (Aly *et al.*, 2010; Kharwar *et al.*, 2011; Dudeja and Giri, 2014). In effect, endophytes of the plants having known anti cancerous properties have also been reported to produce anticancer compounds. Taxol (commercially popular as paclitaxel) is a well-known example of an anticancer agent which was originally derived from the bark of trees of Taxus family, but was later on obtained from the endophytic fungi (such a *Taxomyces andreanae, Taxodiumdistrichum*) of this tree. Since microbes are easy to culture, maintain and reproduce, bulk production of the bioactive compound with pharmaceutical benefits can be easily done. Compounds such as vinblastine, taxol, camptothecin, podophyllotoxin, topotecan and vincristine, are some of the examples of metabolites from endophyte origin used as anticancer agents (Schulz *et al.*, 2002; Strobel and Daisy, 2003).

The marine host microbe interactions, on the other hand are majorly influenced by extreme environments such as low light, high hydrostatic pressure and low temperature environment (Raghukumar, 2008). Moreover, distribution of nutrients in marine sediments is usually non-homogenous for optimal microbial growth, thus several microscale hotspots are frequently generated (Stocker, 2012). Thus, major habitat for microbial fauna is associated with sponges and lower vertebrates. Microbial symbionts in marine conditions, comprises of about 40% of the total volume in the host (Thacker and Freeman, 2012). Similar to plant systems, the endosymbionts provide nutrient supplementation and secondary metabolites to host. These symbionts also enhance host growth rate and competitive abilities, along with nutrient cycling in the ecosystem (Diaz and Rützler, 2001; Erwin and Thacker, 2008; Thacker and Freeman, 2012). These metabolites are often antibiotics, novel anti-inflammatory agents and anticancer agents (Boopathy and Kathirsean, 2010).

3. NATURE OF ENDOSYMBIOTIC ANTICANCER COMPOUNDS

Recent studies indicate that about 51% of the bioactive compounds isolated form endophytes were previously unknown (Kharwar *et al.*, 2011). Since the discovery of Taxol from its host plants (*Taxus* sp) endophyte *Taxomyces andreanae*, a number of novel anticancer compounds have been reported such as camptothecin, ergoflavin, podophyllotoxin, gliocladicillin A&B, cytoskyrins, phomoxanthones A&B, rubofusarian B and epiepoxydon (Stierle *et al.*, 1993; Deshmukh *et al.*, 2009; Pimentel *et al.*, 2011). Bioactive compounds with anti-cancer properties reported so far belong to the class such as quinones, alkaloids, chromone, polyketide, esters, spirobisnaphthalene and terpenes (Table 1) (Guo *et al.*, 2008; Kharwar *et al.*, 2011).

Camptothecin (an alkaloid) is an anticancer compound, which was first isolated from *Camptotheca acuminate,* now was later obtained from the endophytic fungus of the same plant (Kusari *et al.*, 2009). This compound is also a precursor of drugs such as topotecan and irinotecan, which are more soluble in aqueous medium than campto-theca (Kusari *et al.*, 2009). Ergoflavin (xanthane dimer) and secalonic

Table 1: List of Anti-Cancerous Bioactive Compounds Obtained from Various Plant and Marine Symbiotic Microbes

Microbial Source	*Bioactive Compound*	*Structure*	*Reported Against Cancer*	*Stage of Trial*	*Reference*
Alternaria sp.	Reveratrodehydes	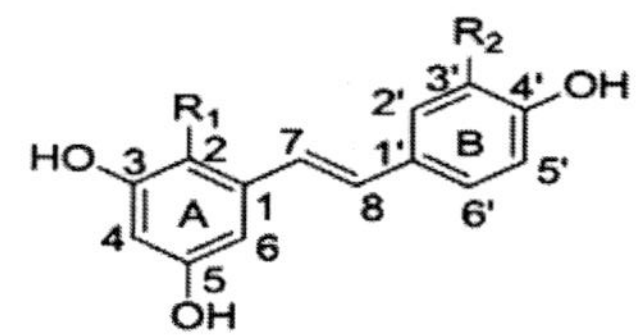	Human breast (MDA-MB-435), human liver (HepG2), and human colon (HCT-116) cell lines	Cell line studies	Wang *et al.*, 2014
Apiospora montagnei	Xanthone derivative (8-hydroxy-3-hydroxymethylxanthone-1-carboxylate)	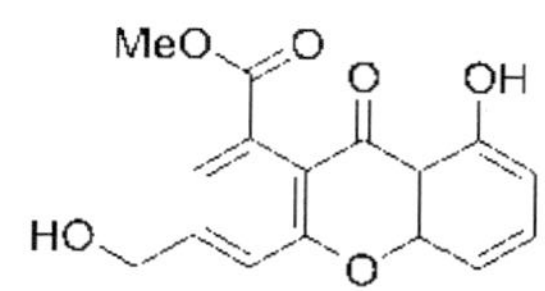	Human breast cancer adenocarcinoma and lung cancer cell line	Cell line studies	Arthan *et al.*, 2017
Aspergillus nidulans	5, 10-dihydrophenazine-1-carboxylic acid	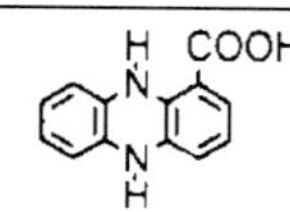	Human cancer cell lines, lung (NCI-H460), breast (MCF-7) and uterine cervix cancer cell line (HeLa)	Cell line studies	Sana *et al.*, 2018

(Table contd...)

(Table 1 contd...)

Microbial Source	*Bioactive Compound*	*Structure*	*Reported Against Cancer*	*Stage of Trial*	*Reference*
Aspergillus sp.	Aspochalasin V	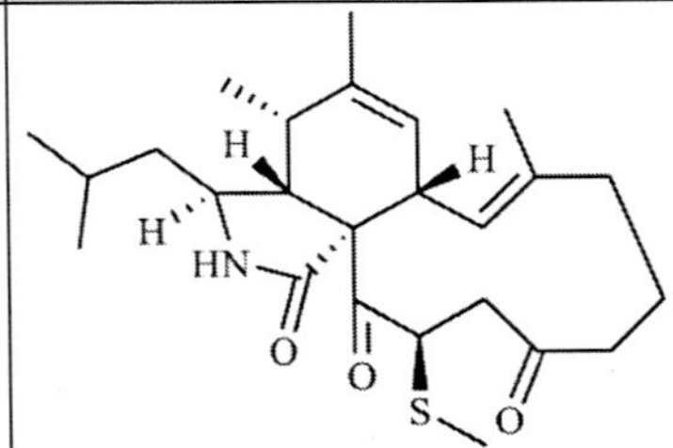	Prostate cancer cell lines (PC3 and HCT116)	Cell line studies	Liu *et al.*, 2014
Aspergillus sp.	Halimide	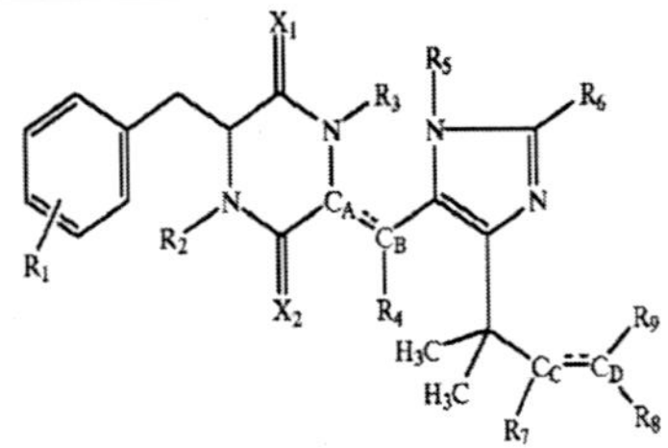	Human colon carcinoma (HCT116) and ovarian carcinoma (A2780) cell line	Cell line studies	Fenical *et al.*, 2000
Aspergillus terreus	Terrein; Butyrolactones	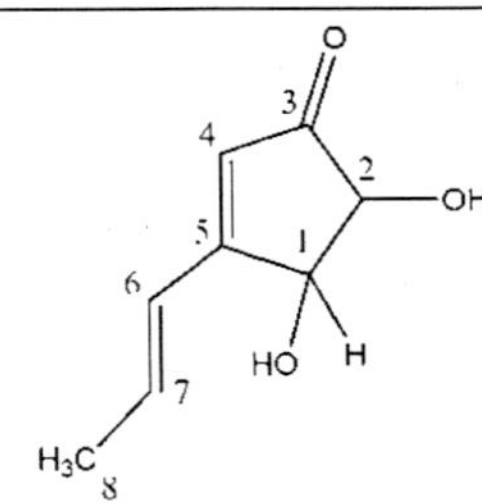	Breast tumor cell lines (MDA-MB-231 and MCF-7)	Cell line studies	Da Silva *et al.*, 2017

(Table contd...)

(Table 1 contd...)

Microbial Source	*Bioactive Compound*	*Structure*	*Reported Against Cancer*	*Stage of Trial*	*Reference*
Bacillus atrophaeus	cyclic lipoheptapeptides	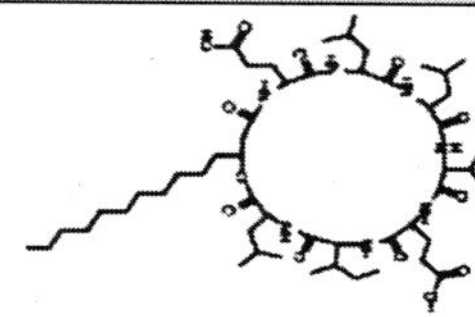	Lung cancer cell line (A549)	Cell line studies	Routhu *et al.*, 2018
Bacillus sp.	HA-21, HA-68, HAMS-105, HAMS-119	Cell extracts composition under study	Hepatocellular carcinoma (HepG2), colon carcinoma (HCT) and Breast carcinoma (MCF-7) cell lines	Cell line studies	Abdoul-Ela *et al.*, 2012
Chaetomiumglobosum	Polysaccharides (GCP-1 and GCP-2)	NMR data available	Lung cancer cell line (A549)	Cell line studies	Wang *et al.*, 2018
Chondrostereum sp.	Chondrostein	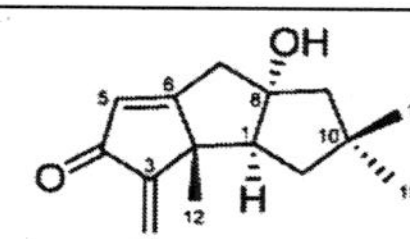	Human lung cancer (A549), human nasopharyngeal carcinoma (CNE2) and human colon cancer (LoVo) cell lines	Cell line studies	Li *et al.*, 2012

(Table contd...)

(Table 1 contd...)

Microbial Source	*Bioactive Compound*	*Structure*	*Reported Against Cancer*	*Stage of Trial*	*Reference*
Curvularia sp.	Tri and dipeptides (N-acetylphenylalanyl-L-phenylalanyl-L-leucine)	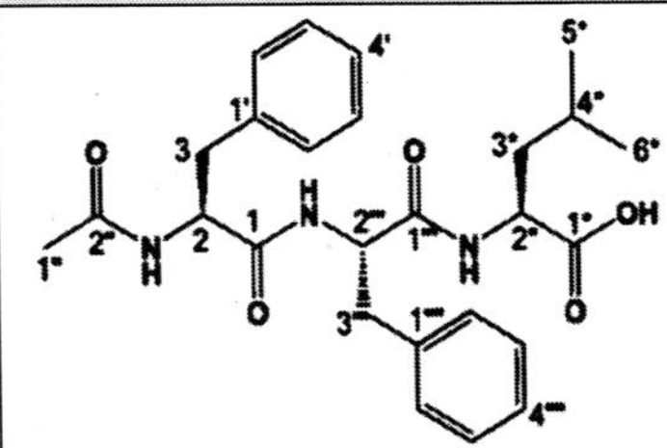	Chronic myelogenous leukemia cell line (K562)	Cell line studies	Tawfike *et al.*, 2018
Diaporthephaseolorum	Chromeno [3,2-c] pyridines	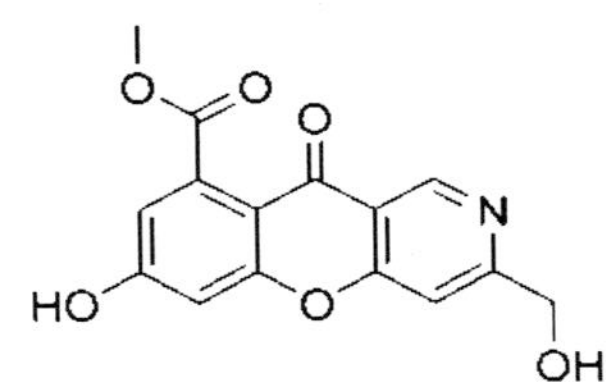	Human breast cancer cell line (MDA-MB-435)	Cell line studies	Cui *et al.*, 2017
Entrasphosporainfrequens	Camptothecin	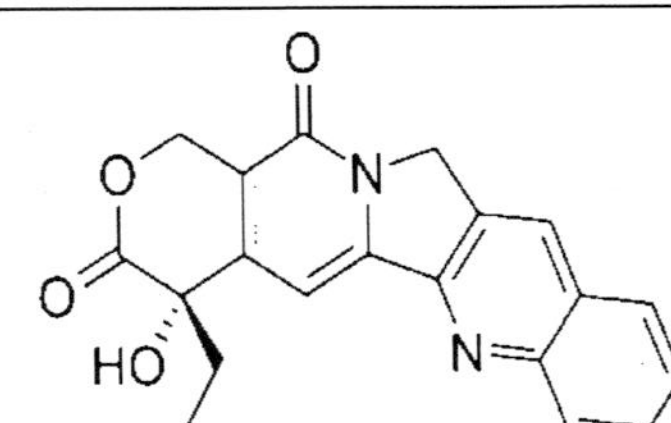	Lung, ovarian, and uterine cancers	Camptothecin commercially available	Amna *et al.*, 2006

(Table contd...)

(Table 1 contd...)

Microbial Source	*Bioactive Compound*	*Structure*	*Reported Against Cancer*	*Stage of Trial*	*Reference*
Eutypella sp.	Scopararane I	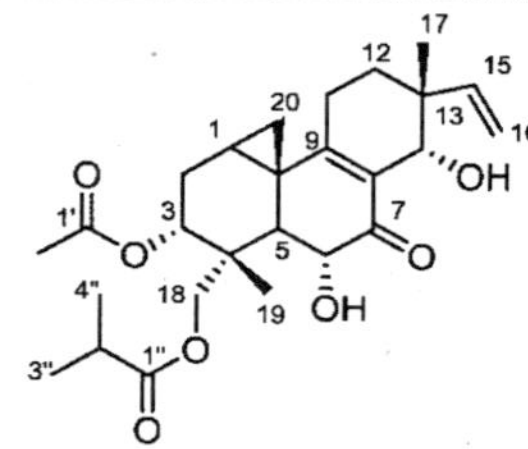	Human breast adenocarcinoma cell line (MCF-7)	Cell line studies	Liu *et al.*, 2017
Lasiodiplodia theobromae	Lasiodiplactone A	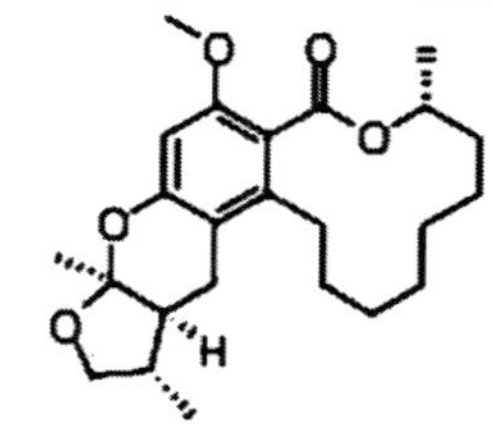	Human lung cancer (A549), Liver cancer (HepG2), Cervical cancer (CNE2), Breast cancer (MCF-7) and Embryonic kidney (HEK 293T) cell lines	Cell line studies	Chen *et al.*, 2017
Neosartorya pseudofischeri	Gliotoxin	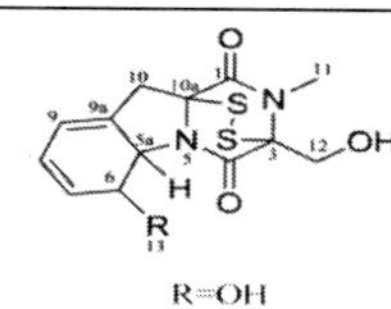	Human embryonic kidney (HEK-293) and human colon cancer (HCT-116) cell lines	Cell line studies	Liang *et al.*, 2014

(Table contd...)

(Table 1 contd...)

Microbial Source	*Bioactive Compound*	*Structure*	*Reported Against Cancer*	*Stage of Trial*	*Reference*
Penicillium purpurogenum	Penicimutanolone Penicimutanin A	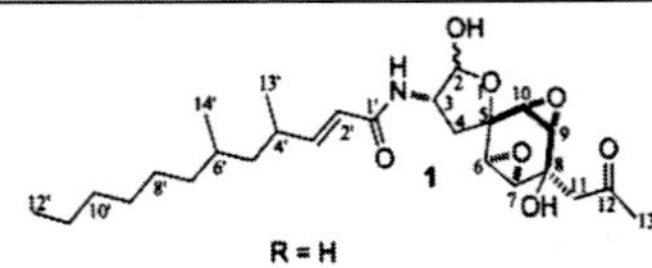 1 R = H	Human myelogenous leukemia (K562), leukemia (HL-60), Uterine cervical cancer (HeLa), gastric cancer (BCG-823) and Breast cancer (MCF-7) cell lines	Cell line studies	Fang *et al.*, 2014
Pestalotiopsis vaccinii	Pestalamine A	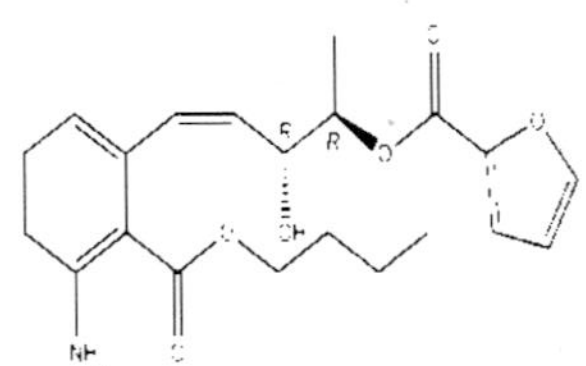	Breast cancer (MCF-7), Uterine cervical cancer (HeLa), and Liver cancer (HepG2) cell lines	Cell line studies	Zhou *et al.*, 2014

(Table contd...)

(*Table 1 contd…*)

Microbial Source	*Bioactive Compound*	*Structure*	*Reported Against Cancer*	*Stage of Trial*	*Reference*
Phomopsis sp.	Cytochalasin H	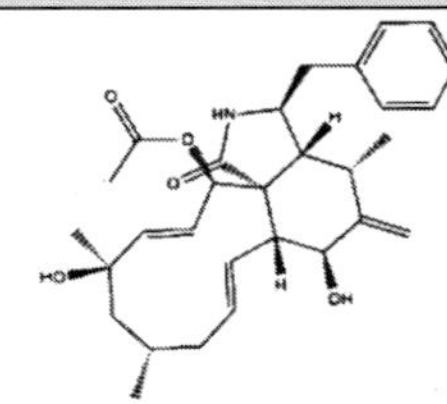	Lung cancer cell line (A549)	Cell line studies	Ma *et al.*, 2018
Phyllosticta sp.	Taxol	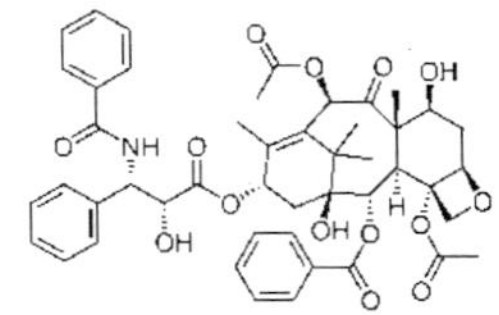	Ovarian and breast cancer	Taxol commercially available	Gangadevi and Muthumary, 2007
Polyporales sp.	Emodin	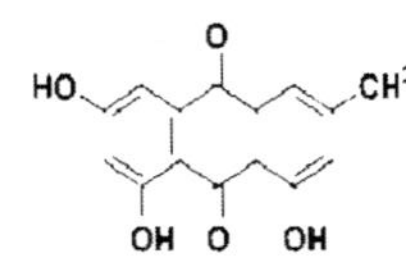	Against human lung (NCI-H322) and human colon (Colo-205) cancer cell lines	Cell line studies	Dar *et al.*, 2017
Trididemnum solidum	Didemnin	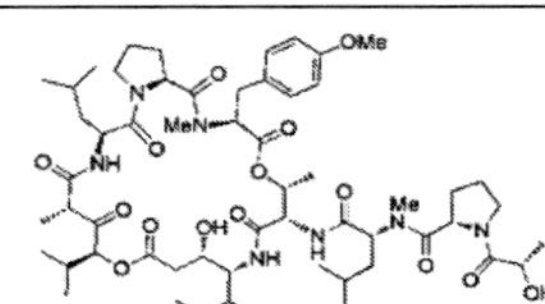	Lymphoid tissue, liver, urinary tract and pancreatic cancer	Pre-clinical trials	Xu *et al.*, 2012 and Lee *et al.*, 2012

acid D (mycotoxin) both belonging to the class of compounds ergochromes, which have also been reported for their anticancer property, are derived from fungus (Deshmukh *et al.*, 2009; Zhang *et al.*, 2009). Phenypropanoid, which is a large group of plant-based secondary metabolites, was isolated from *Penecillium brasilianum*, root endophyte of *Melia azedarach*. This compound is being used for its anticancer, antimicrobial, anti-inflammatory and immunosuppressant activities (Fill *et al.*, 2010).

Another class of compounds with a strong cytotoxic activity is Podophyllotoxin (lignan) and its analogs. Podophyllotoxin was originally obtained from the plant of *Podophyllum* sp. which are among endangered plant species. It is a valuable precursor of anticancer drugs such as teniposide, etoposide and etopophos phosphate (Kour *et al.*, 2008; Kusari *et al.*, 2009). Fungal sources such as *Trametes hirsute*, *Aspergillus fumigatus*, *Fusarium oxysporum*, have opened prospects of mass production for compounds (Kour *et al.*, 2008). Moreover, a potent anti-proliferator depsipeptide was reported with antitumor activity was isolated from *Trididemnum solidum*, a marine zooid, which is the first marine natural product for antitumor clinical trials (Xu *et al.*, 2012).

4. CONCLUSION

The prevalent conditions of multi drug resistance, target specificity, bulk production and cost effectiveness have been the main factors for search of potential drug candidates in microbes associated with terrestrial and marine animals and plants. Medicines derived from such natural sources have always been alluring to humans and this is evident from the fact that today two third of the world population still rely on such medicines for their primary medical care. These novel compounds under trial will be helpful in providing an alternate therapeutic agent against lung cancer. Natural products derived from microorganisms exhibit high potential of bioactive metabolite sources that can be used in medicine and industries. As of today, the world of endophytes and their bioactive compounds is much less explored which can be expedited to learn its full potential.

ACKNOWLEDGEMENT

The authors would like to express their gratitude towards NAM S&T centre for financially supporting participation in the International

Workshop on Drug Development from Herbs and Marine Medicinal Materials held in Hai Phong, Vietnam during 10–12 December, 2018, where the excerpts of this manuscript were presented.

REFERENCES

[1] Aboul-Ela, H.M., Shreadah, M.A., Abdel-Monem, N.M., Yakout, G.A. and van Soest, R.W. (2012). Isolation, cytotoxic activity and phylogenetic analysis of Bacillus sp. bacteria associated with the red sea sponge Amphimedon ochracea. *Advances in Bioscience and Biotechnology,* 3(07), 815.

[2] Aly, A.H., Debbab, A., Kjer, J. and Proksch, P. (2010). Fungal endophytes from higher plants: a prolific source of phytochemicals and other bioactive natural products. *Fungal Diversity,* 41(1): 1–16.

[3] Amna, T., Puri, S.C., Verma, V., Sharma, J.P., Khajuria, R.K., Musarrat, J. and Qazi, G.N. (2006). Bioreactor studies on the endophytic fungus Entrophospora infrequens for the production of an anticancer alkaloid camptothecin. *Canadian journal of microbiology,* 52(3), 189–19.

[4] Are, C., Caniglia, A., Mohammed, M., Smith, L., Cummings, C., Lecoq, C., Berman, R., Audisio, R. and Wyld, L. (2018). Global variations in the level of cancer-related research activity and correlation to cancer-specific mortality: Proposal for a global curriculum. *Annals of Surgical Oncology,* 25(3): 594–603.

[5] Arthan, S., Tantapakul, C., Kanokmedhakul, K., Soytong, K. and Kanokmedhakul, S. (2017). A new xanthone from the fungus Apiosporamontagnei. *Natural product research, 31*(15), 1766–1771.

[6] Behera, D. and Balamugesh, T. (2004). Lung cancer in India. *Indian Journal of Chest Diseases and Allied Sciences,* 46, 269–282.

[7] Bringel, F. and Couée, I. (2015). Pivotal roles of phyllosphere microorganisms at the interface between plant functioning and atmospheric trace gas dynamics. *Frontiers in Microbiology* 6.

[8] Chandra, S. (2012). Endophytic fungi: Novel sources of anticancer lead molecules. *Applied microbiology and biotechnology,* 95(1): 47–59.

[9] Chen, S., Liu, Z., Liu, H., Long, Y., Chen, D., Lu, Y. and She, Z. (2017). Lasiodiplactone A, a novel lactone from the mangrove endophytic fungus Lasiodiplodia theobromae ZJ-HQ1. *Organic & biomolecular chemistry, 15*(30), 6338–6341.

[10] Cragg, G.M. and Newman, D.J. (2005). Plants as a source of anti-cancer agents. *Journal of Ethnopharmacology,* 100(1–2):72–79.

[11] Cui, H., Yu, J., Chen, S., Ding, M., Huang, X., Yuan, J. and She, Z. (2017). Alkaloids from the mangrove endophytic fungus Diaporthephaseolorum SKS019. *Bioorganic and medicinal chemistry letters,* 27(4), 803–807.

[12] Da Silva, I.P., Brissow, E., Kellner Filho, L.C., Senabio, J., de Siqueira, K.A., VandresenFilho, S., Damasceno, J.L., Mendes, S.A., Tavares, D.C., Magalhães, L.G. and Junior, P.A.S. (2017). Bioactive compounds of Aspergillusterreus—F7, an endophytic fungus from Hyptissuaveolens (L.) Poit. *World Journal of Microbiology and Biotechnology*, *33*(3), 62.

[13] Dar, R.A., Majeed, R., Sheikh, A.A., Rehman, S., Hamid, A. and Hassan, Q.P. (2017). Emodin, isolated and characterized from an endophytic fungus Polyporales sp., induces apoptotic cell death in human lung cancer cells through the loss of mitochondrial membrane potential. *The Journal of Phytopharmacology*, 6(5), 288–292.

[14] Deshmukh, S.K., Mishra, P.D., Kulkarni-Almeida, A., Verekar, S., Sahoo, M.R., Periyasamy, G., Goswami, H., Khanna, A., Balakrishnan, A. and Vishwakarma, R. (2009). Anti-inflammatory and anticancer activity of ergoflavin isolated from an endophytic fungus. *Chemistry & biodiversity*, 6(5):784–789.

[15] Dhinakaran, D.I., Manohari, V., Atchya, B., Tamilselvi, K. and Lipton, A.P. (2012). Antifungal and Cytotoxic Activities of Some Marine Sponges Collected from the South East Coast of India.

[16] Diaz, M.C. and Rützler, K. (2001). Sponges: An essential component of Caribbean coral reefs. *Bulletin of Marine Science*, 69(2), 535–546.

[17] Dudeja, S.S. and Giri, R. (2014). Beneficial properties, colonization, establishment and molecular diversity of endophytic bacteria in legumes and non-legumes. *African Journal of Microbiology Research*, 8(15): 1562–1572.

[18] Erwin, P.M. and Thacker, R.W. (2007). Incidence and identity of photosynthetic symbionts in Caribbean coral reef sponge assemblages. *Journal of the Marine Biological Association of the United Kingdom*, *87*(6), 1683–1692.

[19] Fang, S.M., Wu, C.J., Li, C.W. and Cui, C.B. (2014). A practical strategy to discover new antitumor compounds by activating silent metabolite production in fungi by diethyl sulphate mutagenesis. *Marine drugs*, 12(4), 1788–1814.

[20] Farré-Armengol, G., Filella, I., Llusia, J. and Peñuelas, J. (2016). Bidirectional interaction between phyllosphericmicrobiotas and plant volatile emissions. *Trends in plant science*, *21*(10), 854–860.

[21] Fenical, W., Jensen, P.R. and Cheng, X.C. (2000). U.S. Patent No. 6,069, 146. Washington, DC: U.S. Patent and Trademark Office.

[22] Fill, T.P., Da Silva, B.F. and Rodrigues-Fo, E. (2010). Biosynthesis of phenylpropanoid amides by an endophytic Penicillium brasilianum found in root bark of Melia azedarach. *Journal of microbiology and biotechnology*, *20*(3), 622–629.

[23] Goyal, S., Gupta, N., Chatterjee, S. and Nimesh, S. (2017). Natural plant extracts as potential therapeutic agents for the treatment of cancer. *Current Topics in Medicinal Chemistry*, 17(2): 96–106.

[24] Guo, B., Wang, Y., Sun, X. and Tang, K. (2008). Bioactive natural products from endophytes: a review. *Applied Biochemistry and Microbiology,* 44(2): 136–142.

[25] Iqbal, J., Abbasi, B.A., Mahmood, T., Kanwal, S., Ali, B. and Khalil, A.T. (2017). Plant-derived anticancer agents: A green anticancer approach. *Asian Pacific Journal of Tropical Biomedicine.*

[26] Jin, L., Quan, C., Hou, X. and Fan, S. (2016). Potential pharmacological resources: Natural bioactive compounds from marine-derived fungi. *Marine drugs,* 14(4): 76.

[27] Kembela, S.W., O'Connorb, T.K., Arnold, H.K., Hubbell, S.P., Wright, S.J. and Green, J.L. (2014). Relationships between phyllosphere bacterial communities and plant functional traits in a neotropical forest. *PNAS* 111:13715–13720.

[28] Kharwar, R.N., Mishra, A., Gond, S.K., Stierle, A. and Stierle, D. (2011). Anticancer compounds derived from fungal endophytes: Their importance and future challenges. *Natural Product Reports,* 28(7):1208–1228.

[29] Knief, C., Delmotte, N., Chaffron, S., Stark, M., Innerebner, G., Wassmann, R., Mering, C. and Vorholt, J.A. (2012). Metaproteogenomic analysis of microbial communities in the phyllosphere and rhizosphere of rice. *The ISME Journal,* 6:1378–1390.

[30] Knief, C.N.l. Delmotte, S. Chaffron, M. Stark, G. Innerebner, R. Wassmann, C.V. Mering and Vorholt, J.A. (2012). Metaproteogenomic analysis of microbial communities in the phyllosphere and rhizosphere of rice. *The ISME Journal* 6:1378–1390.

[31] Kour, A., Shawl, A.S., Rehman, S., Sultan, P., Qazi, P.H., Suden, P., Khajuria, R.K. and Verma, V. (2008). Isolation and identification of an endophytic strain of Fusarium oxysporum producing podophyllotoxin from Juniperus recurva. *World Journal of Microbiology and Biotechnology, 24*(7), 1115-1121.

[32] Kumari, M., Taritla, S., Sharma, A. and Jayabaskaran, C. (2018). Anti-proliferative and Antioxidative Bioactive Compounds in Extracts of Marine-Derived Endophytic Fungus Talaromycespurpureogenus. *Frontiers in microbiology, 9.*

[33] Kusari, S., Lamshöft, M. and Spiteller, M. (2009). Aspergillus fumigatus Fresenius, an endophytic fungus from Juniperus communis L. Horstmann as a novel source of the anticancer pro-drug deoxypodophyllotoxin. *Journal of applied microbiology, 107*(3), 1019–1030.

[34] Lee, Jisun, Judith N. Currano, Patrick J. Carroll, and Madeleine M. Joullié. "Didemnins, tamandarins and related natural products." *Natural product reports* 29, No. 3 (2012): 404–424.

[35] Li, H.J., Xie, Y.L., Xie, Z.L., Chen, Y., Lam, C.K. and Lan, W.J. (2012). Chondrosterins A–E, Triquinane-Type Sesquiterpenoids from Soft Coral-Associated Fungus Chondrostereum sp. *Marine drugs, 10*(3), 627–638.

[36] Lindow, S.E. and Brandl, M.T. (2003). Microbiology of the Phyllosphere. *Applied and Environmental Microbiology*, 69:1875–1883.

[37] Liu, H., Zhang, L., Chen, Y., Li, S., Tan, G., Sun, Z., Pan, Q., Ye, W., Li, H. and Zhang, W. (2017). Cytotoxic pimarane-type diterpenes from the marine sediment-derived fungus Eutypella sp. FS46. *Natural product research*, 31(4), 404–410.

[38] Liu, Y., Zhao, S., Ding, W., Wang, P., Yang, X. and Xu, J. (2014). Methylthio-aspochalasins from a marine-derived fungus Aspergillus sp. *Marine drugs*, 12(10), 5124–5131.

[39] Ma, Y., Wu, X., Xiu, Z., Liu, X., Huang, B., Hu, L., Liu, J., Zhou, Z. and Tang, X. (2018). Cytochalasin H isolated from mangrove-derived endophytic fungus induces apoptosis and inhibits migration in lung cancer cells. *Oncology reports*, 39(6), 2899–2905.

[40] Pimentel, M.R., Molina, G., Dionísio, A.P., Maróstica Junior, M.R. and Pastore, G.M. (2011). The use of endophytes to obtain bioactive compounds and their application in biotransformation process. *Biotechnology Research International*, 2011.

[41] Raghukumar, C. (2008). Marine fungal biotechnology: an ecological perspective.

[42] Rai, D.K.; Anil Kumar, A.V.; Kumar, Akansha; Kumar, A. Kiran and Thakur, S. (2017). A clinico-radiological and pathological profile of lung cancer patients presented to All India Institute of Medical Sciences (Patna). *Eastern Journal of Medical Sciences*, 2(1): 8–11.

[43] Rajivgandhi, G., Muneeswaran, T., Maruthupandy, M., Ramakritinan, C.M., Saravanan, K., Ravikumar, V. and Manoharan, N. (2018). Antibacterial and anticancer potential of marine endophyticactinomycetes Streptomyces coeruleorubidus GRG 4 (KY457708) compound against colistin resistant uropathogens and A549 lung cancer cells. *Microbial pathogenesis*, 125, 325–335.

[44] Rawat, J., Sindhwani, G., Gaur, D., Dua, R. and Saini, S. (2009). Clinicopathological profile of lung cancer in Uttarakhand. Lung India: official organ of Indian Chest Society, 26(3): 74.

[45] Routhu, S.R., Chary, R.N., Shaik, A.B., Prabhakar, S., Kumar, C.G. and Kamal, A. (2018). Induction of apoptosis in lung carcinoma cells by antiproliferative cyclic lipopeptides from marine algicolous isolate Bacillus atrophaeus strain AKLSR1. *Process Biochemistry*. https://doi.org/10.1016/j.procbio.2018.12.010.

[46] Samant, S.S., Dhar, U. and Palni, L.MS (1998). *Medicinal Plants of Indian Himalaya*. Gyanodaya Prakashan.

[47] Sana, T., Siddiqui, B.S., Shahzad, S., Farooq, A.D., Siddiqui, F., Sattar, S. and Begum, S. (2018). Antiproliferative Activity and Characterization of Metabolites of Aspergillusnidulans: An Endophytic Fungus from Nyctanthesarbor-tristis Linn. against Three Human Cancer Cell Lines.

Medicinal chemistry (Shariqah (United Arab Emirates)). DOI: 10.2174/1573406414666180828124252.

[48] Schulz, B., Boyle, C., Draeger, S., Römmert, A.K. and Krohn, K. (2002). Endophytic fungi: a source of novel biologically active secondary metabolites. *Mycological Research*, 106(9): 996–1004.

[49] Siegel, R., DeSantis, C., Virgo, K., Stein, K., Mariotto, A., Smith, T., Cooper, D., Gansler, T., Lerro, C., Fedewa, S. and Lin, C. (2012). Cancer treatment and survivorship statistics, 2012. *CA: A Cancer Journal for Clinicians*, 62(4): 220–241.

[50] Singh, A., Lal, M. and Samant, S.S. (2009). Diversity, indigenous uses and conservation prioritization of medicinal plants in Lahaul valley, proposed Cold Desert Biosphere Reserve, India. *International Journal of Biodiversity Science & Management*, 5(3), 132–154.

[51] Singh, A.P., Kumar, M., Nagar, B., Pala, N.A. and Bussmann, R.W. (2019). Ethnomedicinal use of plant resources in Kirtinagar Block of Tehri Garhwal in Western Himalaya. *Ethnobotany Research & Applications*, 18(14).

[52] Singh, R. and Dubey, A.K. (2015). Endophytic actinomycetes as emerging source for therapeutic compounds. *Indo Global J. Pharm. Sci.*, 5, 106–116.

[53] Boopathy, S.N. and Kathiresan, K. (2010). Anticancer drugs from marine flora: an overview. *Journal of oncology*, 2010.

[54] Stierle, A., Strobel, G. and Stierle, D. (1993). Taxol and taxane production by Taxomyces andreanae, an endophytic fungus of Pacific yew. Science-New York Then Washington-260: 214–214.

[55] Stocker, R. (2012). Marine microbes see a sea of gradients. *science*, *338*(6107), 628–633.

[56] Tawfike, A.F., Abbott, G., Young, L. and Edrada-Ebel, R. (2018). Metabolomic-Guided Isolation of Bioactive Natural Products from Curvularia sp., an Endophytic Fungus of Terminalialaxiflora. *Plantamedica*, 84(03), 182–190.

[57] Thacker, R.W. and Freeman, C.J. (2012). Sponge–microbe symbioses: recent advances and new directions. In *Advances in Marine Biology* (Vol. 62, pp. 57–111). Academic Press.

[58] Wang, J., Cox, D., Ding, W., Huang, G., Lin, Y. and Li, C. (2014). Three new resveratrol derivatives from the mangrove endophytic fungus Alternaria sp. *Marine drugs*, 12(5), 2840–2850.

[59] Wang, Z., Chen, P., Tao, N., Zhang, H., Li, R., Zhan, X., Wang, F. and Shen, Y. (2018). Anticancer Activity of Polysaccharides Produced from Glycerol and Crude Glycerol by an Endophytic Fungus Chaeto-miumglobosum CGMCC 6882 on Human Lung Cancer A549 Cells. *Biomolecules*, 8(4), 171.

[60] Wingo, P.A., Ries, L.A., Giovino, G.A., Miller, D.S., Rosenberg, H.M., Shopland, D.R., Thun, M.J. and Edwards, B.K. (1999). Annual report to the nation on the status of cancer, 1973–1996, with a special section on

lung cancer and tobacco smoking. *Journal of the National Cancer institute,* 91(8), 675–690.

[61] Xu, W., Yang, Y., Yang, Y., Lu, Z., Lu, Q. and Chen, Y. (2018). Exopolysaccharides from an Ophiopogon japonicus endophyte inhibit proliferation and migration in MC-4 human gastric cancer cells. *Translational Cancer Research*, 7(6), 1567–1576.

[62] Xu, Y., Kersten, R.D., Nam, S.J., Lu, L., Al-Suwailem, A.M., Zheng, H.H., Fenical, W., Dorrestein, P.C., Moore, B.S. and Qian, P.Y. (2012). Bacterial biosynthesis and maturation of the didemnin anti-cancer agents. *Journal of the American Chemical Society,* 134(20): 8625–8632.

[63] Zhang, J.Y., Tao, L.Y., Liang, Y.J., Yan, Y.Y., Dai, C.L., Xia, X.K., She, Z.G., Lin, Y.C. and Fu, L. (2009). Secalonic acid D induced leukemia cell apoptosis and cell cycle arrest of G1 with involvement of GSK-3β/β-catenin/c-Myc pathway. *Cell Cycle*, 8(15), 2444–2450.

[64] Zhou, X., Lin, X., Ma, W., Fang, W., Chen, Z., Yang, B. and Liu, Y. (2014). A new aromatic amine from fungus Pestalotiopsis vaccinii. *Phytochemistry letters*, *7*, 35–37.

Drug Development from Triphala Freeze-Dried Powder

Sam Sam Htu*[1], Thein Zaw Linn[1], Cho Ye Myint[2] and Khin Phyu Phyu[3]

[1]University of Traditional Medicine, Myanmar
[2]University of Pharmacy (Mandalay), Myanmar
[3]Department of Medical Research, Myanmar
*E-mail: samsamhtu@gmail.com

ABSTRACT: Traditionally, powder dosage form of Triphala has been in use for treating diarrhea, dysentery, bleeding pile, digestive agent and blood circulation improving agent. However, dispensing and consumption of raw powder reported to be inconvenient. The present study has made an attempt to prepare the capsule dosage form of Triphala. Aqueous extraction of grinded pericarps of Triphala (1:1:1) was carried out by 150 gm of prepared Triphala with 600 ml of distilled water (DW) using reflux extractor for 3 hours for three times at 60°C. The liquid extract was filtrated using filter paper and filtrate was concentrated by using vacuum rotary evaporator. The concentrated Triphala extract was produced as powder by using freeze-dryer. Freeze-dried powder of Tiphala could provide the solubility and stability of drug. The advantages of freeze-drying as compared with other methods lie in the quality of the dried product. Phytochemical analysis showed the presence of flavonoids, carbohydrates, glycosides, reducing sugars, tannins, amino acids, steroids, phenolic compounds and saponins were present. In each capsule, 300 mg of freeze-dried powder was filled. The capsule filling process was carried out by manual filling machine. The capsules were kept in containers (60 capsules/container) and sealed with the aluminium foil. The plastic containers were stored in refrigeration temperature. Throughout the study, the capsules color and the content color were not changed. The Mean ± SD the uniformity of Triphala capsules weight (n = 20) was 307.75 ± 7.1963 mg. All capsules disintegrated in 27.866 ± 1.5 min. Disintegration times of all capsules were within the standard range (30 minutes for hard gelatin capsule) for the capsules in accordance with the British Pharmacopoeia, 2009.

Keywords: Triphala, Freeze-Dried Powder, Capsule.

1. INTRODUCTION

Triphala (in Sanskrit; tri = three and phala = fruits) is composed of the three myrobalans; *Phyllanthus emblica* Linn. (Zee-Phyu), *Terminalia chebula* Retz. (Phan-Khar) and *Terminalia belerica* Roxb. (Thit-Saint). The formulation generally consists of equal proportions of pericaps of these myrobalans. Triphala is regarded as an important *rasayana* and good purgative in the Traditional Ayurvedic Texts such as; the Charak Samhita and Susruta Samhita which date back to 1500 B.C. (Gupta, 2010). The present study was attempted to introduce the Triphala as freeze-dried powder and prepare the capsule dosage. The capsule is the popular type of pharmaceutical dosage form and is intended for oral administration.

2. MATERIALS AND METHODS

2.1 Materials

1. The seedless pericarps of *Phyllanthus emblica* Linn, *Terminalia chebula* Retz. and *Terminalia belerica* Roxb., collected from Mandalay Division
2. Reflux extractor
3. Rotary evaporator
4. Distilled water
5. Freeze-dryer (model FD-1, Japan)
6. Mortar and pestle
7. Hard gelatin capsules
8. Manual capsule filling machine (Zuma 1012, Italy)
9. The polishing machine
10. Analytical balance (OHASUS)
11. Electronic calculator
12. Disintegration apparatus (Pharma test 16678, Germany).

2.2 Methods

2.2.1 *Preparation of Triphala Freeze-Dried Powder*

Three kinds of Triphala fresh fruits were collected from Mandalay Division and the authentic identification of the fruits was carried out. The seedless dried pericarps of Triphala were prepared as 1:1:1 ratio.

Aqueous extraction of Triphala was prepared by 150 gm of Triphala with 600 ml of distilled water using reflux extractor for 3 hours for three times at 60°C. The liquid extract was filtrated and filtrate was concentrated by using vacuum rotary evaporator.

Freeze dryer (model FD-1, Japan) was used in this study to get the powder. 100 ml of Triphala extract filled flasks were immersed and turned in the ethanol 95% pre-freeze bath (minus 50°C) to get the layer of frozen solution inside the flask. The flasks containing layer of frozen solution were immediately attached the drying chamber through the vacuum pumps (Figure 1). This process took at most eight hours to get the dry layer. The dried layer was scraped and made powder.

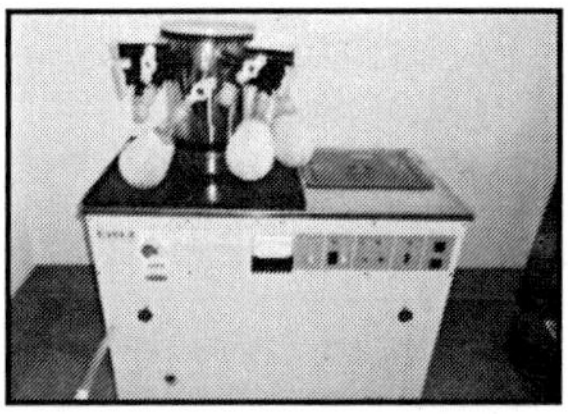

Fig. 1: Freeze-drying Process of Triphala Aqueous Extract

2.2.2 *Phytochemical Analysis of Triphala*

Phytochemical screening of Triphala freeze-dried powder was carried out as stated in physiochemical standards of UNANI formulations.

2.2.3 *Preparation of Triphala as the Capsule Dosage Form*

In this study, with the purpose of easy to administer and to obscure the bitter and astringent taste of dried powder of Triphala, the capsules dosage form was prepared. According to the required amount (300 mg), 0 size capsule was selected in this study. The characteristics of selected capsule in this study are:

Capsule size = 0 size
Capsule weight = 96 ± 6 mg
Capsule length = 21.7 ± 0.3 mm
Capsule content = 450 mg (Aulton, 1988)

2.2.4 *Triphala Capsule Filling Process*

The empty capsules were filled into the capsule loading tray which was then placed over the bed with 150 holes of the manual capsule filling machine.

The weighed amount of the Triphala powder (45 gm for 150 capsules) was filled in powder tray. Triphala powder was spreaded with help of a powder spreader. The caps were pressed with the help of plate and operated the lever to unlock the cap and body of the capsules. The loading tray was removed and collected the filled Triphala capsules in tray.

Small amount of adhered powder after filling was polished by polishing machine. Then, 60 capsules were put in each container and a silica gel pack was added to prevent the moisture (Figure 2). Finally, the containers were sealed with aluminium foil and stored in refrigeration temperature.

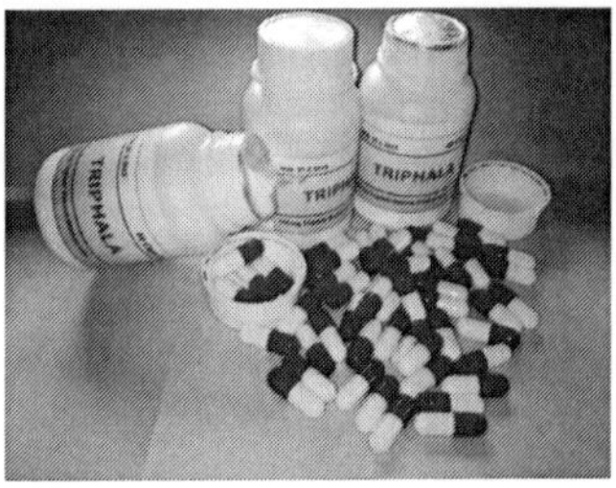

Fig. 2: Triphala Capsules

2.2.5 *Evaluation of Triphala Capsules*

The following tests were carried out on the prepared Triphala capsules to comply with the requirements of the official compendia (British Pharmacopoeia, 2009).

1. ***Determination of Uniformity of Fill Weight Test of Capsules:*** The random sample of 20 capsules was weighed individually by an electronic balance. Then, the average weight and limited weight range were calculated.

   The uniformity of fill weight test was involved four steps as; weighing a specified number of capsules, emptying out their contents, reweighing the shells and calculating the weight of the filled.

2. ***Determination of Disintegration Test of Capsules:*** Disintegration test was performed by using the digital microprocessor based disintegration apparatus (Pharma test 16678, Germany).

This test used a transparent tube with a metal mesh base. Five capsules were tested in this test. One capsule was introduced into each tube and one tube was controlled. Sets of these tubes were oscillated up and down in the test medium (1000 ml of distilled water at 37°±2°C). The end point was taken as the time at which all the contents have passed through the mesh.

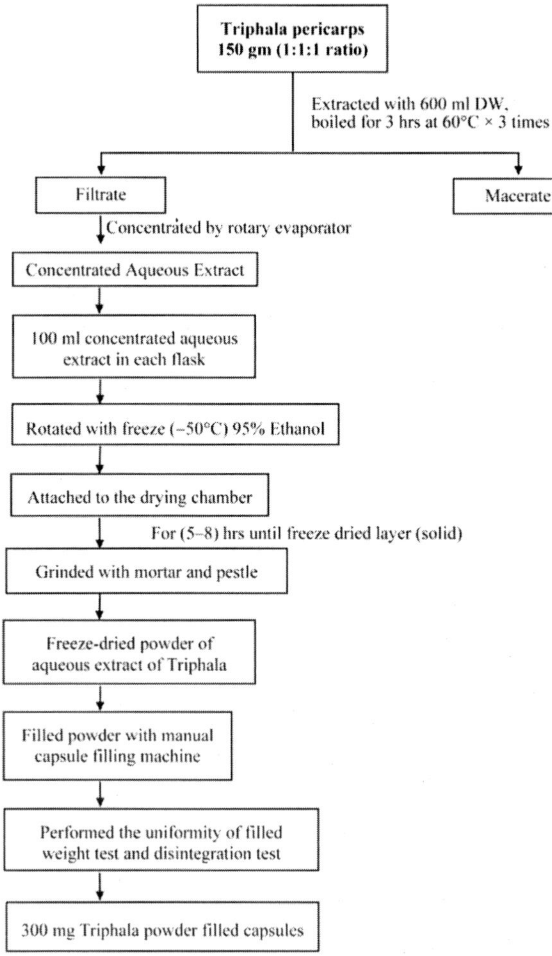

Fig. 3: Flow Diagram of Extraction of Triphala and Freeze-Drying Process

3. RESULTS AND DISCUSSION

3.1 Yield Percentage of Aqueous Extract of Triphala

The result of yield percentage (w/w) of aqueous extract of Triphala was 33.33%.

3.2 Physical Characteristics

Triphala freeze-dried powder was in yellow color, good retention of flavor, taste stay in fresh and could provide the solubility and stability of drug. The freeze-dried powder was stored in a clean and dry well-closed container. Condensation and moisture were prevented by adding the silica gel packs.

3.3 Phytochemical Analysis

Phytochemical analysis of the freeze-dried powder of Triphala was carried out qualitatively. Analysis of the tests showed the presence of carbohydrates, reducing sugar, glycosides, flavonoids, tannins, amino acids, steroid, phenolic compounds and saponin. The results are presented in Table 1.

Table 1: Phytochemical Constituents of the Freeze-Dried Powder of Triphala

No.	*Constituents Determined*	*Reagents Used*	*Observation*	*Present (+)/ Absent (–)*
1.	Alkaloids	1.Dragendroff's reagent 2.Mayer reagent 3.Wagener reagent	Orange ppt White ppt Yellow or brown ppt	– – –
2.	Flavonoids	Con: HCl and Mg	Brown color	+ +
3.	Carbohydrate	10% Naphthol	Red ring	+
4.	Glycosides	10% lead acetate solution	White ppt	+++
5.	Starch	Iodine, Potassium iodide	Blue color	–
6.	Reducing sugar	Benedict's test	Brick red ppt	+
7.	Tannins	10% Ferric chloride solution	Deep blue color	+++
8.	Amino acids	Ninhyrin reagent	Purple spot	++
9.	Steroid	Con: H_2SO_4	Red color	++
10.	Terpenoids	Chloroform, acetic anhydrate and Con: H_2SO_4 (Liebermann-burchard test)	Pink color	–
11.	Phenolic compounds	10% Ferric chloride	Deep blue color	+++
12.	Saponins	Distilled water	Frothing	+
13.	Cyanogenic glycoside	Sodium picrate paper	Brick red color	–

+++ = Abundant + = Poor

++ = Fair – = Absent

3.4 Evaluation of Triphala Capsules

The uniformity of Triphala freeze-dried powder filled capsules weight (n = 20) was tested and Mean ± SD was found to be 307.75 ± 7.1963 mg. The results are shown in Table 2. All tested capsules (n = 5) disintegrated in 27.866 ± 15 min. Disintegration times of all capsules were within the standard range (30 minutes for hard gelatin capsules) for the capsule in accordance with BP 2009. The results are presented in Table 3.

Table 2: Determination of Uniformity of Filled Weight Test of Capsules (n = 20)

No.	*Weight of Capsules (mg)*	*Weight of Shells (mg)*	*Weight of Medicament (mg)*
1.	410	101	309
2.	415	098	317
3.	405	097	308
4.	407	097	310
5.	409	100	309
6.	392	097	295
7.	410	096	314
8.	408	097	311
9.	410	100	310
10.	403	103	300
11.	398	099	299
12.	392	098	294
13.	419	099	320
14.	400	099	301
15.	404	095	309
16.	414	100	314
17.	401	093	308
18.	416	100	316
19.	402	103	299
20.	412	100	312
Mean			307.75
SD			± 7.1963

Upper limit = 330.08 mg

Lower limit = 284.67 mg

Table 3: Determination of Disintegration Test of Capsules (n = 5)

Capsule No.	*Disintegration Time (min)*
1	28:43
2	29:13
3	29:52
4	26:12
5	26:13
Mean	27.866
SD	± 1.5

4. DISCUSSION

Triphala is the most widely used and easily available herbal remedy in Myanmar. Many researchers reported that Triphala had antioxidant activity, cholesterol lowering activity and having balancing and rejuvenating effects (Suman, 2011). The three kinds of fruits were collected from August to October and were dried. The aqueous extract freeze-dried powder of Triphala was stored in a clean and dry well-closed container. Condensation and moisture of dry powder were prevented by adding the silica gel packs. The powder was in yellow color and good retention of flavor and taste stay in fresh throughout the study. The powder could provide the solubility and stability of drug. Therefore, freeze-drying method will be useful for long term saving of the other Traditional Medicinal Powder without reducing the product quality.

Phytochemical analysis of the freeze-dried powder of Triphala revealed that the presence of carbohydrates, reducing sugar, glycosides, flavor-noids, tannins, amino acids, steroid, phenolic compounds and saponin. But, starch, alkaloids, terpenoids and cyanogenic substances were absent. In this study, qualitative detection of the freeze-dried powder of Triphala showed the presence of phenols and flavonoids.

The present study was attempted to prepare the capsule dosage form of Triphala. The capsules are kept in containers and stored in refrigeration temperature. Throughout the study, the capsules color and the content color were not changed. The uniformity of Triphala capsules weight (n = 20) was tested and Mean ± SD was found to be 307.75 ± 7.1963 mg. All capsules disintegrated in 27.866 ± 1.5 min. Disintegration times of all capsules were within the standard range (30 minutes for hard gelatin capsule) for the capsules in accordance with the British Pharmacopoeia, 2009. Throughout the study period, the capsules color and the content (Triphala freeze-dried powder) color were not changed. Triphala freeze-dried powder preserved freshness, color, taste and aroma. Triphala capsule dosage form may improved patient compliance and acceptability, which otherwise are poor due to obscure unpleasant taste. The stability of capsule dosage form should be studied to predict the real shelf-life of the capsule dosage form.

5. CONCLUSION

In conclusion, Triphala freeze-dried powder is rich in phytochemical constituents. Triphala capsules have met the standard limits for weight uniformity and disintegration times in accordance with the British Pharmacopoeia, 2009. The capsules color and the content color have not changed and no interaction between capsule and Triphala powder was recorded. This study may be useful for the improvement of patient compliance and acceptability on Triphala capsule dosage form.

ACKNOWLEDGEMENT

The authors would like to thank Dr. Than Maung (Ret: Rector, UTM), Dr. San San Nwet (Ret: Rector, UOP, Ygn), Dr. Kyaw Oo (Ret: Director, Socio-Medical Research, DMR, UM), U Thaung Nyunt (Ret: Manager, TM Factory, Ygn) and other staff, U Maung Maung Oo (MD, Great Wall TM Manufacturing Co., Ltd.), Daw Hnin Hnin Htun (Lecturer, Dept. of Botany, U TM), Dr. Hla Moe (AP, Dept. of Physiology, UMM).

REFERENCES

[1] Aulton, M.E. (1988). The science of dosage form design. Churchill Livingstone, Edinburgh, New York, London.

[2] British Pharmacopoeia (2009). The General Medical Council, London, The Pharmaceutical Press: HMSO.

[3] Gupta, M. (2010). Therapeutic uses of the polyherbal drug triphala in geriatric diseases. *Int J Pharma Bil Sci*; 1: pp. 1–13.

[4] Physicochemical standards of UNANI formulation (1987). Central Council for Research in Unani Medicine (Ministry of Health and Family Welfare). Government of India, Nice printing press, New Delhi.

[5] Suman, R. (2011). A study on comparative hypolipidemic activity of different ratios of Triphala. Master of Pharmacy (Pharmacology). Dissertation, Rajiv Gandhi University of Health Sciences, Karnataka, Bangalore.

Anti-Allergic Property-based Screening and Validation of Medicinal Plants Described in *Ayurveda*

Daya N. Mani[1,5,*], Amit Kaushik[1,2,5], Harshika Khanna[1], Dewasya P. Singh[1,2,5], Ajay Kumar[1], Manish K. Patel[1], Maneesha Mall[2], Pallavi Pandey[3], V. Sundaresan[4], Karuna Shanker[3], Ashutosh K. Shukla[2,5] and Kamal Sachdev[6]

[1]Herbal Medicinal Product Department, CSIR—Central Institute of Medicinal and Aromatic Plants, P.O. CIMAP, Lucknow-226015, India

[2]Biotechnology Division, CSIR—Central Institute of Medicinal and Aromatic Plants, P.O. CIMAP, Lucknow-226015, India

[3]Chemical Sciences Division, CSIR—Central Institute of Medicinal and Aromatic Plants, P.O. CIMAP, Lucknow-226015, India

[4]Plant Biology and Systematics Department, CSIR—Central Institute of Medicinal and Aromatic Plants, Research Centre, Allalasandra, GKVK Post, Bengaluru-560065, India

[5]Academy of Scientific and Innovative Research (AcSIR), Ghaziabad-201002, India

[6]Department of Kayachikitsa, State Ayurvedic College, Lucknow-226001, India

*E-mail: dn.mani@cimap.res.in; dayanandanm@yahoo.com

ABSTRACT: Due to the moderate increase in the rate of morbidity and mortality in cases of anaphylaxis in the past few decades, the question that has arisen is - how to prevent this disease? Anaphylaxis and asthma are type-I hypersensitivity reaction and mast cells are the key mediators. In the classical texts of Ayurveda, various medicinal plants are reported to be useful in the treatment of allergy and upper respiratory tract disorders, but their role in mast cell-mediated allergic anaphylaxis has not yet been fully investigated. Therefore, our aim was to screen those medicinal plants, which have the potential to inhibit vascular permeability, leukocyte migration and allergic mediator (cytokines and mast cells) production. The anti-histaminic activity analysis was carried out by determining the percentage mortality in mice that received mast cell degranulator (compound-48/80) and studying the effect of test plant extracts on the elevated histamine level upon mast cell degranulation. Test plant extracts, when administered orally 1-h before compound-48/80 injection at 200 mg/kg body weight dose, inhibited the induced anaphylactic shock. Decrease in histamine level in blood confirmed that the test plant extracts stabilized mast cell degranulation. The present study also showed an improved survival rate in mice. Results suggested that some of the selected plant extracts were found to be highly effective against the release of histamine from mast cells. Further, identification of the leads from the shortlisted plants will provide a potential remedy for treating allergic disorders in future.

Keywords: Mast Cells, Degranulation, Anaphylaxis, Ayurveda, Allergy, Compound-48/80.

1. INTRODUCTION

Allergy, specifically immediate-type hypersensitivity reaction including bronchial asthma, systemic anaphylaxis, rhinoconjunctivitis, atopic dermatitis, and eczema, is the most common human disease and, its prevalence has been continuously increasing over the past few years (Choi and Yan, 2009). Bronchial asthma is an inflammatory disorder of airways, which affects about 300 million people worldwide irrespective of the age group and is expected to increase by ~50% every decade (Balaha *et al.*, 2012). Asthma is a critical health problem, whereby the exact mechanism of disease progression is not yet fully understood but antigen induced-antibody production, inflammation of bronchioles and airway hyper-responsiveness are the hallmarks, which have been well studied documented (Lee *et al.*, 2006). In asthma, there is a complex mechanism such as narrowing of arteries associated with the modulation of mast cell levels, lymphocytes, cytokines, and other inflammatory mediators (Kumari and Dutta, 2013). National Institute of Health defines asthma as a chronic inflammatory disease in which different cells and cell contents play a vital role. Allergic airway inflammation causes an increase in bronchial hyper-responsiveness to a variety of stimuli (Balaha *et al.*, 2012). Allergic airway hyper-responsiveness is often driven by the imbalance of Th_1/Th_2 (T-helper cells) cytokines, which leads to the development of increased IgE and eosinophil levels in the airways. On the basis of growing understanding related to the pathogenesis of allergic asthma, various management strategies have been developed, which include inhaled corticosteroids and β2 agonists that mainly focus on reducing inflammation and relaxing bronchoconstriction. However, these therapies result in undesired systemic and local side effects on high doses or repeated consumption for long term use. Thus researchers are trying to seek and validate other therapies, which have negligible or fewer side effects, preferably taken from natural sources for the treatment of allergy and asthma (Shin *et al.*, 2014). Moreover, mast cells are important inflammatory mediators in allergy, allergic asthma and anaphylaxis. Upon activation, these mast cells secrete vasoactive and proinflammatory mediators such as histamine, serotonin, TNF, cytokines and, proteases. Previous studies have proved that mast cells play a crucial role in the pathogenesis of inflammatory disorders (Balaji *et al.*, 2014).

Several medicinal plants mentioned in *Ayurveda* texts possess the potential to treat upper respiratory tract diseases. These herbal medicines are useful in relieving bronchial asthma as well as convulsive bronchitis. Most anti-asthmatic herbal drugs act on β-adrenergic receptors causing relaxation of bronchial smooth muscles or act as bronchodilators. Some of the herbal medicines act as mast cell stabilizers, anti-allergic, anti-inflammatory, anti-anaphylactic, anti-spasmodics and inhibitory mediators including cytokines, leukotrienes, lipooxygenase and, cyclooxygenase. Here, on the basis of Indian traditional knowledge, we tried to screen and validate the anti-allergic activity of some medicinal plants like, *Albizia lebbeck*, *Clerodendrum serratum* (synonym, *Rotheca serrata*), *Curcuma longa*, *Ephedra gerardiana*, *Ocimum sanctum* (synonym, *Ocimum tenuiflorum*), *Onosma bracteatum* (synonym, *Onosma bracteata*), *Solanum surattense* (synonyms, *Solanum virginianum*, *Solanum xanthocarpum*), on compound 48/80-induced systemic anaphylaxis in mice.

2. MATERIAL AND METHODS

2.1 Drugs and Chemicals

Compound-48/80 (2-[4-methoxy-3, 5-bis[[2-methoxy-5-(2-methylaminoethyl) phenyl] methyl] phenyl] - N-methylethanamine) (Figure 2) was obtained from Sigma Aldrich Co. (St. Louis, MO, USA), mouse histamine ELISA kit was procured from QAYEE-BIO (Shanghai, China) and other chemicals were purchased from Hi-Media Laboratories Pvt. Ltd., India.

2.2 Plant Collection and Authentication

Fresh plant materials were collected and authenticated by Dr. V. Sundaresan, CRC (CSIR-CIMAP Research Centre), Bengaluru, who also provided their voucher specimen numbers (Table 1).

Table 1: Voucher Specimen Numbers of all the Selected Plants

S. No.	*Plant Name*	*Part Used*	*Common Name*	*Family*	*CSIR-CIMAP Voucher No.*
1.	*Albizia lebbeck* (L.) Benth	Bark	*Sirish*	Fabaceae	CIMAP – 122
2.	*Clerodendrum serratum* (L.) Moon	Root	*Bharangi*	Lamiaceae	CIMAP – 126
3.	*Curcuma longa* L.	Rhizome	*Haldi*	Zingiberaceae	CIMAP – 123
4.	*Ephedra gerardiana* Wall. ex. Stapf	Stem	*Somlata*	Ephedraceae	CIMAP – 130
5.	*Ocimum sanctum* (syn.)	Leaves	*Tulsi*	Lamiaceae	CIMAP – 124
6.	*Onosma bracteatum*	Leaves	*Gojihva*	Boraginaceae	CIMAP – 128
7.	*Solanum surattense* Burm. f.	Whole plant	*Kantkari*	Solanaceae	CIMAP – 127

2.3 Preparation of Plant Extracts

All the plants were freshly collected and, cold infusion (*hima*) was prepared after washing and grinding the plant material. Cold infusion extracts were prepared by soaking the shade-dried plant material overnight in distilled water and filtering using muslin-cloth. Thereafter, the extracts were concentrated on a rotary evaporator (BUTCHI; R-210, Switzerland) and lyophilized (Martin & Christ).

2.4 Standardization of Prepared Extracts

The extracts were standardized as per the WHO guidelines for quality standards. The following parameters were performed: organoleptic properties, total ash value, alcohol- and water-soluble extractives, loss on drying, pH value, heavy metal analysis and, preliminary phytochemical screening.

2.5 Experimental Animals

Sixty *Swiss albino* mice (20–25 g) were used in the study. All the animals were acclimatized for a week before the experiment and maintained at normal laboratory conditions of humidity, temperature and light. The animals were provided with the commercial standard diet and water *ad libitum*. The protocol for the experiment (CIMAP/IAEC/2016-19/27) was approved by the Institutional Animal Ethics Committee constituted under the CPCSEA (Committee for the Purpose of Control and Supervision of Experiments on Animals), New Delhi, India. Six animals were used per group making a total of sixty animals for the ten groups.

2.6 Compound-48/80-induced Systemic Anaphylaxis

Mice received an intraperitoneal injection of compound-48/80 (8 mg/kg, body weight) as mast cell degranulator. All the test plant extracts were administered 1 hr before the injection of compound-48/80 (n = 6/group) at the dose of 200 mg/kg, body weight, orally. Another group was orally administered ketotifen at 10 mg/kg body weight as a positive control drug. Mortality was recorded for 1 hr after the induction of anaphylactic shock in mice (El-Agamy 2012). Blood was collected from the retro-orbital plexus of all the mice and the serum was separated for further histamine analysis.

2.7 Statistical Analysis

Statistical analysis performed with the help of InStat GraphPad software (version 3.0, USA). Difference between means was calculated by one-way analysis of variance followed by Student's t-test (n = 6 mice/group). Results were considered statistically significant when $P < 0.05$.

3. RESULTS

3.1 Short Listing of Anti-allergic Plants on the basis of Traditional Knowledge of *Ayurveda*

In *Ayurveda,* the term *Kasa* is frequently used for cough or bronchitis. In classical texts of *Ayurveda* like, *Charak Samhita Chikitsasthana* Chapter 18; *Sushruta Samhita,* Volume 6: *Uttara-tantra* Chapter 52;

Astanghridyam Chikitsasthana Chapter 3; and *Madhavnidan Kasnidan*, detailed discussion is available on *Kasa roga* and its *chikitsa* (treatment). *Kasa roga* is a disease of the *Prana Vaha Srotas* (respiratory system), which occurs due to imbalance (vitiation) of *Kapha* and *Vata doshas*. *Kasa* occurs when *Apana Vayu* (originating from kidney) is obstructed resulting in an increase in upward motion. Vitiation of *Udana Vayu* (originating from throat) propels the air upward and out of the body. *Vata* may however lodge in the chest, back, or head, resulting in pain and repeated coughing. *Kasa* begins with the vitiation of *Apana Vayu* in the *Purishavaha Srota* (large intestine). *Vata* eventually overflows into circulation *(Raktavaha Srota)* and relocates to the *Prana Vaha Srota* (respiratory system). *Kasanat Kasa*, the vitiated *Vayu* moves forcefully upwards through the *Kanth* (throat) producing a sound typical of a broken bronze vessel (*bhinna Kansya*). As per *Charak*, five types of *Kasa* have been described in *Ayurveda* - *Vataja Kasa* (*Vata* vitiation), *Pittaja Kasa* (*Pitta* vitiation), *Kaphaja Kasa* (*Kapha* vitiation), *Ksataja Kasa* (due to injuries in chest), and *Ksaya Kasa* (due to diseases like tuberculosis). According to the *Charak Samhita*, various factors causing the *Kasa roga* are *Dhooma* (smoke, smokers cough), *Raja* (dust), *Ati Ruksha Annasevan* (dry food, chips, French fries), *Ativyayama* (excess exercise, heavy weight lifting, running, jumping beyond your capacity), *Diwaswapna* (daytime sleeping), *Ati maithuna* (excessive sexual activity), excessive *Guru, Sheeta* (both food and environment), and *Kashayaja Kasa* (tubercular cough). For the treatment of *Kasa roga, Kapha Vata Shamak Chikitsa and Ushn prakriti* (hot nature) medicinal plants have been prescribed in *Ayurveda*.

कसति शिरः कंठाधूर्वे गच्छति वायुरिति कासः।
कस-गतौ इत्यस्मात् कस्नात् कासः।। *Charka Samhita, Shlok-1*

In the process of respiration, if any foreign particulate matter is present in the respiratory tract then the disturbed air present in respiratory system tries to forcefully evacuate it. During the process of evacuation, swelling occurs in the respiratory tract, causing a disturbing sound known as *Kasa*.

In the present study, we have used the aforementioned knowledge described in classical Ayurvedic texts regarding treatments for *Kasa roga* based on medicinal plants and tried to select some of them for proper scientific validation based on modern parameters (Tables 1–3).

Table 2: Standardization of Plant Materials

S. No.	*Test Parameters*	*Albizia lebbeck*	*Clerodendrum serratum*	*Curcuma longa*	*Ephedra gerardiana*	*Ocimum sanctum*	*Onosma bracteatum*	*Solanum surattense*
1.	*Aq. Extract yield (%)	21.50	16.16	21.85	12.02	5.2	14.69	10.65
2.	Color	Brown	Cream	Yellow	Brown	Green	Green	Green
3.	Odour	Bitter	Bitter	Bitter	Bitter	Bitter	Bitter	Bitter
4.	Loss on drying (%)	14	9	8	21	15	15	24
5.	Total ash values (%)	13	7	11	37	24	42	12
6.	Acid-insoluble ash (%)	2	2	2	4	5	14	3
7.	Water soluble extractives (%)	0.13	0.29	0.38	0.29	0.64	0.23	0.11
8.	Alcohol-soluble extractives (%)	0.11	0.2	0.73	0.15	0.47	0.06	0.04
9.	pH	5.6	7.7	6.4	5.6	6.1	7.0	5.2

*(% w/w)

Table 3: Preliminary Phytochemical Screening

S. No.	*Tests*	*Albizia lebbeck*	*Clerodendrum serratum*	*Curcuma longa*	*Ephedra gerardiana*	*Ocimum sanctum*	*Onosma bracteatum*	*Solanum surattense*
1.	Alkaloids	+	+	+	+	+	+	+
2.	Glycosides	+	+	–	+	+	+	+
3.	Flavonoids	+	+	+	+	+	+	+
4.	Terpenoids	+	+	+	+	+	+	+
5.	Steroids	+	+	+	+	+	+	–
6.	Saponins	+	+	–	+	+	–	+
7.	Phenolics	+	+	–	+	+	+	+
8.	Tannins	+	+	–	+	+	+	+

+ Present, – Absent

3.2 Plant Extracts Reduce the Effect of Compound-48/80-Induced Anaphylactic Shock

Compound-48/80 is a prominent reagent to study anaphylaxis as it causes an immediate hypersensitivity reaction. The intraperitoneal injection of compound-48/80 caused 100% mortality in the negative control group. In comparison, treatment with plant extracts an hour before compound-48/80 challenge protected the mice against the anaphylactic shock and reduced the mortality. Complete (100%) mortality was observed after compound-48/80 challenged group was administered with 200 mg/kg of *O. sanctum* extract, whereas mice survived in all other plant extract groups at 200 mg/kg dose (Figure 1).

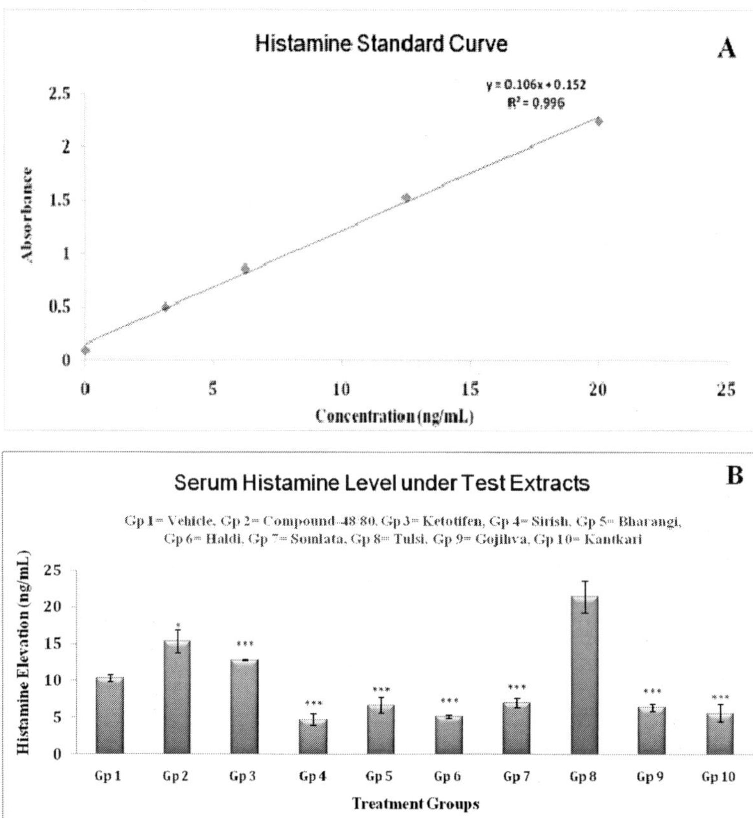

Fig. 1: Effect of selected plant extracts on compound-48/80-induced anaphylactic shock in mice. **A.** Histamine standard curve. **B.** Effect of test extracts on the elevated histamine level in blood-serum histamine level in blood-serum after compound-48/80-induced anaphylactic shock. Above data are represented as mean ± SEM where *** = $p < 0.001$ and * = $p < 0.05$.

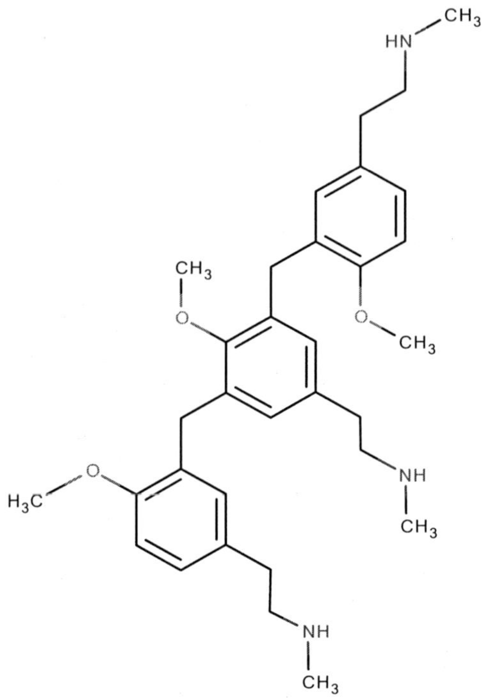

Fig. 2: Chemical Structure of Compound-48/80

4. DISCUSSION

Phytochemical screening of plant extracts indicated the presence of major phytochemicals, such as saponins, flavonoids, alkaloids, and glycosides (Table 3). Previous studies reported that saponins possess mast cell stabilizing, antiallergic, and antihistaminic potential. Glycosides exhibit antihistaminic activity through spasmolytic activity by relaxing the smooth muscle of trachea and also show bronchodilator activity. Flavonoids are known to attenuate basophil histamine release and neutrophil beta-glucuronidase release. They also inhibit the release of histamine-induced by compound-48/80 administration and therefore, possess in *vivo* antiallergic activity (Taur and Patil, 2011). Allergies are caused due to inappropriate functions of the immune system, which often occur due to the presence of various allergens such as pollen, animal dung, fast foods, paints and insects. Presently, the problem related to immune dysfunction, has moderately increased. Allergic disorders include allergic rhinitis, systemic anaphylaxis, pruritis, and asthma. Mast cells are the primary mediators of allergic reactions, which are activated by coupling with high affinity IgE (immunoglobulin-E) receptors. Mast cell-derived pro-inflammatory mediators, particularly TNF-α, IL-1β and, IL-6 play a crucial role in promoting the inflammation and allergic response. The pre-stored cytokines are released but upon activation of mast cells cytokines are also newly synthesized for release. TNF-α triggers inflammation, leukocyte infiltration and, tissue fibrosis and also acts as an initiator of cytokine associated inflammatory condition by the stimulation of cytokine production. IL-1β is an important mediator in the cytokine family, which administers the inflammatory and immune functions. IL-6 is produced by mast cells and its accumulation causes skin allergic disease (Chai *et al.*, 2013). Primary cause of anaphylaxis is IgE-mediated hypersensitivity reaction. Hence its treatment might involve the use of immunotherapeutic agents that decrease the production of IgE. The standard drug ketotifen is an H1-antihistaminic with some crymoglycate-like action (stimulation of immunogenic and inflamematory cells and release of other mediators is inhibited). The anti-anaphylactic and mast cell stabilizing effect of plant extracts might be attributed to the suppression of IgE antibody production, which causes mast cell degranulation. Besides, mast cell stabilization and anti-allergic activity of medicinal plants might be due to the presence of major phytochemicals (Balaji *et al.*, 2014). Since the need of the day was to find out solutions for the treatment of allergy and its related disorders, in this study, we screened some medicinal plants mentioned in *Ayurveda* texts and found that they attenuate the allergic symptoms in compound-48/80-induced systemic anaphylaxis in mice. Anaphylactic allergic reactions are immediate-type allergic reactions induced by compound-48/80, which result in the activation of histamine release through the mast cells and also activate the G-proteins, follow extrusion of β-hexosaminidase, histamine and, various cytokines. Histamine released from mast cells is stored in secretory granules. Compound-48/80 and various other agents induce mast cell degranulation, which results in anaphylactic shock in humans and mammals (Chai *et al.*, 2013). Initially, we standardized the occurrence of allergic reactions due to the administration of compound-48/80 at the dose of 8 mg/kg body weight, intraperitoneally. Later, we validated the effect of test extracts at the dose of 200 mg/kg, body weight, orally against anaphylactic shock induced by compound-48/80 administration. The results obtained showed that our test extracts protected the mice from mortality after anaphylactic shock induced by mast cell degranulator (compound-48/80), which was revealed in the histamine analysis of blood-serum (Figure 1). Previous studies reported that mast cell-mediated allergy is associated with an increase in Th_2 cytokines and, production of IgE. IL-4 (Th_2 cytokine) supports B-cell differentiation to plasma cells, which secrete antigen-specific IgE and facilitate proliferation of mast cells. It has been observed that IgE binds to the receptors present on the surface of mast cells and subsequently release allergic mediators that promote immediate-type hypersensitivity reactions, mucus secretion, extrusion of cell followed by an increase in vascular permeability. It is well established that compound-48/80 releases histamine from the mast cells following depletion of tissue histamine level (Lee *et al.*, 2010). Most of the plant extracts tested by us were found to inhibit histamine release, thereby indicating that they possessed an inhibitory potential against the anaphylactic shock induced by compound-48/80 in the mouse model.

5. CONCLUSION

It is important to scientifically validate traditional knowledge using modern parameters in order to increase its acceptability and broaden the horizons for traditional systems of medicine like *Ayurveda* (Shukla *et al.*, 2013). In this direction, the present study contributes towards the scientific validation of the anti-allergic property of selected Ayurvedic plants. The results in the current study revealed that all the test extracts inhibit histamine release as shown in mouse serum analysis. Thus, chemical compounds present in the test extracts might be used to prevent dysfunction of the immune response caused due to allergic reactions. Still, it remains to be elucidated as to what type of chemical compounds and signal factors are modulated by the test extracts. Further studies are required to analyze role of membrane receptors and gene expression in allergic disorders.

ACKNOWLEDGEMENT

Authors are thankful to Director CSIR-CIMAP, Lucknow, for providing necessary laboratory facilities and financial assistance.

CONFLICT OF INTEREST

There is no conflict of interest.

REFERENCES

[1] Balaha, M.F, Tanaka, H., Yamashita, H., Abdel Rahman, M.N. and Inagaki, N. (2012). Oral *Nigella sativa* oil ameliorates ovalbumin-induced bronchial asthma in mice. *International Immunopharmacology* 14: 224–231.

[2] Balaji, G., Chalamaiah, M., Hanumanna, P., Vamsikrishna, B., Jagadeesh Kumar, D. and Venu Babu, V. (2014). Mast cell stabilizing and anti-anaphylactic activity of aqueous extract of green tea (*Camellia sinensis*). *International Journal of Veterinary Science and Medicine* 2: 89–94.

[3] Chai, O.H., Shon, D.H., Han, E.H., Kim, H.T., Song, C.H. (2013). Effects of *Anemarrhena asphodeloides* on IgE-mediated passive cutaneous anaphylaxis, compound 48/80-induced systemic anaphylaxis and mast cell activation. *Experimental and Toxicologic Pathology* 65: 419–426.

[4] Choi, Y.H. and Yan, G.H. (2009). Anti-allergic effects of scoparone on mast cell-mediated allergy model. *Phytomedicine* 16: 1089–1094.

[5] El-Agamy, D.S. (2012). Anti-allergic effects of nilotinib on mast cell-mediated anaphylaxis like reactions. *European Journal of Pharmacology* 680: 115–121.

[6] Kumari, S. and Dutta, A, (2013). Protective effect of *Eleteria cardamomum* (L.) Maton against Pan masala induced damage in lung of male Swiss mice. *Asian Pacific Journal of Tropical Medicine* 6: 525–531.

[7] Lee, D.-H., Kim, S.-H., Eun, J.-S. and Shin, T.-Y. (2006). *Mosla dianthera* inhibits mast cell-mediated allergic reactions through the inhibition of histamine release and inflammatory cytokine production. *Toxicology and Applied Pharmacology,* 216: 479–484.

[8] Lee, M.Y., Lee, N.H., Jung, D., Lee, J.A., Seo, C.S., Lee, H., Kim, J.H. and Shin, H.K. (2010). Protective effects of allantoin against ovalbumin (OVA)-induced lung inflammation in a murine model of asthma. *International Immunopharmacology* 10: 474–480.

[9] Shin, I.-S., Park, J.-W., Shin, N.-R., Jeon, C.-M., Kwon, O.-K., Kim, J.-S., Kim, J.-C., Oh, S.-R., Ahn, K.-S. (2014). Melatonin reduces airway inflammation in ovalbumin-induced asthma. *Immunobiology* 219: 901–908.

[10] Shukla, A.K., Mall, M., Rai, S.K., Singh, S., Nair, P., Parashar, G., Shasany, A.K., Singh, S.C., Joshi, V.K. and Khanuja, S.P.S. (2013). A transcriptomic approach for exploring the molecular basis for dosha-balancing property-based classification of plants in Ayurveda. *Molecular Biology Reports* 40: 3255–3262.

[11] Taur, D.J. and Patil, R.Y. (2011). Mast cell stabilizing and antiallergic activity of *Abrus precatorius* in the management of asthma. *Asian Pacific Journal of Tropical Medicine* 4: 46–49.

Efficacy of Mosquito Repellent Formulations from Clove, Citronella, Eucalyptus Essential Oils and Neem Oil

Gadae Maung Maung[1], Maung Maung Mya[2], Mar Mar Myint[3], Yu Yu Nwe Oo[4], Kay Thi Kyaw[5], Myat Chaw Su[6] and Phyu Phyu Win[7]

[1, 3–6] Pharmaceutical Research Department, Chemical Technology Research Centre, Dept. of Research and Innovation, Myanmar

[2]Department of Medical Research, Ministry of Health and Sport, Myanmar

[7]Chemical Technology Research Centre, Department of Research and Innovation, Ministry of Education, Myanmar

E-mail: [1]gadaemgmg.gd@gmail.com; [2]dr.mgmgmya@gmail.com; [3]zeroamber@gmail.com; [4]yuyunweooo@gmail.com; [5]kaythikyaw.ygn@gmail.com; [6]chawsu.myat@gmail.com: [7]dripphyuwin@gmail.com

ABSTRACT: This study aims to assess the repellent efficacy of the formulations of mosquito repellents including clove, citronella, eucalyptus essential oils and neem oil. Vector-borne diseases such as dengue and malaria are health problems in Myanmar, hence, vegetable oils and essential oils from herbal plants are used in herbal mosquito repellent formulation. In this research work, clove essential oil was extracted by hydro-distillation. Other essential oils such as citronella essential oil and eucalyptus essential oil and ingredients such as neem oil, virgin coconut oil, soybean oil and olive oil were bought from market. Clove, citronella, eucalyptus essential oils and neem oil were used as active ingredients in formulations. Virgin coconut, olive and soybean oils were used to prevent evaporation of essential oils. Efficacy of two formulations was evaluated by using World Health Organization Guidelines for efficacy testing mosquito repellents for human skins. Laboratory reared female mosquito, Aedesaegypti, was used for repellent test. The results showed that formulation (1) provided 100%, 98%, 94%, 80%, 72% and 47% protection for 30, 60, 90, 120, 150 and 180 minutes and formulation (2) provided 100%, 100%, 94%, 85%, 83% and 79% protection for 30, 60, 90, 120, 150 and 180 minutes against

Aedesaegypti respectively. The longest duration of 100% repellency of formulation (2) was 60 minutes and 30 minutes for formulation (1). Formulation (2) provided higher efficacy than formulation (1).

Keywords: Repellent Efficiency, Clove Oil, Eucalyptus Oil, Neem Oil, Citronella Oil, Aedesaegypti.

1. INTRODUCTION

Mosquito-borne diseases or mosquito-borne illnesses are diseases caused by bacteria, viruses or parasites transmitted by mosquitoes. They can transmit disease without being affected themselves. Nearly, 700 million people get a mosquito-borne illness each year resulting in over one million deaths.[2] Diseases transmitted by mosquitoes include malaria, dengue, West Nile virus, chikungunya, yellow fever, lymphatic filariasis and Zika fever.[10] Dengue is carried by *Aedes* mosquitoes. *Aedesaegypti* is the main vector of dengue virus in urban areas and *Aedesalbopictus* is the vector in rural areas. The main vector of dengue virus in Myanmar is *Aedesaegypti* and secondary vector is *Aedesalbopictus.*[7]

A number of interventions to control and prevent mosquito-borne diseases exist. Some interventions currently in use include using long-lasting insecticidal nets, indoor residual spraying, outdoor spraying, addition of chemicals to water and other insect repellents.[10]

Insect repellent may be divided into 2 basic chemical classes: 1) the synthetic chemicals, such as DEET (N, N-Diethyl-meta-toluamide), picaridin (KBR-3023), and ethylbutylacetyl-aminopropionate (IR3535); and 2) the plant-derived oils and synthetics, such as oil of lemon, eucalyptus, oil of citronella and permethrin.[6]

The field of repellent development from plants is extremely fertile due to wealth of insecticidal compounds available in plants, which act as defences against various pathogens.[5] The plant products that are in use include a wide range of substances from crude plant extracts to essential oils and isolated compounds. Synthetic derivatives of many plant compounds with repellent properties are also in use. It is well known that the essential oil repellents from plants are potential sources of compounds with bioactivities against vector mosquitoes.[9]

Essential oils being complex mixtures of volatile organic compounds are generally produced as secondary metabolites in plants. They are constituted of hydrocarbons (terpenes and susquiterpenes) and oxygenated compounds (alcohol, esters, ethers, aldehydes, ketones, lactones and phenols). Essential oils extracted from different families that are Myrtaceae, Verbenaceae, Lamiaceae, Poaceae and Caesalpiniceae have shown high repellency against arthropod species.[1]

Recently, commercial repellent products containing plant-based ingredients have gained increasing popularity among consumers, as these are commonly perceived as "safe" in comparison to long-established synthetic repellents although this is sometimes a misconception.[12]

2. MATERIALS AND METHODS

2.1 Hydrodistillation of Clove Essential Oil

Clove essential oil was extracted by hydrodistillation.[4] 200 g of dried clove (*Syzygiumaromaticum*) buds in 1 L flask was submitted to hydrodistillation for 8 hours. The distillate was separated into oil and hydro layer using a separating funnel.

2.2 Collection of Ingredients

Eucalyptus and citronella essential oil, neem oil, soybean oil, olive oil and virgin coconut oil were bought from market.

2.3 Preparation of Active Ingredient Mixture

2.5 percentage of total active ingredient mixture was prepared with ethanol as detailed.

Citronella essential oil	1.87%
Clove essential oil	0.13%
Eucalyptus essential oil	0.31%
Neem oil	0.19%

2.4 Mosquito Repellent Activity Testing

The repellent activity test was done by the method of World Health Organization (2009). In this method, estimation of effective dose and estimation of complete protection time include. In these tests, 5 to 7 days old female mosquitoes are put into 35–40 cm per side mosquito cage. The mosquito density is 50 to 100 mosquitoes. Equal ratio of male and female volunteers is suitable. To find effective dose, the arm applied with control solvent and the test solution are inserted into the cage for 30 seconds and the test is continued until the effective dose is found. For estimation of complete protection time, the procedure is the same but the control and treated arm are put for 3 minutes.

2.4.1 *Dose Effect Analysis of Active Ingredient Mixture*

Three to five day old 50 female mosquitoes (*Aedesaegypti*) were starved for 24 hours before testing, and kept in a steel net cage (59 cm × 59 cm × 59 cm). Four volunteers' forearm area of volunteers (n = 4 individuals) were used as test areas or exposed areas. The untreated areas that were fingers were protected with gloves and tied with rubber bands to prevent mosquito biting. The volunteers' left forearm areas were used as control. The right forearm exposed area was applied with 1 milliliter of the test solution mixture (2.5 g/100 ml ethanol). The treated forearm was inserted into mosquito filled cage for 30 seconds and recorded the number of biting or landing mosquito during 30 seconds. The incremental dose was applied until the dose that protected mosquito biting within 30 seconds was observed.

2.4.2 *Mosquito Repellent Activity of Active Ingredient Mixture*

After finding the 30 second protection dose of active ingredients, the repellency test for active ingredient mixture was done. The procedure for repellency test was nearly the same like procedure in searching dose. The control area was also inserted into cage for 3 minutes after swabbing 1 ml of ethanol solution. The resulting dose was prepared to dissolve in ethanol. 1 ml of this solution was applied to the right forearm area. It was inserted into mosquito filled cage for 3 minutes to record the number of landing or biting mosquitoes. The control area was inserted into the mosquito cage again to get the average number of landing or biting mosquitoes. The percentage protection was calculated by using the following formula:

$$P = \frac{C - T}{C} \times 100$$

Where, P is percent protection, T is the number of landing or biting mosquitoes on treated arm and C is the number of landing or biting mosquitoes on the control arm of the same individual. C is the average number of landing or biting mosquitoes on the untreated arm.

2.4.3 *Formulations of Mosquito Repellents*

Formulation (1) was prepared according to the 30 seconds protection dose. The concentrations of active ingredients for formulation (2) were 2 times of that of formulation (1). The ingredients for formulation (1) and (2) were as follows:

(a) *Ingredients of formulation (1)*

Clove essential oil	(1%)
Citronella essential oil	(15%)
Neem oil	(1.5%)
Eucalyptus essential oil	(2.5%)
Virgin coconut oil	(30%)
Soybean oil	(30%)
Olive oil	(10%)
Ethanol	(10%)

(b) *Ingredients of formulation (2)*

Clove essential oil	(2%)
Citronella essential oil	(30%)
Neem oil	(3%)
Eucalyptus essential oil	(5%)
Virgin coconut oil	(20%)
Soybean oil	(20%)
Olive oil	(10%)
Ethanol	(10%)

2.4.4 *Repellent Activity Testing of Mosquito Repellent Formulations*

In this procedure, 50 female mosquitoes (*Aedesaegypti*) starved for 24 h were used for repellency test. The exposed area was the volunteer's right forearm area and the control area was the left forearm. 1 ml of ethanol was applied to the left forearm area and inserted into the cage for 3 minutes. The number of landing or biting mosquitoes within 3 minutes was recorded. 0.5 ml of formulations was swabbed on the right forearm area. After that, the right forearm was inserted into the mosquito cage and let it in cage for 3 minutes to check the number of landing or biting mosquitoes. The procedure was repeated every 30 minutes until the repellency was declined under 50%. The left arm was inserted into the mosquito cage again to get the average number of landing or biting mosquito. The percentage protection of mosquito repellent was calculated by the above formula.

In every repellency test, four volunteers participated. The tests were done three times and the results were calculated by mean of three tests.

3. RESULTS AND DISCUSSION

The only active ingredient mixture protected 67%, 50%, 34%, 22% against *Aedesaegypti* for 30, 60, 90 and 120 minutes. Mosquito repellent formulation (1) provided 100%, 98%, 94%, 80%, 72% and 47% for 30, 60, 90, 120, 150 and 180 minutes. Mosquito repellent formulation (2) provided 100%, 100%, 94%, 85%, 83% and 79% for 30, 60, 90, 120, 150 and 180 minutes.

Mosquitoes alone transmit diseases that are malaria, filaria, dengue haemorrhagic fever, dengue fever, zika and yellow fever to more than 700 million people annually.[3] Therefore, the control of mosquitoes is an important public health problem around the world. Chemicals and synthetic insecticides used for control of vectors are causing irreversible damage to the ecosystem and human beings and animals.[7]

Many researchers have shown that plant essential oils have better repellent efficacy rather than plant extracts. However, all the essential oils are highly volatile and this contributes to their poor longevity as mosquito repellents.[8] This is a big problem for mosquito repellent containing essential oils as active ingredients. Reducing of evaporation of essential oils is a solution for this problem. In this study, the oils that are soybean oil, virgin coconut oil and olive oil are used to prevent evaporation without harmful effects to humans.

In this study, formulation (1) containing 20% active ingredients (0.5 ml used in repellency test for formulation (1) showed 100% repellency for 30 minutes and formulation (2) containing 40% active ingredients (0.5 ml used in repellency test for formulation (2) showed 100% repellency for 60 minutes.

Studies have shown that repellents based on essential oils generally do not provide sufficient repellent effect against mosquito bites (in terms of 100% repellent effect maintained for a long duration) compared to what is provided by DEET, which provides between 6–8 h of complete (100%) repellent effect. It is well understood that such limitation is caused by the high volatile nature of the essential oils.[8] In order to overcome this limitation, the techniques applied in the production of plant-based repellents are making use of fixative materials such as vanillin, polymers, and adjuvant to control the volatility of the essential oils. Although, such fixative materials were shown to have helped in increasing the repellent effect of the formulations (compared to their pure oil form), the duration of the repellent effect achieved is yet to match the duration of the synthetic repellent. Most of the plant-based repellent products in the market have < 2 h of 100% repellent effect. Hence several formulation techniques have been developed to improve current techniques such as the microencapsulation technique.[13] This study reports that instead of the use of microencapsulation, carrier oils that are olive oil, soybean oil and virgin coconut oil are used to prolong the protection.

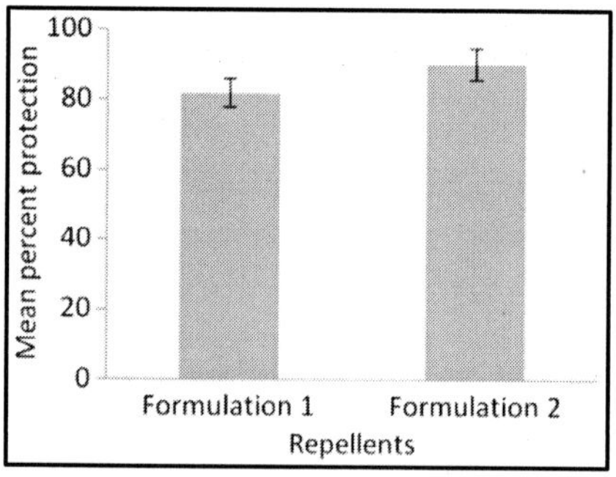

Fig. 1: Mean Percent Protection of Repellents (Two formulations)

4. CONCLUSION

In this study, the formulation (1) provided 100% protection for 30 minutes while the formulation (2) provided 100% protection for 60 minutes. Only active ingredient mixture protected 67% but formulation (1) could do 100% for 30 minutes because other ingredients that were olive oil, virgin coconut oil and soybean oil could reduce evaporation of active ingredients. The non-active ingredients used in formulations were natural and also good for skin.

ACKNOWLEDGEMENTS

I would like to express my special thanks of gratitude to Ministry of Education for financial support. I sincerely thank to Dr. Kyaw Zin Thant (Director General, retired) who allowed mosquito repellent efficacy testing at Department of Medical Research. My thanks also go to staff from Medical Entomology Research Division, Department of Medical Research for their valuable help in my research work.

REFERENCES

[1] Kalita, Bhupen; Bora, Somi and Sharma, Anil Kumar (2013). Plant Essential Oils as Mosquito Repellent—A Review. *International Journal of Research and Development in Pharmacy and Life Sciences;* Vol. 3, No. 1, pp. 741–747, ISSN: 2278-0238.

[2] Caraballo and Hector (2014). Emergency Department Management of Mosquito-Borne Illness: Malaria, Dengue, and West Nile Virus. *Emergency Medicine Practice;* May 2014, 16(5).

[3] Govindarajan, M., Jebanesan, A., Pushpanathan, T. and Samidurai, K. (2008). Studies on effect of Acalyohaindisa L. (Euphorbiaceae) leaf extract on the malaria vector *Anopheles stephensi* Liston (Diptera: Culicidae). Parasitology Research 2008; 103(3): 691–695.

[4] Guan, Wenqiang; Li, Shufen; Yan, Ruixiang; Tang, Shaokun and Quan, Can. (2007). Comparison of essential oils of clove buds extracted with supercritical carbon dioxide and other three traditional extraction methods. *Food Chemistry,* 101 (2007), 1558–1564.

[5] Harrewijn, P., Minks, A.K. and Mollema, C. (1995). Evolution of plant volatile production in insect-plant relationships. *Chemoecology,* 1995, 5:55–73.

[6] James, H. Diaz, M.D., MPH&TM, Dr P.H. (2016). Chemical and Plant-Based Insect Repellents: Efficacy, Safety, and Toxicity, *Wilderness & Environmental Medicine,* 27, 153–163.

[7] Maung, Maung Mya; Zar, Zar Aung; Chit, That New; Aye Win, Oo, Than, Myat Htay, *Sein Thaung and Yan Naung Maung Maung,* 2017. Larvicidal, Ovicidal and Repellent Effect of *Citrus hystrix* DC (Kaffir lime) fruit, peel and internal materials extracts on *Aedesaegypti* mosquitoes. *Journal of Biological Engineering Research and Review;* 4(1): 34–43.

[8] Phasomkusolsil, S. and Soonwera, M., Insect repellent activity of medicinal plant oils against Aedesaegypti (Linn.), Anopheles minimus (Theobald) and Culexquinquefasciatus Say based on protection mean biting rate. *Southeast Asian J Trop Med Public Health* 2010; 41: 831–40, 23.

[9] Tiwary, M., Naik, S.N., Tewary, D.K., Mittal, P.K. and Yadav, S. (2007). Chemical composition and larvicidal activities of essential oil of

Zanthoxylumaromatum DC (Rutaceae) against three mosquito vectors. *J vector Borne Dis.* 2007; 44:198–204.

[10] World Health Organization (2014). A Global Brief on Vector-Borne Diseases, WHO 2014. WHO/DCO/WHD/2014.1.2014.1.

[11] World Health Organization Guidelines for efficacy testing mosquito repellents for human skins. 2009. WHO Geneva 2009. WHO/HTM/NTD/WHOPES/2009.4.

[12] Martar, Ferreira Maia and Sarah J., Moore (2011). Plant-based insect repellents: A review of their efficacy, development and testing. *Maia and Moore Malaria Journal.*

[13] Zurainee, M. Nor and Rohani, Ahmad. Repellent effect of micro-encapsulated essential oil in lotion formulation against mosquito bites. *Journal of vector borne diseases,* March 2017.

The Role of Apigenin in Different Zones of Porcine Articular Cartilage

P.Y. Sikosana and K.S.C.M. Motaung*

Tshwane University of Technology, Faculty of Science,
Department of Biomedical Sciences, Pretoria, South Africa
*E-mail: smotaung@gmail.com

ABSTRACT: Articular cartilage is a tissue which cannot repair itself after injury because it lacks neural, cellular and blood supply. Once damaged, it leads to osteoarthritis which is an irreversible disease with defective integrity of articular cartilage. The researcher explored the regenerative effects of the flavonoid compound called apigenin in the different zones of articular cartilage before damage. These were explored on the tissue's resident cells called chondrocytes by using microculture tetrazolium assay, CyQUANT cell proliferation assay, glycosamino-glycans assay, gene expression, histology and immunolocalisation of collagen type II. Apigenin successfully regenerated articular cartilage zones by stimulating collagen type II, aggrecan and cartilage oligomeric matrix protein which are fundamental for the tissue regeneration. In description, apigenin significantly stimulated chondrocyte proliferation in both superficial and middle zones of articular cartilage in microculture tetrazolium assay, CyQUANT cell proliferation assay, collagen type II immunolocalisation and histology analysis. Moreover, this flavonoid enhanced glycosaminoglycan content on both zones. Gene expression was more accumulated on day four than day seven. This study revealed the potential role of apigenin in articular cartilage injury.

Keywords: Apigenin, Articular Cartilage, Collagen Type II, Anti-Inflammatory, Growth Factors, Flavonoids.

1. INTRODUCTION

Articular cartilage (AC) is a highly specialised, resilient connective tissue that covers the ends of the articulating joints. Its function is to provide a smooth and frictionless contact surface, lubricate the joints and bear mechanical loads on them (Fox, Bedi & Rodeo, 2009; Milner, Robert & Gibson, 2012). It contains the extracellular matrix (ECM), which is a functional component, providing hydration required for lubrication. The ECM comprises a single cell line, the chondrocytes, contributing 2–3% of the tissue mass and playing a role in the synthesis and maintenance of the ECM. Water (contributing up to 80%); collagen (contributing between 12–21%), proteoglycans (contributing in the range of 6–10%) are the other major components of ECM. The remaining 2–3.5% is contributed by lipids, phospholipids, non-collagenous proteins and glycoproteins (Fox, Bedi & Rodeo, 2009; Moreira-Teixeira *et al.*, 2011; Mobasheri *et al.*, 2014).

Water plays a distinct role in the transportation and circulation of nutrients to chondrocytes for lubrication (Fox, Bedi & Rodeo, 2009). Collagen provides shear and tensile strength of the tissue (Lotz *et al.*, 2010). Proteoglycans are responsible for resistance to compressive forces and supply the cartilage with its osmotic properties (Pearle *et al.*, 2005; Fox, Bedi & Rodeo, 2009). Articular cartilage is made up of four distinct zones, namely the superficial, middle, deep and calcified zones, with varying functional and structural components (Pearle *et al.*, 2005). This connective tissue is deprived of nerves, lymphatic and blood vessels, thus restricting the repair mechanism after injury (Lewis & Smith, 2012). The chondrocytes of the normal AC synthesize and maintain the ECM, which is activated by anabolic (growth) factors such as bone morphogenic proteins (BMPs), transforming growth factor beta (TGF-β) and insulin-like growth factor (IGF). Imbalance in AC homeostasis is initiated by elevated synthesis of catabolic factors (cytokines) such as interleukin 1 beta (IL-1β) and tumour necrosis factor alpha (TNF-α), which are associated with AC degradation, in turn leading to commencement and development of osteoarthritis (OA) (Sandel & Aigner, 2001; Clouet *et al.*, 2009).

In description, OA is a chronic musculoskeletal disease characterised by the progressive disintegration of AC, as well as other joint tissues, causing affliction to the whole joint (Neogi, 2012, Mobasheri *et al.*, 2014). The effects associated with it involve pain, debilitated functionality and tissue destruction due to the stimulation of ECM degrading enzymes and inflammatory molecules (Lotz *et al.*, 2010; Waittenauer, Smith & Aden, 2013). In addition, this chronic disease is concomitant with necrosis, contributing to mechanical and cellular alterations in the structure and components of AC, causing stringency between the articulating joints due to synovitis (Lewis & Smith, 2012; Makela, Huttu & Korhonen, 2012; Mobasheri *et al.*, 2014).

Tchetina (2011) elucidated the AC zonal changes in early, mild and late OA. In early OA, changes take place in the zonal up-regulation of chondrocytes differentiation-related genes and matrix metalloproteinases (MMPs), which are responsible for ECM destruction, particularly in the superficial and middle zones, where initial AC destruction takes place.

In mild OA, changes in the superficial zone show evidence of low proteoglycan content and chondrocyte apoptosis (Pfander *et al.*, 2001; Dumond *et al.*, 2004; Fernandes *et al.*, 1998; Tchetina *et al.*, 2007). There are high levels of IL-1β in this zone. The superficial zone is gradually lost with clusters of chondrocytes. In the middle zone and deep zone the up-regulation of annexin VI and VIII antigens with chondrocyte clusters occurs. In late OA, there is severe fibrillation owing to the tissue degradation from the superficial zone descending to the calcified zone, with characteristic fractures and clefts (Pfander *et al.*, 2001; Wu *et al.*, 2002; Hollander *et al.*, 1995). There is evident collagen destruction surrounding the chondrocytes. Moreover, the up-regulation of MMP-13,-2,-11, adisintegrin and metalloprotease with thrombospondin motifs (ADAMTS) as well as collagen type I, II, III, VI, and X, is evident next to the surface of the AC, with extreme expression of IL-1β and tumour necrosis factor-α (TNF-α). In addition, in late OA, annexin VIII and osteocalcin are expressed in the middle and deep zone (Tchetina, 2011).

There is no documented effective cure for OA. The available treatment in the market and health sectors namely: pharmacological, regenerative treatment, osteochondral transplant, arthroscopy, osteotomy and joint replacement therapy among others, are associated with complications such as renal, hepatic, gastrointestinal and cardiovascular dysfunction, immunological reactions, fibrous cartilage aftermath, high costs, haemorrhage and infection (Clouet *et al.*, 2009; Wittenauer, Smith & Aden, 2013; Velden *et al.*, 2015; Gidwani & Fairbank, 2004; Ickinger & Tikly, 2011). Thus effective treatment is required, which can target and arrest the action of cellular pathways and molecules involved in the inflammatory events in the AC without detrimental outcomes.

It is reputed that a phytochemical, apigenin, has anti-inflammatory properties that mediate a series of events thereby instigate down-regulation of inflammatory enzymes such as cyclooxygenase-2 (COX-2) and nitric oxide synthase (NOs), which are involved in OA (Kang *et al.*, 2005). In addition, it has been found to have inhibitory activity against collagenase (matrix metalloproteinase-1), which degrades collagen and proteoglycan matrices in the joints (Lee *et al.*, 2007). Furthermore, in their study, Lee *et al.* (2007) proposed that direct injection of apigenin into inflammatory joints might allow inhibition of collagenase without causing cytotoxicity and concluded that apigenin may be useful as a functional food component and as an alternative medicine to help treat inflammatory symptoms (Lee *et al.*, 2007).

Apigenin is commonly found in parsley, chamomile, celery, grapefruit and apples; vegetables such as onions and spinach, as well as in red wine. Moreover, apigenin can safely be taken in the daily diet with no documented side effects (Shukla & Gupta, 2010). Lim *et al.* (2011) stated that apigenin has the potential to protect collagen matrix breakdown by facilitating down-regulation of the destructive matrix metalloproteins-13 (MMP-13) in the cartilage of diseased tissues such as those found in arthritic disorders (Lim *et al.*, 2011). Moreover, it is alleged that apigenin consumption as juice from celery and parsley has the potential to maintain electrolyte balance and reduce breast cancer tumours respectively (Kordich & Kordich, 2013).

2. MATERIALS AND METHODS

2.1 Sample and Tissue Acquisition

Porcine stifle (knee joint) from three-month-old piglets (n = 6) were obtained from abattoir and dissected under aseptic conditions to expose the femoral condyles as described previously in our laboratory (Motaung *et al.*, 2011). The superficial zone cartilage (100 μm) of the femoral condyles was harvested using a model B electric dermatome (Phoenix Surgical, Cape Town, S.A.). Thereafter, osteochondral plugs were removed from the femoral condyles using a coring reamer. The middle zone (1.25 mm slices) was removed from each plug using a custom cutting jig. Petri dishes were first weighed before sample collection. Dissected cartilage slices were collected from the superficial and middle zone of the AC under aseptic conditions. The cartilage slices were then weighed and the weight of the petri dishes was subtracted from the cartilage weight. The difference was used to determine how much collagenase-P (Roche diagnostics, Indianapolis, USA) had to be added to the cartilage slices for digestion.

Ethics

Vertebrate Animals: Not applicable. Only vertebrate (non-human) cadaveric materials were used in this study.

2.2 Monolayer Cell Culture

The cartilage slices were washed three times with phosphate buffered saline (PBS) (GIBCO, Life Technologies, Johannesburg, SA) and transferred to 15 mℓ tubes with 1 mℓ of 0.05% Trypsin-EDTA (Life Technologies, Johannesburg, SA) to induce cartilage permeability. The tubes were then placed in an orbital shaker (Forma Scientific Inc., California, USA) for 30 minutes at 230 rpm. Trypsin-EDTA was removed and collagenase-P was added according to the relevant calculation and digested for 2.5 hours in the orbital shaker. 10 mℓ of 10% foetal bovine serum (FBS) (Separations Scientific, Johannesburg, S.A.), diluted with Dulbecco Modified Eagles Medium (DMEM/F12 containing 50 µg/mℓ ascorbic acid 2-phosphate, 100 µg/mℓ sodium pyruvate, 0.1% bovine serum albumin, 100 units/mℓ penicillin, 100 µg/mℓ streptomycin and 25 mM HEPES) (GIBCO, Life Technologies, Johannesburg, SA) was added to the digested cartilage and mixed thoroughly. The cells were then filtered through a 70 µm cell strainer and centrifuged for 5 minutes at 1000 rpm. The supernatant was discarded and the sediment (chondrocytes) was washed three times with PBS centrifuged between washes at 1000 rpm for 5 minutes. After the last wash, 1 mℓ of 1% FBS was added to the cells for cell counting in a T20 automated cell counter (Bio-Rad, Hercules, CA) using trypan blue exclusion assay. Isolated chondrocytes were cultured in 96-well plates for microculture tetrazolium (MTT) cell viability/proliferation (1×10^4 cells/well), 48-well plates for CyQUANT cell proliferation (5×10^4 cells/well) and 12-well plates for real-time polymerase chain reaction (RT-PCR) (1×10^5 cells/well) assays. Thereafter, the cell culture plates (Corning Life Sciences, New York, USA) were placed in a humidified incubator under 95% air and 5% CO_2 at 37°C. Chondrocytes were incubated overnight in DMEM/F12 medium containing 1% FBS for cell attachment. After the incubation period, the media were changed to serum-free DMEM/F12/ITS media. Cells were treated with apigenin (Sigma-Aldrich, Missouri, USA) at concentrations of 5, 10, 20, 50 and 100 μM; and cultured for one, four and seven days for MTT assay; as well as four and seven days for gene expression. Untreated cells served as negative controls and were allocated to each set of experiments without apigenin. Transforming growth factor beta 1 at 3 ng/mℓ (Sigma-Aldrich, Missouri, USA) was used as positive control, based on studies carried out by Motaung, Reddi and Di Cesare (2011) and Maepa *et al.* (2016).

2.3 Micromass Culture

For assays requiring cell pellets - GAG assay, histology and collagen type II immunolocalisation - chondrocytes were further cultured using the micromass culture method as adapted from Tare *et al.* (2005), with slight modifications. Briefly, chondrocytes were firstly cultured as a monolayer at a density of 1×10^6 cells/well in six-well plates in a humidified atmosphere at 37°C and 5% CO_2. After 24 hours at confluence, the cells were detached with 0.05% trypsin-EDTA and 1.5 mℓ of 10% FBS was added. The cells were transferred into 15 mℓ centrifuge tubes. The suspension was centrifuged at 400 g for 10 minutes at 4°C. The supernatant was removed, 1 mℓ of DMEM/ITS was added to the tubes and the cells were counted in a T20 automated cell counter (Bio-Rad, Hercules, CA) using trypan blue assay. The cell count harvest was 5.06×10^6 cells/mℓ for the surface zone and 5.54×10^6 cells/mℓ for the middle zone. The suspension was further transferred into microcentrifuge tubes and centrifuged at 400 g for 10 minutes. The chondrocytes were then cultured as pellets for 14 days for GAG assay and 21 days for histology and immunohistochemistry. The cultured chondrocytes were treated with apigenin at 5, 10, 20, 50 and 100 μM concentrations (Sigma-Aldrich, Missouri, USA). Untreated cells served as negative controls. TGF-β1 at 3 ng/mℓ was used as positive control.

2.4 Microculture Tetrazolium Assay

Microculture tetrazolium (MTT) assay was performed to evaluate cell proliferation by means of determining the viable cell number of proliferating chondrocytes. The assay was performed on days one, four and seven in 96-well plates using the CellTiter 96® Non-Radioactive Cell

Proliferation Assay (Promega, Madison, USA) following the manufacturer's instructions. The CellTiter 96® assay principle outlines the cellular conversion of tetrazolium salt into a formazan product that is easily detected using a 96-well plate reader. The method includes aspirating media out, washing cells with PBS, adding 15 μℓ of the MTT dye solution (3-(4, 5-dimethylthiazol-2-yl)-2, 5-diphenyltetrazolium bromide), incubating for 4 hours, followed by adding stop/solubilisation solution to each well (100 μℓ), mixing and further incubation for 1 hour. Absorbance was read at 570 nm wavelengths using the microplate reader (Thermofisher Scientific, Waltham, UK).

2.5 CyQUANT® Cell Proliferation Assay

The CyQUANT® cell proliferation assay was used to assess cell proliferation by determining the accurate amount of deoxyribonucleic acid (DNA) produced by proliferating chondrocytes. Briefly, media were aspirated, followed by washing with PBS, and chondrocyte pellets were resuspended in 50 μℓ of 1× cell lysis buffer supplemented with 180 mM NaCl and 1 mM EDTA. Thereafter, DNase-free RNase A (Roche Diagnostics, Indianapolis, USA) was added to a final concentration of 1.35 K units (27 μℓ per well) and samples were incubated at room temperature for 1 hour (this was done to free the samples from RNA, leaving only DNA in the sample). Subsequently, 173 μℓ of 2× concentration of CyQUANT GR dye diluted in cell lysis buffer was added in each sample and then incubated for 3 minutes. Lastly, fluorescence was measured using a GloMax ®-Multi Detection System (PROMEGA, Madison, USA) at an excitation of 480 nm and emission of 520 nm. The DNA standard curve was prepared at a range of 10 ng/mℓ to 1 μg/mℓ, following the manufacturer's instructions. Briefly, 100 μg/mℓ bacteriophage λ DNA standards was first diluted to 1 μg/mℓ by mixing 10 μℓ of the stock solution with 990 μℓ of CyQUANT GR/cell-lysis buffer. Further dilution was performed, ranging from 0 to 1000 ng/mℓ final DNA concentration.

2.6 Glycosaminoglycan Assay

GAG assay was performed for the evaluation of the GAG disaccharide amount present in the chondrocyte pellets. Media were aspirated from samples and washed with PBS. The pellets were then treated with 250 μℓ of proteinase K solution (Celtic Molecular Diagnostics,

Mowbray, SA) at 200 μg/mℓ concentration and incubated overnight at 56°C in a dry bath (Bio-Rad, Hercules, CA). This was followed by increasing the temperature to 90°C before analysis. The dye solution was prepared as follows: 16 mg of 1, 9 Dimethyl-Methylene Blue (DMMB) dye was dissolved in 1 L water containing 3.04 g glycine, 1.6 g NaCl and 95 mℓ of 0.1 M acetic acid (Sigma-Aldrich, Missouri, USA). The dye solution was filtered using Whatman filter paper (Sigma-Aldrich, Missouri, USA). A standard curve was prepared by first using 100 μg/mℓ working solution of bovine chondroitin sulphate, which was further diluted with PBE to a range of 10 μg/mℓ to 50 μg/mℓ. For cell pellet samples, 5 μℓ of the pellet digest was diluted with 25 μℓ of PBE. Thereafter, 10 μℓ of the sample and standards were transferred into 96-well microplates in triplicate. This was followed by the addition of 250 μℓ DMMB dye right before reading. Subsequently, an equal volume of water to samples was added to the plates as blank in triplicate. Absorbance was read at 525 nm immediately in the microplate reader (Thermo Fisher Scientific, Waltham, UK).

2.7 Quantitative Real-Time Polymerase Chain Reaction

Quantitative real-time polymerase chain reaction (qRT-PCR) was performed to evaluate the expression of collagen type II, COMP and aggrecan mRNAs. To achieve this, the cultured chondrocytes were prepared and counted. Total RNA was isolated from cultured monolayer cells using the Nucleospin RNA kit (Macherey-Nagel, Düren, Germany) with on-membrane DNase1 (Qiagen) digestion to avoid genomic DNA contamination. The quality and quantity of isolated RNA were checked using a Qubit 2.0 fluorometer instrument (Life Technologies). Total RNA was reverse transcribed into cDNA using the iScript cDNA synthesis kit (Bio-Rad, Hercules, CA) in the Veritis Thermal Cycler (Life Technologies). Real-time qPCR was performed in triplicate on cDNA with the StepOne Plus Real-Time PCR sequence detector system and Taq Man gene expression reagents (Life Technologies). Collagen type II, aggrecan and COMP mRNA levels were normalised to glyceraldehydes 3-phosphate dehydrogenase (GAPDH) levels and expressed relative to the untreated control culture levels (ΔCT methods; Life Technologies) (Livak and Schmittgen, 2001). The forward and reverse primers for collagen type II, aggrecan and COMP were predesigned by InqabaBiotec (Hatfield, RSA) as shown in Table 1.

Table 1: Primer Sequences

Primer	*Forward Sequence*	*Reverse Sequence*
Porcine GAPDH	5'-TCCCTGCTTCTACTGGTGCT-3'	5'-TGAGCTTGACAAAGTGGTCG-3'
Porcine Collagen type II	5'-TGTTCTGAGAGGTCTTCCTGGCAA-3'	5'-CAGGAGCTCCAGCTTCACCA-3'
Porcine Aggregan	5'-AGCCTGAGGAGCCTTTACATTTG-3'	5'-ACACTGCTCGTAGCCTGCTTC-3'
Porcine COMP	5'-GGACAGTGATGGTGATGGTATAG-3'	5'-TCACATGCATCTCCCACAAA-3'

2.8 Histological Analysis

Histology was used to evaluate the micro-anatomy of the cartilage and its inherent components by using different stains specific for AC. Formalin-fixed, paraffin-embedded and sectioned samples were stained with Sirius red, Alcian blue and Safranin O (Cell Path Services, Randburg, RSA). Images were acquired on a Leica DMIL LED biological microscope at 40× magnification. Sample pellets were fixed with 10% neutral buffered formalin (Sigma-Aldrich, Missouri, USA), followed by a 13-hour processing schedule using Tissue-Tek VIP 5 Junior. Subsequently, sample pellets were embedded in paraffin wax, sectioned at 5 μm thickness and mounted on AutoFrost microscope slides. Sections were deparaffinised by incubating in xylene for 6 minutes, followed by incubations in 100%, 95% and 70% ethanol respectively, for 10 minutes. Lastly, the sections were further incubated in distilled water for 5 minutes and in PBS for 5 minutes.

2.8.1 *Sirius Red*

This staining method was used for the evaluation of collagen content, which is expressed by the red discoloration of collagen fibres. Sections were de-waxed in xylene for 6 minutes before being hydrated in three changes of decreasing concentrations of ethyl alcohol (+/– 10 dips in each). Thereafter, samples were washed with tap water and nuclei stained with Weigert's haematoxylin for 10 minutes before being washed in running tap water for 10 minutes. Slides were then stained in picro-sirius red for one hour and washed in two changes of acidified water. Lastly, section slides were dehydrated with three changes of increasing concentrations of ethyl alcohol (+/– 10 dips in each), cleared with two changes of xylene (+/– 10 dips in each) and mounted with entellan.

2.8.2 *Alcian Blue*

This staining technique was used for the evaluation of proteoglycans, which stain blue in colour. Sections were de-waxed in xylene for 6 min and hydrated in three changes of decreasing concentrations of ethyl alcohol (+/– 10 dips in each) before being washed with tap water and rinsed in a 3% acetic acid solution. Thereafter, slides were stained in filtered Alcian blue staining solution for 1 hour and washed in distilled water. Sections were counter-stained with 1% neutral red for 45 seconds and washed in distilled water. Lastly, sections were dehydrated with three changes of increasing concentrations of ethyl alcohol, cleared with two changes of xylene and mounted with entellan.

2.8.3 *Safranin O*

This staining procedure was used for the evaluation of ECM of the cartilage, staining orange to red in colour. Sections were de-waxed in xylene for 6 minutes before being hydrated in three changes of decreasing concentrations of ethyl alcohol (+/– 10 dips in each). Thereafter, samples were washed in running tap water for 10 minutes. Subsequently, slides were stained with fast green solution for 5 minutes and were rinsed quickly with 1% acetic acid solution for 10–15 seconds. This was followed by staining in 0.1% Safranin O solution for 5 minutes. Lastly, samples were dehydrated with three changes of increasing concentrations of ethyl alcohol, cleared with two changes of xylene and mounted with entellan.

2.9 Collagen Type II Immuno-Localisation

Immunohistochemistry was used to evaluate collagen type II immuno-localisation on cell pellet sections with the novolink min polymer detection system kit (Leica Microsystems, USA). Sections were de-paraffinised with proteinase K for 10 minutes and washed by dipping 20 times in PBS. This was followed by incubating sections in 1%

hydrogen peroxidase (Blocking buffer) for 5 minutes at room temperature and then washing sections with PBS by dipping 10–15 times. Thereafter, sections were incubated overnight at 4°C with a primary antibody at 1:30 dilution of novacastra rabbit polyclonal collagen type II antibody (Leica Microsystems, USA). The following day sections were dipped 15 times in PBS. Sections were then incubated with link antibody for 1 hour at room temperature and dipped 15 times in PBS. This was followed by incubating sections with streptavidin-HRP for 1 hour at room temperature and then washed by dipping in PBS 15 times. One drop of 3, 3'- diaminobenzidine (DAB) chromogen (dilution: 1 drop of DAB chromogen + 1 mℓ of substrate) was filtered on each section at a time for antibody-biotin conjugate detection. Lastly, sections were counterstained with haematoxylin for 1 minute and washed with the tap water. For each set of treatment groups, one section was exposed to collagen type II (Col2) primary antibody and the other one was without a collagen type II.

2.10 Statistical Analysis

All data (n = 6) was expressed as the mean and standard deviation (SD) for each experiment. Statistical analysis was performed using Microsoft Office Excel 2013 (Redmond, WA, USA). A one-way analysis of variance (ANOVA) with Tukey's HSD (honestly significant differences) to account for multiple comparisons was used to determine the effects of apigenin on collagen type II, aggrecan and COMP in the surface and middle zones of the AC. A significance change of * represents a p value = 0.05 and ** p value = 0.01.

3. RESULTS

3.1 Influence of Apigenin on Cell Viability using MTT Assay

3.1.1 *Superficial Zone*

The MTT CellTiter 96® non-radioactive cell proliferation assay evaluated the viability of chondrocytes from the superficial zone of porcine AC after one, four and seven days of treatment with apigenin at 5, 10, 20, 50 and 100 μM concentrations. TGF-β1 at 3 ng/mℓ concentration was used as a positive control while untreated chondrocytes served as negative control (Figure 1A). On day one, apigenin treatment showed increased cell proliferation at 5, 20 and 50 μM concentrations by 2%, 5% and 1% respectively. The positive control, TGF-β1 (3 ng/mℓ), increased cell proliferation by 1% compared to negative control. However, apigenin treatment decreased cell proliferation at 100 μM and significantly at 10 μM by 2% and 24% respectively, compared to the negative control. The effect of apigenin on cell proliferation using MTT CellTiter 96® assay was biphasic as it showed two different effects on different apigenin treatment concentrations.

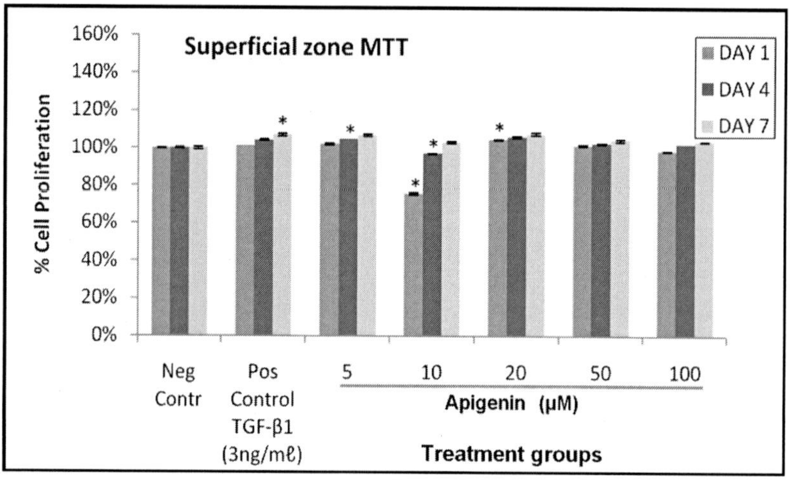

Fig. 1(A): Effect of apigenin on chondrocyte proliferation in the superficial zone for days one, four and seven by MTT assay. All significant changes are shown as (*= $p < 0.05$, **= $p < 0.01$).

On day four, there was an evident increase in cell proliferation on chondrocytes treated with apigenin concentrations of 20 μM, 50 μM and 100 μM by 6%, 3% and 2% respectively compared to the negative control. In addition, apigenin showed a significant increase at 5 μM by 5% and treatment with positive control TGF-β1 (3 ng/mℓ) showed an increase in cell proliferation by 4%, compared to the negative control. Conversely, a 3% decline in cell proliferation was observed at an apigenin concentration of 10 μM; however, this was higher than day one proliferation, which was 24%.

On day seven, there was a further increase in cell proliferation in response to apigenin treatment at 5, 10, 20, 50 and 100 μM concentrations by 7%, 3%, 7%, 4%, 3% respectively, compared to the negative control. Treatment with 3 ng/mℓ of positive control TGF-β1 significantly increased cell proliferation by 7%, as shown in Figure 1A.

3.1.2 *Middle Zone*

The MTT CellTiter 96® non-radioactive cell proliferation assay evaluated the viability of chondrocytes from the middle zone of porcine AC after one, four and seven days of treatment with apigenin at 5, 10, 20, 50 and 100 μM concentrations. TGF-β1 at 3 ng/mℓ concentration was used as a positive control while untreated chondrocytes served as negative control (Figure 1B). On day one, treatment with apigenin stimulated chondrocyte proliferation at 5 μM concentration by 3% and significantly at 20 μM and 50 μM concentrations by 5% and 4% respectively, compared to the negative control. Positive control TGF-β1 (3 ng/mℓ) treatment showed increased cell proliferation by 3%. However, apigenin treatment displayed a decrease in cell proliferation at 100 μM by 3% and significantly at 10 μM by 4%, compared to the negative control. Day four displayed increased cell proliferation in response to treatment with apigenin concentrations of 5 μM by 9%, 10 μM by 6%, 50 μM by 10% and 100 μM by 4% and 20 μM showed a significant increase by 8%, compared to the negative control. In addition, positive control TGF-β1 (3 ng/mℓ) treatment increased cell proliferation by 5%. On day seven, there

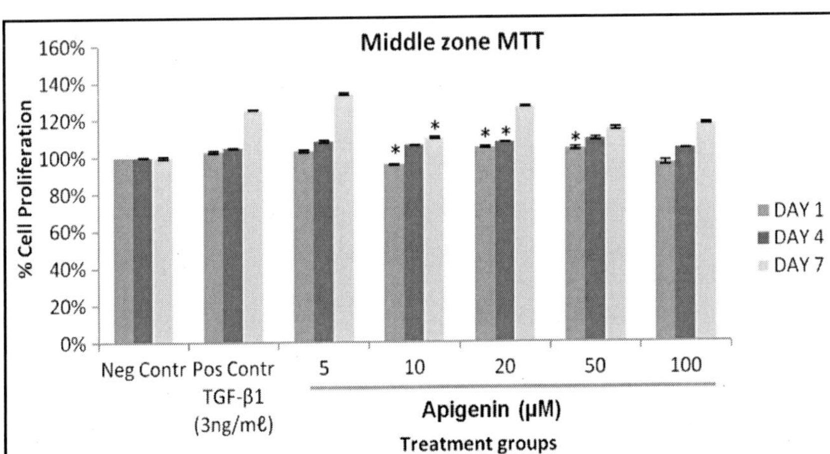

Fig. 1(B): Effect of Apigenin on Chondrocyte Proliferation from the Middle Zone for Days One, Four and Seven by MTT Assay. All Significant Changes are Shown as (*= $p < 0.05$, **= $p < 0.01$).

was an increase in chondrocyte proliferation in reaction to treatment with apigenin concentrations of 5 µM by 34%, 10 µM by 10%, 20 µM by 27%, 50 µM by 15%, and 100 µM by 18%, compared to the negative control. Moreover, positive control TGF-β1 (3 ng/mℓ) treatment showed increased cell proliferation by 26%, as shown in Figure 1B.

3.2 Effect of Apigenin on DNA Analysis using CYQUANT® Cell Proliferation Assay

This highly sensitive, fluorescence-based microplate assay evaluated chondrocyte proliferation by measuring the amount of DNA present in cultured chondrocytes. The CyQUANT GR reagent was added to cells, which produced fluorescence upon binding to the DNA of proliferating chondrocytes from the superficial and middle zone in the Promega GloMax Multi-Detection System (Promega, Madison USA). The amount of DNA was assessed afterone, four and seven days of treatment with 5, 10, 20, 50 and 100 µM apigenin concentrations; 3 ng/mℓ of TGF-β1 was used as a positive control and untreated cells served as negative control. The amount of DNA in response to apigenin treatment was increased in a dose- and time-dependent manner. Moreover, the middle zone stimulated a higher DNA amount than the superficial zone and this effect was more

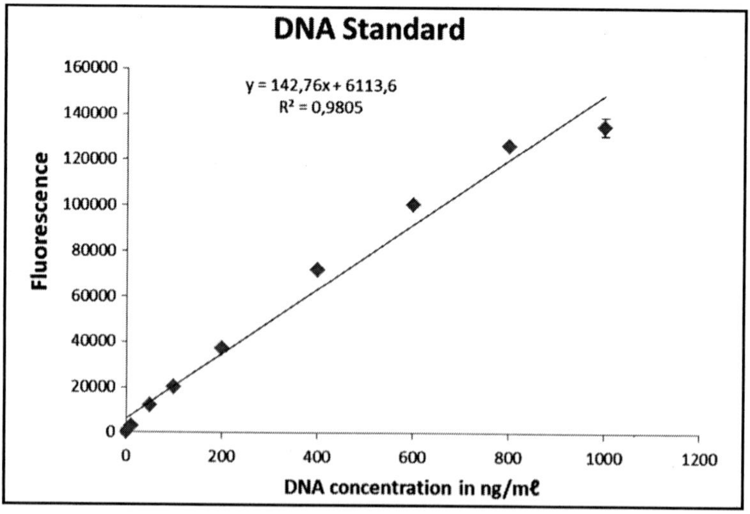

Fig. 2(A): The Bacteriophage λ DNA Standard Curve

evident on day seven. The DNA standard curve (Figure 2A) was prepared by diluting bacteriophage lambda (λ) DNA in CyQUANT GR/cell-lysis buffer to give a range covering 10 ng/mℓ to 1 μg/mℓ, following the manufacturer's instructions. The standards were also processed and treated similarly to the test samples.

3.3 Influence of Apigenin on Porcine Superficial Zone Chondrocytes using CyQUANT Assay

Treatment of chondrocytes with apigenin on day one revealed an increase in DNA amount at 5 μM by 19% and 20 μM by 68%, compared to the negative control. Furthermore, the amount of DNA was significantly enhanced at apigenin concentrations of 10 μM by 21%, 50 μM by 35% and 100 μM by 41%, compared to the negative control. A similar effect was detected on chondrocytes treated with the positive control TGF-β1 (3 ng/mℓ), which increased the DNA amount by 47%. On day four, there was an increase in the DNA amount in response to chondrocyte treatment with apigenin concentrations of 5 μM by 12%, 10 μM by 17%, 20 μM by 16%, 50 μM by 5% and 100 μM by 6%, compared to the negative control. A further increase in DNA amount was observed in positive control TGF-β1 (3 ng/mℓ) treatment by 31%. On day seven, the amount of DNA was increased after chondrocyte exposure to apigenin concentrations of 5 μM by 15%, 10 μM by 0.5%, 20 μM by 16% and50 μM by

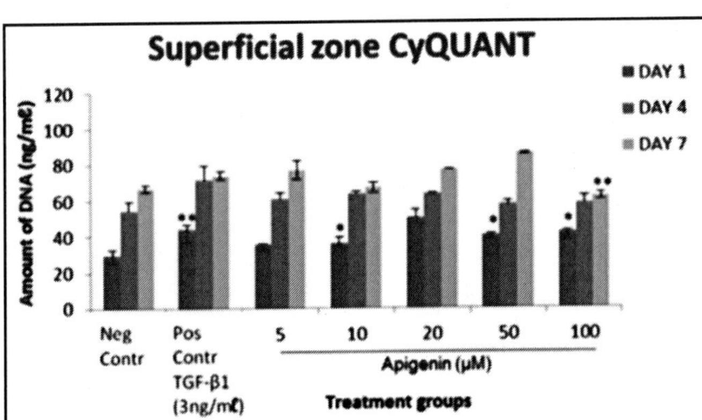

Fig. 2(B): Effect of apigenin on superficial zone DNA analysis using CyQUANT cell proliferation. The amount of DNA was extrapolated from the bacteriophage λ DNA standard curve. All significant changes are shown as (*= $p < 0.05$, **= $p < 0.01$).

29%, compared to the negative control. Treatment with positive control TGF-β1 (3 ng/mℓ) increased the DNA amount by 11%. However, a significant decrease in the DNA amount was evident at an apigenin concentration of 100 μM by 7%, as shown in Figure 2B.

3.4 Influence of Apigenin on Porcine Middle Zone Chondrocytes using CyQUANT Assay

On day one of chondrocyte treatment, there was an increase in the DNA amount in response to treatment with apigenin at 5 μM by 43% and 20 μM by 8%, compared to the negative control. This effect was also evident for positive control TGF-β1 (3 ng/mℓ) treatment by a 10% increase. Conversely, on day one, a reduction in the DNA amount was evident at apigenin concentrations of 10 μM by 2%, 50 μM by 3% and 100 μM by 11%, compared to the negative control. On day four, the DNA amount was significantly increased at positive control TGF-β1 (3 ng/mℓ) by 7% and at apigenin concentrations of 10 μM by 23%, compared to the negative control. Contrarily, apigenin lowered DNA production at 5 μM by 14%, and 100 μM by 2% and a significant decrease was observed at 20 μM by 19% and at 50 μM by 24%, compared to the negative control. Interestingly, on day seven, the DNA amount was increased in reaction to treatment with all apigenin concentrations of 5, 10, 50 and 100 μM by 23%,

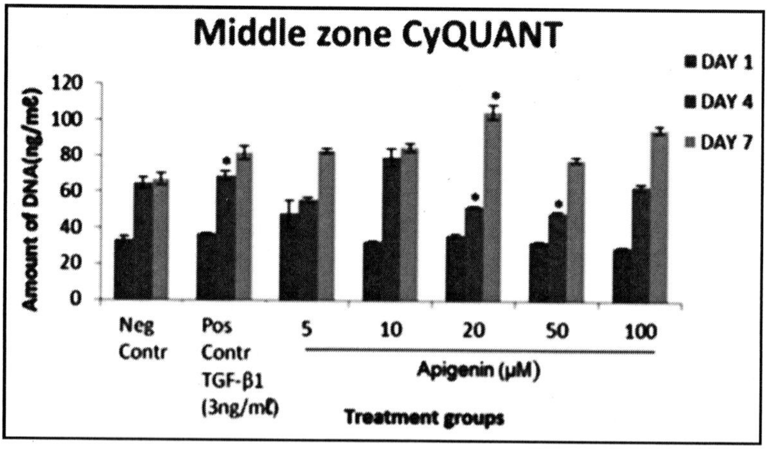

Fig. 2(C): Effect of apigenin on middle zone DNA analysis using CyQUANT cell proliferation. The amount of DNA was extrapolated from the bacteriophage λ DNA standard curve. All significant changes are shown as (*= $p < 0.05$, **= $p < 0.01$).

27%, 16% and 42%, with 20 µM showing a significant increase by 58% compared to the negative control. Moreover, positive control TGF- β1 (3 ng/mℓ) treatment increased the DNA amount by 22%, as shown in Figure 2C.

3.5 Effect of Apigenin on Porcine Chondrocytes using the GAG Assay

The present study investigated the synthesis of GAG on day 14 using DMMB dye on superficial and middle zone chondrocytic pellets, which were cultured following a micromass method. Apigenin efficacy on GAG production was explored at concentrations of 5, 10, 20, 50 and 100 µM; 3 ng/mℓ of TGF-β1 was used as a positive control and untreated pellets served as negative control. Results revealed that GAGs

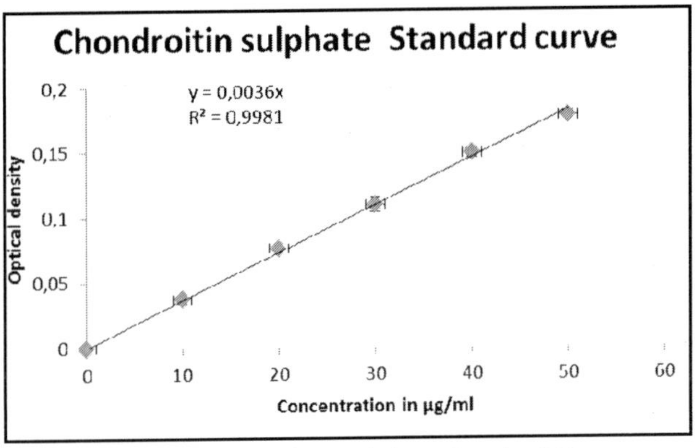

Fig. 3(A): Chondroitin Sulphate Standard Curve

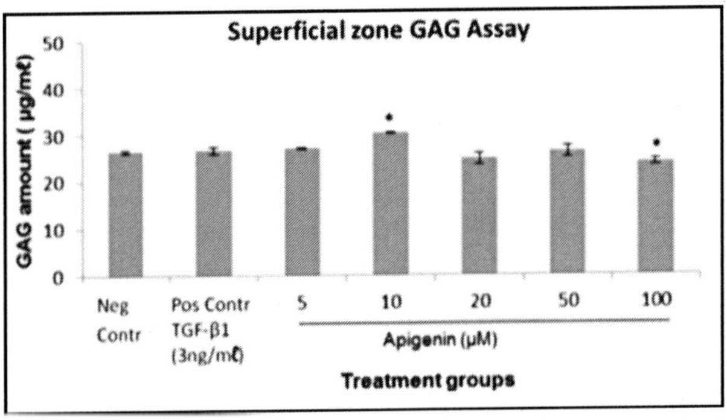

Fig. 3(B): Effect of apigenin on day 14 superficial zone GAG synthesis. The amount of GAG was extrapolated from the bovine chondroitin sulphate standard curve. All significant changes are shown as (*= p < 0.05, **= p < 0.01).

were synthesised in a dose-dependent manner, in response to different apigenin treatments. Furthermore, apigenin-treated middle zone cell pellets produced the highest amount of GAGs compared to superficial zone cell pellets (Figure 3B and 3C). Chondroitin sulphate was used to create a standard curve, as shown in Figure 3A.

In the superficial zone (Figure 3B), accumulation of the GAG amount was evident in chondrocyte pellets treated with apigenin at 5 μM concentration by 3%, and with TGF-β1 (3 ng/mℓ) by 1%, compared to the negative control. Moreover, apigenin at 10 μM significantly increased GAG synthesis by 15%, compared to the negative control. On the contrary, GAG synthesis was decreased when treated with apigenin at 20 μM and 50 μM by 6% and 0.8% respectively, and was significantly decreased at 100 μM by 9% compared to the negative control, as shown in Figure 3B.

In the middle zone (Figure 3C), there was an increase in GAG production in chondrocyte pellets treated with apigenin at 10 μM concentration by 1% and a significant increase of 8% was observed at an apigenin concentration of 100 μM, compared to the negative control. On the contrary, apigenin showed a decrease in GAG content at apigenin concentrations 5, 20 and 50 μM by 6.5%, 7% and by 8% respectively, compared to the negative control. The positive control TGF-β1 (3 ng/mℓ) significantly decreased GAG synthesis by 11% compared to the negative control, as shown in Figure 3C.

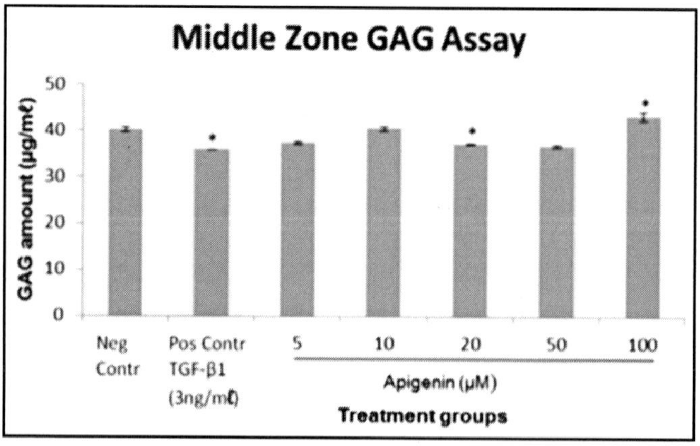

Fig. 3(C): Effect of apigenin on day 14 middle zone GAG synthesis. The amount of GAG was extrapolated from the bovine chondroitin sulphate standard curve. All significant changes are shown as (*= $p < 0.05$, **= $p < 0.01$).

3.6 Influence of Apigenin on Collagen Type II mRNA Expression

3.6.1 *Superficial Zone Day Four*

Superficial zone chondrocyte exposure to apigenin for four days significantly enhanced collagen type II mRNA expression at 5 µM, 10 µM and 20 µM concentrations to 1.1-fold, 1.4-fold and 2.3-fold respectively, compared to the negative control (Figure 4A). Positive control TGF-β1 (3 ng/mℓ) treatment enhanced collagen type II mRNA expression to 2.1-fold. Contrarily, apigenin down-regulated collagen type II mRNAat concentrations of 50 µM to 0.3-fold and 100 µM to 0.2-fold, compared to the negative control, as shown in Figure 4A.

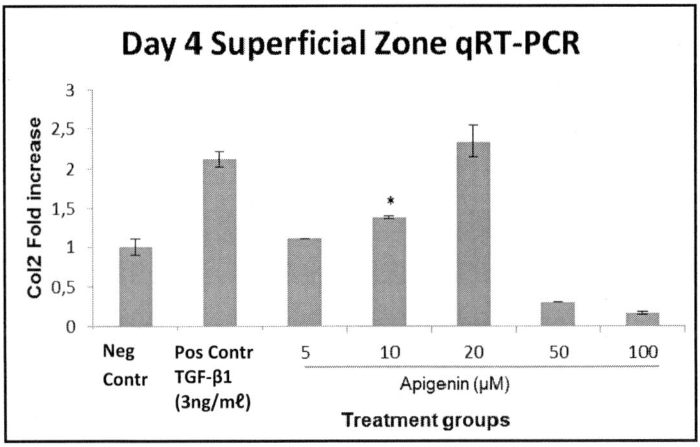

Fig. 4(A): Increase in collagen type II mRNA after four days of treatment with different concentrations of apigenin in the superficial zone. All significant changes are shown as (*= $p < 0.05$, **= $p < 0.01$).

3.6.2 *Superficial Zone Day Seven*

Superficial zone chondrocyte exposure to apigenin for seven days stimulated an increase in collagen type II mRNA expression at concentrations of 20 µM by up to 1.7-fold and at 100 µM by up to 1.4-fold. An analogous result was observed at the positive control TGF-β1 (3 ng/mℓ) with an increase of up to 1.6-fold, compared to the negative control (Figure 4B). Moreover, apigenin significantly up-regulated collagen type II mRNA at 50 µM concentration by up to 1.4-fold, compared to negative control. On the contrary, apigenin significantly down-regulated collagen type II mRNA expression at 5 μM 0.4-folds and at 10 μM 0.5-folds, compared to the negative control, as shown in Figure 4B.

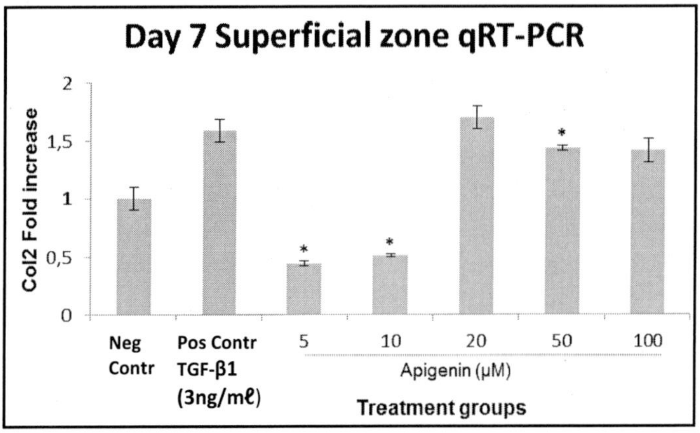

Fig. 4(B): Increase in collagen type II mRNA after seven days of treatment with different concentrations of apigenin in the superficial zone. All significant changes are shown as (*= $p < 0.05$, **= $p < 0.01$).

3.6.3 *Middle Zone Day Four*

Treatment of middle zone chondrocytes with apigenin for four days enhanced collagen type II mRNA expression at 50 μM concentration

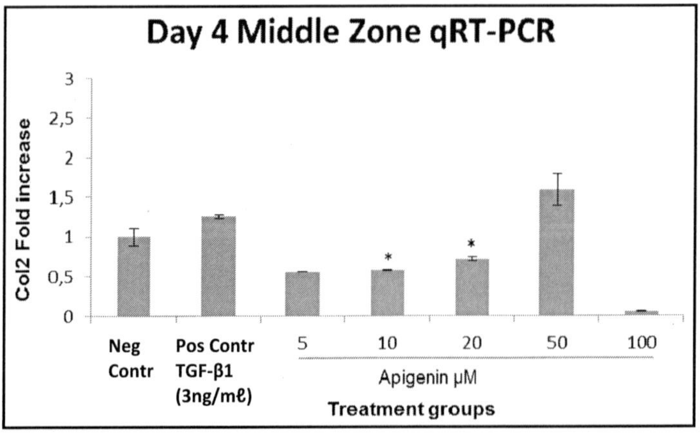

Fig. 4(C): Increase in collagen type II mRNA after four days of treatment with different concentrations of apigenin in the middle zone. All significant changes are shown as (*= $p < 0.05$, **= $p < 0.01$).

1.6-folds compared to the negative control (Figure 4C). Positive control TGF-β1 (3 ng/mℓ) up-regulated collagen type II mRNA 1.3-fold. Down-regulation of collagen type II mRNA was identified after treatment with apigenin at concentrations of 5 μM and 100 μM 0.6-folds and 0.06-fold respectively. A further significant decrease was evident at 20 μM concentration with 0.7-fold and 10 μM with 0.6-fold compared to the negative control, as shown in Figure 4C.

3.6.4 *Middle Zone Day Seven*

Collagen type II mRNA expression on middle zone chondrocytes was enhanced on day seven in response to apigenin treatment at a concentration of 20 μM by up to 1.2-fold, compared to the negative control. Positive control TGF-β1 (3 ng/mℓ) significantly increased collagen type II mRNA expression by up to 1.5-fold, compared to the negative control (Figure 4D). Collagen type II mRNA down-regulation 0.9-fold was observed at an apigenin concentration of 10 μM and a significant decrease in expression was observed at 5, 50 and 100 μM concentrations, with expression being reduced 0.6-, 0.26- and 0.3-fold respectively, when compared to the negative control, as shown in Figure 4D.

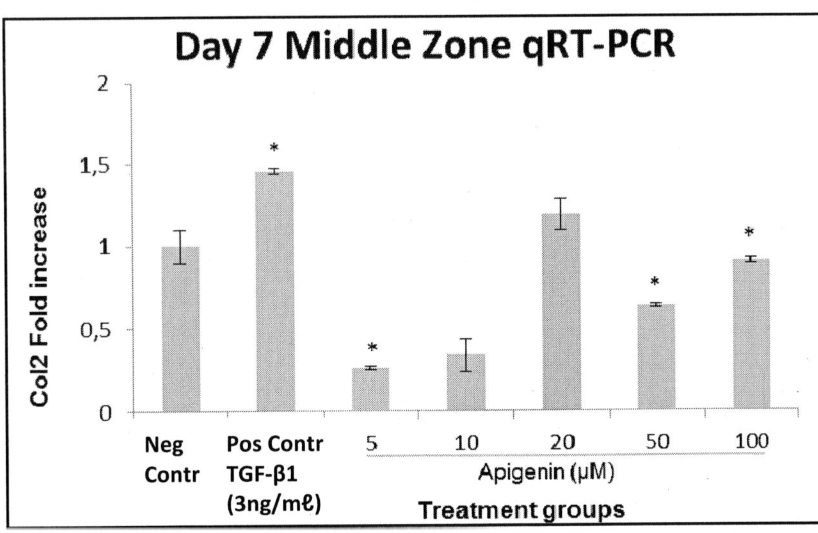

Fig. 4(D): Increase in collagen type II mRNA after seven days of treatment with different concentrations of apigenin in the middle zone. All significant changes are shown as (*= $p < 0.05$, **= $p < 0.01$).

3.7 Influence of Apigenin on Aggrecan mRNA Expression

3.7.1 *Superficial Zone Day Four*

Treatment of superficial zone chondrocytes with apigenin for four days enhanced aggrecan mRNA expression up to 2.6-fold at 20 µM concentration, compared to the negative control (Figure 5A). A significant increase in aggrecan mRNA expression was observed at an apigenin concentration of 10 µM and 5 µM with 4.4- and 1.1-fold increases, respectively. Positive control TGF-β1 (3 ng/mℓ) significantly up-regulated aggrecan mRNA 2.6-fold compared to the negative control. Conversely, aggrecan mRNA was down-regulated at apigenin treatment of 50 µM and 100 µM concentrations to 0.5-fold and 0.1-fold respectively, compared to the negative control, as shown in Figure 5A.

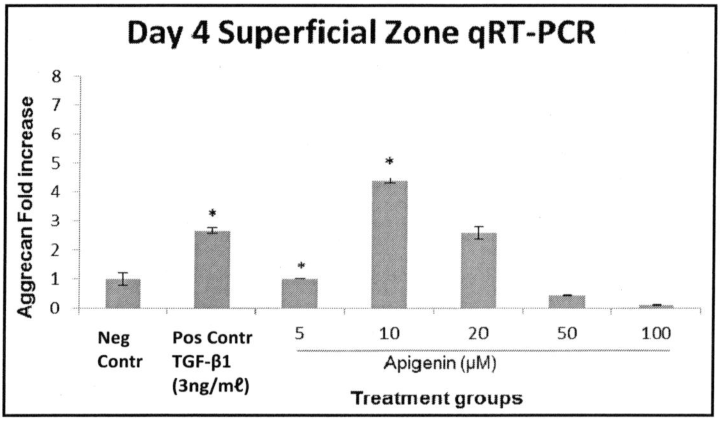

Fig. 5(A): Increase in aggrecan mRNA expression after four days of treatment with different concentrations of apigenin in the superficial zone. All significant changes are shown as (*= $p < 0.05$, **= $p < 0.01$).

3.7.2 *Superficial Zone Day Seven*

Superficial zone chondrocyte exposure to apigenin for seven days stimulated an increase in aggrecan mRNA expression at concentrations of 20 µM up to 2.5-fold and at 50 µM up to 1.5-fold, compared to the negative control (Figure 5B). In addition, aggrecan mRNA expression was significantly increased at apigenin concentrations of 5 µM up to 1.7-fold and at 10 µM up to 2.7-fold, compared to the negative control. Down-regulation of aggrecan mRNA was observed on chondrocytes treated with apigenin at 100 μM to 0.8-fold and at positive control TGF- β1 (3 ng/mℓ) to 0.6-fold, as shown in Figure 5B.

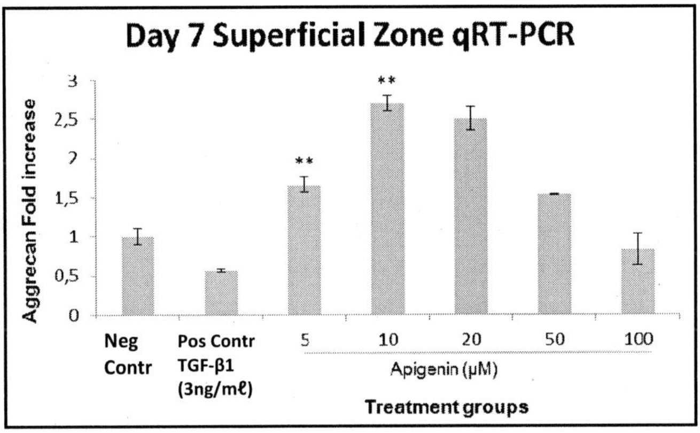

Fig. 5(**B**): Increase in aggrecan mRNA expression after seven days of treatment with different concentrations of apigenin in the superficial zone. All significant changes are shown as (*= $p < 0.05$, **= $p < 0.01$).

3.7.3 *Middle Zone Day Four*

Treatment of middle zone chondrocytes with apigenin for four days enhanced aggrecan mRNA expression at concentrations of 10 and 100 μMup to 1.1-fold and 4.6-fold respectively, compared to the negative control (Figure 5C). Furthermore, apigenin significantly up-

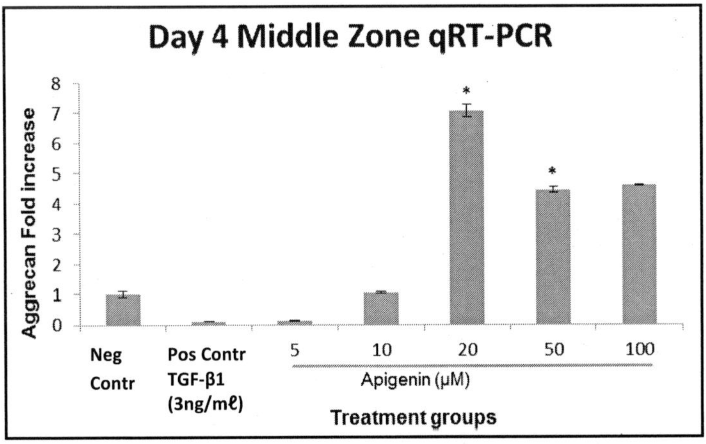

Fig. 5(**C**): Aggrecan mRNA expression after four days of treatment with different concentrations of apigenin in the middle zone. All significant changes are shown as (*= $p < 0.05$, **= $p < 0.01$).

regulated aggrecan mRNA at concentrations of 20 and 50 µM up to 7.0- and 4.5-fold respectively, compared to the negative control. Down-regulation of aggrecan mRNA was observed on chondrocytes treated with apigenin at 5 µM to 0.1-fold and significantly at positive control TGF-β1 (3 ng/mℓ) to 0.1-fold when compared to the negative control, as shown in Figure 5C.

3.7.4 *Middle Zone Day Seven*

In the middle zone, on day seven (Figure 5D), results revealed that treatment of chondrocytes with apigenin at concentrations of 20 µM and 100 µM enhanced aggrecan mRNA expression 1.1-fold and 1.3-fold respectively, and significantly at 10 µM up to 1.3-fold, compared to the negative control. Conversely, aggrecan mRNA was down-regulated at apigenin concentrations of 50 µM to 0.6-fold. Further significant down-regulation was witnessed at an apigenin concentration of 5 µM to 0.7-fold and at positive control TGF-β1 (3 ng/mℓ) treatment to 0.3, compared to the negative control, as shown in Figure 5D.

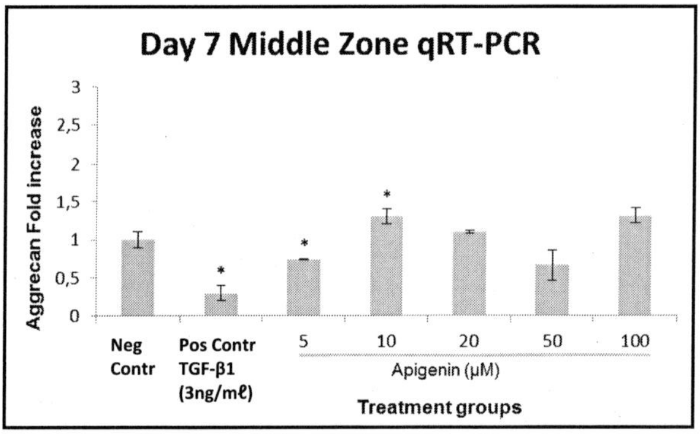

Fig. 5(D): Increase in aggrecan mRNA expression after seven days of treatment with different concentrations of apigenin in the middle zone. All significant changes are shown as (*=p < 0.05, **= p < 0.01).

3.8 Influence of Apigenin on COMP mRNA Expression

3.8.1 *Superficial Zone Day Four*

Treatment of superficial zone chondrocytes with apigenin at a concentration of 100 µM enhanced COMP mRNA expression to 2.0-fold and a further significant increase was observed at apigenin concentrations of 5 µM up to 1.6-fold and at 20 µM up to 2.0-fold, compared to the negative control (Figure 5A). A similar effect was observed at positive control TGF-β1 (3 ng/mℓ) treatment up to 7.1-fold, compared to the negative control. However, COMP mRNA expression was decreased at apigenin treatment of 10 µM to 0.6-fold and significantly at 50 µM to 0.4-fold, compared to the negative control, as shown in Figure 6A.

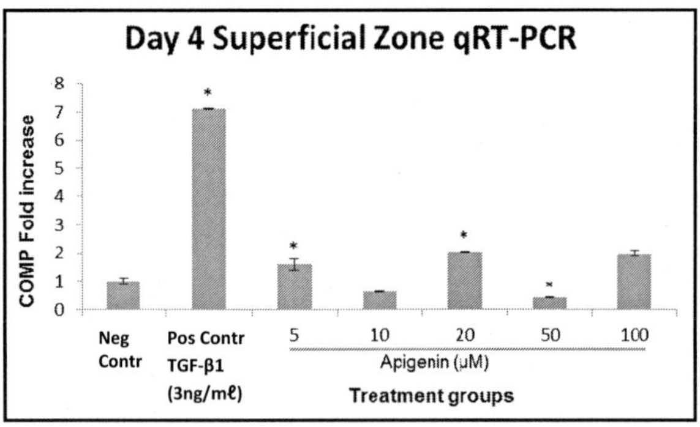

Fig. 6(A): Increase in COMP mRNA expression after four days of treatment with different concentrations of apigenin the superficial zone. All significant changes are shown as (*= $p < 0.05$, **= $p < 0.01$).

3.8.2 *Superficial Zone Day Seven*

On day seven in the superficial zone, there was an increase in COMP mRNA expression in response to apigenin treatment at concentrations

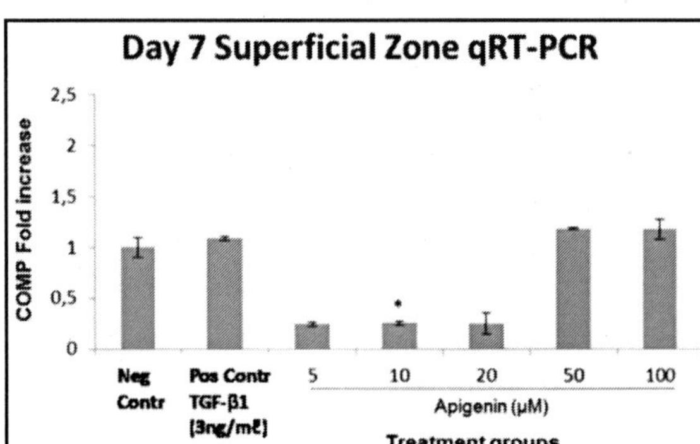

Fig. 6(B): Increase in COMP mRNA expression after seven days of treatment with different concentrations of apigenin in the superficial zone. All significant changes are shown as (*= $p < 0.05$, **= $p < 0.01$).

of 50 μM and 100 μM, both by up to 1.2-fold compared to negative control. A similar effect was observed at positive control TGF-β1 (3 ng/mℓ) treatment up to 1.1-fold, compared to the negative control (Figure 6B). Conversely, COMP mRNA was down-regulated at apigenin treatment of 20 μM to 0.2-fold and at 5 μM to 0.3-fold and significantly at 10 μM to 0.2-fold, compared to the negative control, as shown in Figure 6B.

3.8.3 *Middle Zone Day Four*

Treatment of middle zone chondrocytes with apigenin for four days at 5 μM and 50 μM concentrations stimulated COMP mRNA up-regulation to 4.3-fold and 1.1-fold respectively, compared to the negative control (Figure 6C). Moreover, COMP mRNA expression was significantly increased at positive control TGF-β1 (3 ng/mℓ) treatment up to 4.5-fold, compared to the negative control. Treatment of chondrocytes with apigenin concentrations of 10 μM, 20 μM and 100 μM down-regulated COMP mRNA expressions 0.1-fold, 0.2-fold and 0.04-fold respectively, compared to the negative control, as shown in Figure 6C.

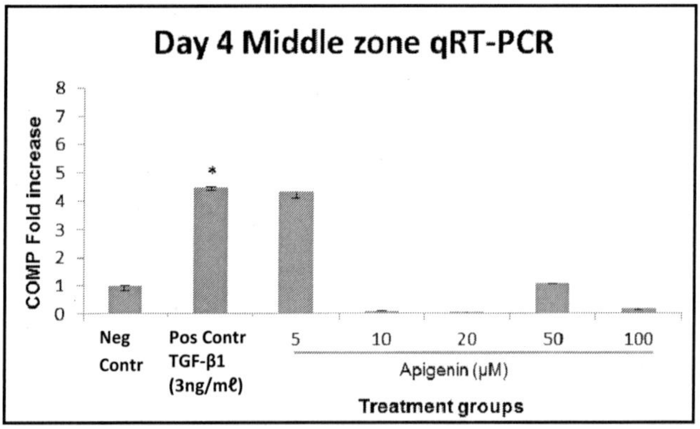

Fig. 6(C): Increase in COMP mRNA expression after four days of treatment with different concentrations of apigenin in the middle zone. All significant changes are shown as (*= $p < 0.05$, **= $p < 0.01$).

3.8.4 *Middle Zone Day Seven*

COMP mRNA expression in middle zone chondrocytes was enhanced on day seven in response to apigenin at a concentration of 20 μM up to 1.3-fold, with positive control TGF-β1 (3 ng/mℓ) treatment showing an increase up to 2.1-fold compared to the negative control (Figure 6D). Down-regulation of COMP mRNA was observed on treatment with apigenin concentrations of 50 µM and 100 µM to 0.7-fold and 0.9-fold respectively, compared to the negative control. Furthermore, COMP mRNA was significantly down-regulated at apigenin concentration of 5 and 10 µM both to 0.1-fold, compared to negative control, as shown in Figure 6D.

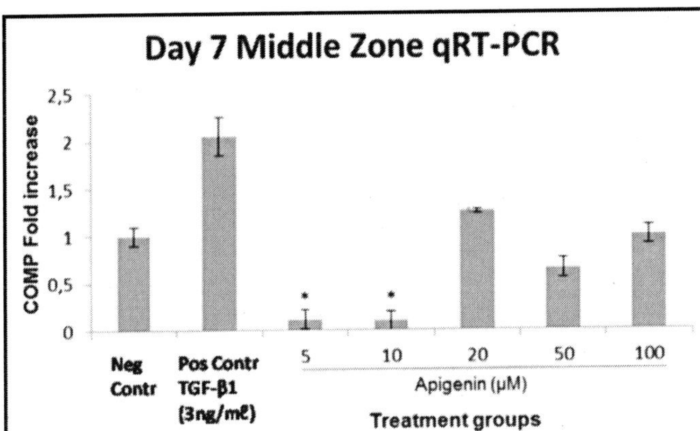

Fig. 6(D): Increase in COMP mRNA expression after seven days of treatment with different concentrations of apigenin in the middle zone. All significant changes are shown as (*= $p < 0.05$, **= $p < 0.01$).

3.9 Effect of Apigenin in Histology of Porcine Articular Cartilage

Articular chondrocytes, isolated from porcine femoral heads, were cultured as a monolayer until confluence before being cultured as cell pellets for 21 days using a micromass culture technique adapted from the Tare *et al.* (2005) method, with slight modifications. The pellet sections were treated with apigenin concentrations of 5, 10, 20, 50 and 100 µM; TGF-β1 (3 ng/mℓ) was used as a positive control and untreated pellets served as negative control groups. Cartilage microanatomy and constituents in these pellets were assessed, employing histology staining procedures (Sirius red, Alcian blue and Safranin O). Interestingly, it was discovered that the overall histology of the cell pellets resembled the AC structure with apparent chondrocytes in the ECM, as observed in Sirius red stain (Figures 7A and

7B); Alcian blue stain (Figures 7C and 7D) and Safranin O stain (Figures 7E and 7F).

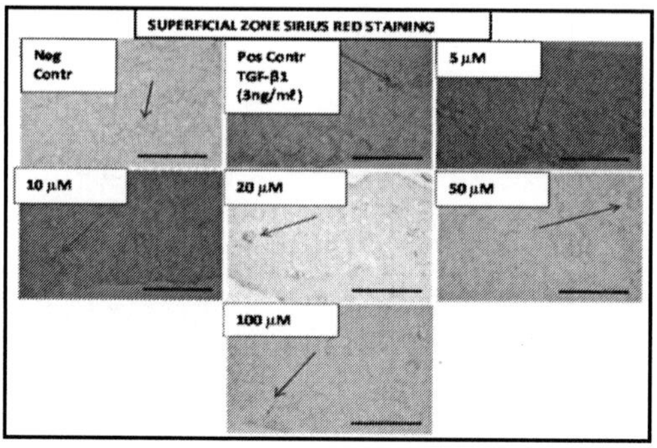

Fig. 7(**A**): Sirius red stained chondrocytic pellets from the superficial zone; arrows indicate fusion of collagen threads. Scale bar - 100 µm.

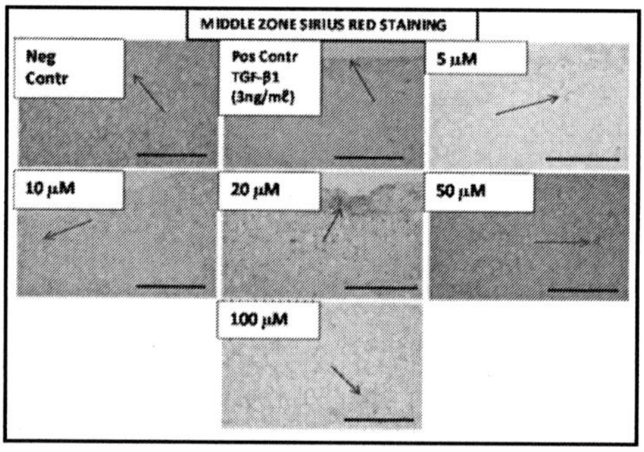

Fig. 7(**B**): Sirius red stained chondrocytic pellets from the middle zone; arrows indicate fusion of collagen threads. Scale bar - 100 µm.

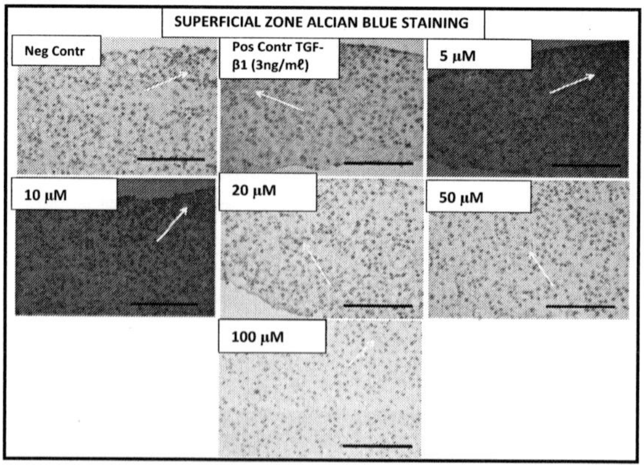

Fig. 7(**C**): Alcian blue-stained chondrocytic pellets from the superficial zone; arrows indicate proteoglycans content. Scale bar - 100 µm.

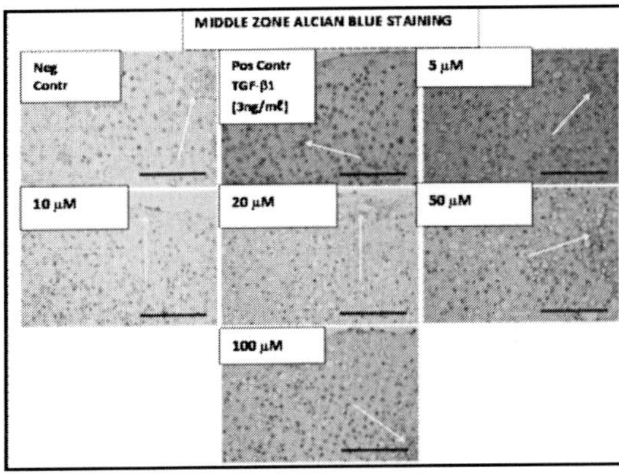

Fig. 7(D): Alcian blue-stained chondrocytic pellets from the middle zone; arrows indicate proteoglycans content. Scale bar - 100 μm.

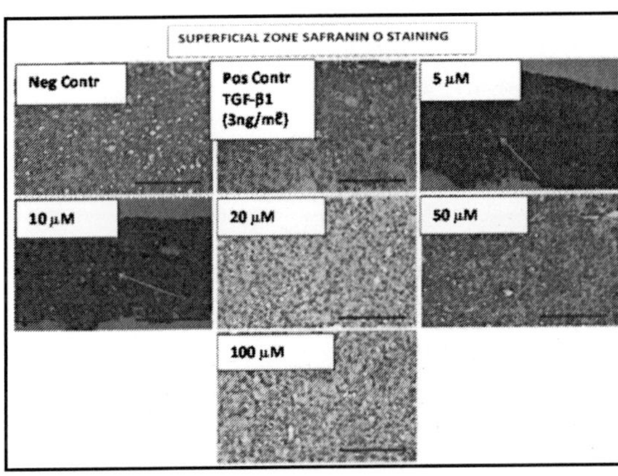

Fig. 7(E): 0.1% Safranin O stained chondrocytic pellets from the superficial zone; arrows indicate ECM production. Scale bar - 100 μm.

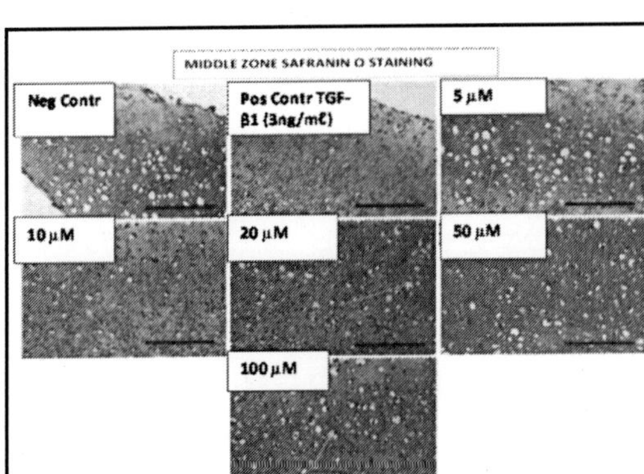

Fig. 7(F): 0.1% Safranin O stained chondrocytic pellets from the middle zone; arrows indicate ECM production. Scale bar - 100 μm.

3.9.1 *Sirius Red*

The Sirius red staining method was used to evaluate the collagen content present in the chondrocytic pellets. The accumulation of red-stained threads across the chondrocytes was reminiscent of collagen fibrils. Chondrocytes stained yellowish in response to Weigert's haematoxylin counterstaining (Figures 7A and 7B). Staining of cell pellets with Sirius red at apigenin concentrations of 5, 10 and 20 μM and at 3 ng/mℓ of positive control TGF-β1 in the superficial zone showed intense staining. The intensity of staining is directly proportional to the collagen content. The middle zone Sirius red stained pellets showed more intense staining at apigenin concentrations of 5, 20 and 100 μM, compared to the negative control and at positive control TGF-β1 (3 ng/mℓ) treatment. Moreover, it was observed that superficial zone pellet sections (Figure 7A) stimulated more intense staining than those from the middle zone (Figure 7B).

3.9.2 *Alcian Blue*

The Alcian blue staining technique was used to assess proteoglycan content confined in the cell pellets. The chondrocyte pellets stained with Alcian blue showed a fundamental area of firm matrix proteoglycans, which stained blue in colour, and the chondrocytes stained pink in response to 1% neutral red counter-stain (Figures 7C and 7D). Apigenin-treated pellet sections showed intense staining at concentrations of 5, 20 and 50 μM, and this was true for 3 ng/mℓ of positive control TGF-β1 treatment, on both the superficial and middle zone (Figures 7C and 7D). However, the middle zone pellet sections (Figure 7D) were stained more intensely than those of the superficial zone (Figure 7C).

3.9.3 *Safranin O*

The 0.1% Safranin O staining method was used to demonstrate the presence of cartilaginous matrix surrounding chondrocytes. Interestingly, chondrocytic pellets stained with Safranin O exhibited production of cartilage ECM that was marked by intense orange-pink staining and chondrocyte nuclei stained black (Figures 7E and 7F). Apigenin-treated pellet sections displayed intense staining at 5 μM and 100 μM concentrations in the superficial zone (Figure 7E) and more intense staining was observed at 5, 20 and 50 μM concentrations in the middle zone (Figure 7F). It is evident that more intense staining with Safranin O was observed in the middle zone than in the superficial zone.

3.10 Effect of Apigenin on Collagen Type II Immunolocalisation

Immunolocalisation of collagen type II was evaluated from the apigenin-treated pellet sections after 21 days of incubation following micromass culture. TGF-β1 (3 ng/mℓ) was used as positive control and untreated pellets served as negative controls. For each set of treatment groups, was collagen type II primary antibody (Col2 Ab) exposed pellet and the other group without the antibody (Figures 8A and 8B). All tissue sections exposed to collagen type II primary antibody were positive for collagen type II, staining brown. The sections without the primary antibody showed no staining, demonstrating the validity and consistency of this method. Intense staining was highly evident in the middle zone compared to the superficial zone (Figures 8A and 8B), with apigenin 20 μM and 50 μM being intensely stained compared to negative controls and other apigenin-treated sections.

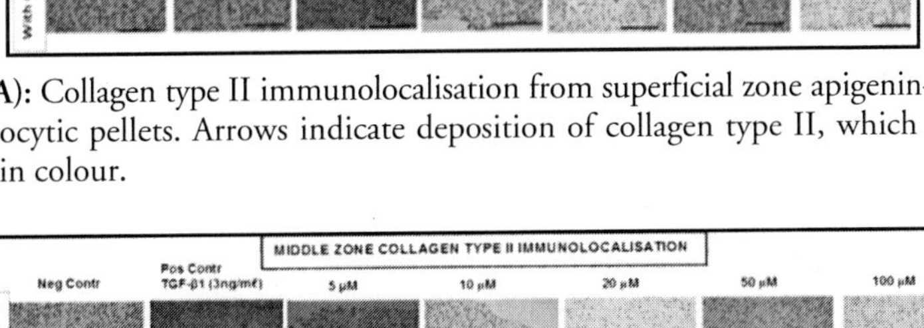

Fig. 8(A): Collagen type II immunolocalisation from superficial zone apigenin-treated chondrocytic pellets. Arrows indicate deposition of collagen type II, which stained brown in colour.

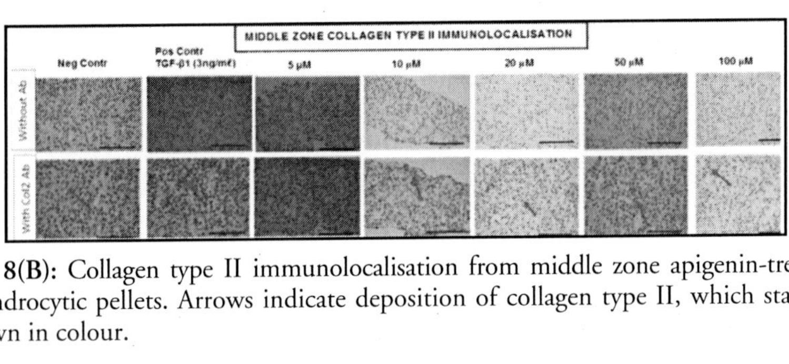

Fig. 8(B): Collagen type II immunolocalisation from middle zone apigenin-treated chondrocytic pellets. Arrows indicate deposition of collagen type II, which stained brown in colour.

4. DISCUSSION

Articular cartilage is a resilient tissue that covers the articulating joint surfaces and functions to provide a smooth, frictionless contact surface and lubrication and to bear mechanical loads on the joints (Fox, Bed & Rodeo, 2009; Milner, Robert & Gibson, 2012). This connective tissue is embedded predominantly with chondrocytes, collagens and proteoglycans in the ECM; these are crucial for the tissue characteristic function. It is well documented that AC has limited capacity for self-renewal because of its avascular, aneural and alymphatic properties (Moreira-Teixeira *et al.*, 2011; Mobasheri *et al.*, 2014; Caldwell & Wang, 2015). The deviations in AC homeostasis is initiated by elevated synthesis of tissue degradation factors, which are associated with AC damage, in turn leading to commencement and development of OA, a chronic disease of the AC characterised by distinctive necrosis in the joints with resultant compromised functionality (Sandel & Aigner, 2001; Clouet *et al.*, 2009). The regulation and synthesis of zonal genes such as collagen type II, aggrecan and COMP are critical for the understanding of cartilage homeostasis in health and disease. The researcher therefore, investigated effects of apigenin in the superficial and middle zone chondrocytes of porcine AC to determine whether it would have the ability to stimulate chondrocyte proliferation in different zones of porcine AC.

In this study, the effect of apigenin in chondrocyte proliferation was investigated using MTT assay. Subsequently, chondrocytes were treated with apigenin at 5, 10, 20, 50 and 100 μM concentrations on days one, four and seven. Results proved apigenin to be effective in inducing cell proliferation from day one to day seven. Apigenin increased chondrocyte proliferation in a time-dependent manner from day one to day seven, on different concentrations. However, apigenin showed a biphasic effect among different concentrations. Proliferation rate was more observed in the middle zone compared to superficial zone compared to the superficial zone, with 5 μM, 20 μM and 50 μM showing higher proliferation than other apigenin concentrations. These results corroborate with the findings of an in study of Kang *et al.* (2005), based on *in vitro* results on rabbit cartilage which showed effect of apigenin in preventing cytotoxicity and anti-proliferation which was observed at 30 μM and 100 μM using MTT assay. In addition, apigenin was found to have proliferative effect of about 10 to 20% at 1 to 10 μM concentrations. In the *in vivo* cultures of New Zealand white rabbits, apigenin displayed chondroregenerative effect at about 0.1 to 100 μM and preferably at concentrations between 1 μM and 80 μM. In another *in vitro* study conducted by Park *et al.* (2016), which evaluated effect of apigenin on proliferation of rabbit chondrocytes cultured for 72 hours using Sulforhodamine B (SRB) Assay, apigenin showed no cytotoxicity on chondrocytes at concentrations of 1, 10, 50 and 100 μM.

In order for a cell to survive, it must divide after its genetic information has doubled (Zaritsky & Woldringh, 2015). Studying the extent of DNA produced by chondrocytes is fundamental for the assessment of the proliferative capability of chondrocytes which is vital for AC regeneration. In the present study, the researcher explored the influence of apigenin at 5, 10, 20, 50 and 100 μM concentrations on proliferating chondrocytes by evaluating the amount of DNA produced on days one, four and seven. The study revealed that apigenin enhances DNA synthesis in a time-dependent manner, and more DNA production was observed on day seven in both the superficial and middle zone. There was a distinct proliferative activity between superficial and middle zone. However, higher DNA amount was observed on middle zone compared to the superficial zone and this was evident on day seven. Similarly, to MTT assay observations, the middle zone stimulated a higher DNA amount when compared to the superficial zone and this effect was more evident on day seven. This finding validates the credence that the middle zone has higher chondro proliferative characteristics than the superficial zone (Iwamoto *et al.*, 2013). Nonetheless, no information has been reported on the effects of apigenin on DNA production on chondrocytes. Nevertheless, wogonin, aflavone analogous to apigenin showed strong binding with chondrocytes genomic DNA and exerted chondroprotective effects *in vitro* using Ethidium bromide fluorescence (Khan *et al.*, 2017). In addition to chondrocyte survival for optimal proliferation, the normal AC function relies on high aggrecan content, high GAG substitution and large aggregate size. In brief description, GAGs are disaccharide molecules that provide the high anionic charge density essential for the distinctive osmotic properties of aggrecan (Roughley, 2006). To evaluate the synthesis of GAGs, chondrocytes were treated with apigenin at 5, 10, 20, 50 and 100 μM concentrations and incubated for 14 days as micromass pellets. It was found that apigenin stimulates the synthesis of GAGs in the middle zone more than in the superficial zone. Furthermore, apigenin enhanced the production of GAGs in a biphasic manner, with 10 μM and 100 μM showing more synthesis compared to other apigenin concentrations, the negative control and positive control (3 ng/mℓ) TGF-β1. Influence of apigenin in cartilage was demonstrated in a study conducted by Durigova, Roughley & Mort (2008) where the flavone, at 100 mM significantly protected proteoglycan aggregate degradation in bovine cartilage explants stimulated with cytokines by inhibiting the action of hyaluronidase on hyaluronic acid using Dimethylmethylene Blue (DMMB) colorimetric assay after six days of culture, a component that non-covalently binds aggrecan in the extracellular matrix non-covalently attaching aggrecan. Chondroprotective effect of apigenin on *in vitro* rabbit chondrocyte explants was displayed in the study carried out by Lim, Park & Kim (2011), where apigenin significantly inhibited the degradative activity of MMP-13, thus preventing ECM breakdown of cartilage explants, notably at 10 μM. These findings were possible through the measurement of released GAG using the Blyscan sulphated glycosaminoglycan assay kit after three days of culture, where apigenin prevented the release of glycosaminoglycans in rabbit cartilage explants treated with IL-1β. The amount of GAG was decreased at the positive control TGF-β1 (3 ng/mℓ) treatment in the middle zone, compared to the negative control. In justification of these findings, Mi *et al.* (2003) and Moulharat *et al.* (2004) proved that TGF-β1 triggers the synthesis of aggrecanases (ADAMTS-4), which are responsible for aggrecan degradation.

Collagen type II provides the tensile strength of the AC (Bhosale & Richardson, 2008). In this study, collagen type II mRNA expression was up-regulated in response to apigenin treatment in biphasic manner and 20 μM showed more expression in both zones AC. On day four, more collagen type mRNA was observed on superficial zone, compared to middle zone. This was also observed on day seven. In support of this, the superficial zone is understood to retain a high concentration of collagen fibrils (Lotz *et al.*, 2010; Muller *et al.*, 2014; Tiku & Sabaawy, 2015). The effect of apigenin in collagen was studied by Lim, Park & Kim (2011), where apigenin effectively protected collagen by inhibiting the action of collagen degradation enzyme (MMP-13) in cultured

SW1353 cells (human chondrosachoma cell line) at concentrations of 5–25 μM after 24 hours of incubation. This result was observed using PT-PCR and Western blotting. In light of TGF-β1, our findings correlate with previous studies which proved TGF-β1 to induce collagen type II expression on rat chondrocytes (Joyce *et al.*, 1990), on porcine chondrocytes (Maepa *et al.*, 2016) and on human chondrocytes (Yoon *et al.*, 2015).

Aggrecan is responsible for major resilience and stress distribution in AC (Temenoff & Mikos, 2000). The present study revealed that apigenin stimulated more aggrecan mRNA expression in the middle zone on day four compared to superficial zone. On day 7, apigenin stimulated more mRNA expression, compared to middle zone. Overall, when comparing the degree of up-regulation on number of culture days, it was noted that on day four accumulated more aggrecan mRNA expression than in day seven. The possible reason for this phenomenon is that structural modifications occur with time, such as the reduction of the monomer weight and shortening of the chondroitin sulphate chains, are common are common to sulphated proteoglycan monomers synthesized by in vitro chondrocytes as well as those synthesised by freshly excised cartilage (Pacifici, Fellini & Holtzer 1981). Furthermore, the extent of expression showed a biphasic effect and it was noted that 10 μM and 100 μM apigenin treatment results from GAG assay corroborate with aggrecan mRNA results. In support of the efficacy of apigenin, in a previous study conducted by Durigova, Roughley and Mort (2008), it was discovered that apigenin significantly protected cartilage from the catabolic activity of cytokines, thereby stimulating the aggrecan in bovine cartilage explants at concentration of 100 mM. The effects of apigenin in chondrocytes was also studied by Park *et al.* (2016), and it was discovered that apigenin inhibited IL-1β-induced MMP-3 gene expression, which targeted proteoglycans aggrecates using, 10% sodium dodecyl sulphate-polyacrylamide gel electrophoresis assay after 2 hours in growth medium with 1, 10, 50, or 100 μM of apigenin, followed by incubition in the presence or absence of IL-1β (10 ng/mℓ) for 24 hours. In the aspect of the positive control TGF-β1 (3 ng/mℓ) down-regulated aggrecan mRNA. These outcomes on TGF-β1 correlate with those of previous studies, which proved this growth factor to stimulate the synthesis of aggrecanases (ADAMTS-4), which are responsible for aggrecan degradation (Mi *et al.*, 2003; Moulharat *et al.*, 2004).

Cartilage oligomeric matrix protein is an AC constituent responsible for the maintenance of chondrocyte phenotype, cell growth and matrix development (Shen *et al.*, 1995; Motaung, DiCesare & Reddi, 2011).Cartilage oligomeric matrix protein is an AC constituent responsible for the maintenance of chondrocyte phenotype, cell growth and matrix development (Shen *et al.*, 1995; Motaung, DiCesare & Reddi, 2011). In this study, the researcher explored the effect of apigenin in COMP regulation and discovered that COMP mRNA expression was up-regulated more distinctly in the superficial zone than in the middle zone on both days four and day seven. Moreover, it was evident that more enhanced COMP mRNA expression was observed on day compared to day seven. The degree of COMP expression was presented in a dose- and time-dependent manner. This was also true for positive control TGF-β1 (3 ng/mℓ), with higher expression in the superficial zone on day four. Cartilage oligomeric matrix protein plays an important role in matrix assembly (Motaung, DiCesare & Reddi, 2011; Acharya, DiCesare *et al.*, 2014) through interaction with a number of cartilage ECM proteins, including collagens, as well as proteoglycans such as aggrecan and others (Thur *et al.*, 2001; Briggs & Chapman, 2002; Di Cesare *et al.*, 2002; Budde *et al.*, 2005; Chen *et al.*, 2007). The effect of apigenin in cartilage matrix is fairly positive according to the outcomes displaying that this flavone inhibits the exploitation activity of hyaluronidase enzyme in the ECM of bovine cartilage explants using Dimethylmethylene Blue (DMMB) colorimetric assay after six days of culture (Durigova, Roughley & Mort, 2008). In light of TGF-β1, the findings of this study correlate with those of a previous study by Motaung *et al.* (2011) on the influence of TGF-β1 in COMP mRNA expression, which proved substantial up-regulation of COMP in bovine chondrocytes. However, more expression was observed on day seven compared to day four. Conversely, the previous findings are distinct to the observations of this study on the basis that COMP mRNA expression was reduced on day seven in contrast to day four in both the TGF-β1 and apigenin treatment groups.

For the documented reason that articular cartilage is a tissue that cannot restore itself after injury because of its avascular, aneural and alymphatic nature (Caldwell & Wang, 2015), numerous cell lines have been used well to engineer tissues with properties analogous to inherent cartilage. In addition, the field of tissue engineering intends to revive the AC and mimic the ECM with interlinked collagen, proteoglycans and glycoproteins. Consequently, tissue engineering envisages the restoration of intricate cartilage defects (Responte, Natoli & Athanasiou, 2007; Kumar, Griffin & Butler, 2016). The use of natural compounds in tissue engineered models, because of their novel properties in anti-inflammation treatment and in a wide range of remedies, with minor side effects (Jalil, Shuid & Muhammad, 2012), raises the hope of restoration of AC after damage. This study has substantiated the effectiveness of the natural flavonoid, apigenin, when administered to chondrocytes and cultured as micromass to form pellets, mimicking AC. The grading method for intensity of sating was adopted from Sun *et al.*, (2012).

Following 21-day culture and after apigenin treatment, the histology of the cell pellets efficiently revealed the resemblance of the AC structure to apparent chondrocytes in the ECM as observed in Sirius red stain, Alcian blue stain and Safranin O stain. Sirius red revealed the collagen content and the most effective treatments were 5 μM and 10 μM; as well as at 3 ng/mℓ of TGF-β1, in the superficial zone, while the middle zone showed more intense staining at apigenin concentrations of 5 μM, 20 and 100 μM, compared to the negative control and at TGF-β1 (3 ng/mℓ) treatment. Middle zone showed more staining compared to superficial zone staining. The Sirius red staining method in micromass culture has been established to intensify the collagen content as proved by Tare *et al.* (2005) in human chondrocytes and in a separate study by Prante *et al.* (2006). This validates the efficacy of this culture and staining method.

Alcian blue stain in chondrocytic pellets revealed proteoglycans production and more intense staining was observed at apigenin concentrations of 5, 20 and 50 μM, and this was true for 3 ng/mℓ of TGF-β1 treatment, on both the superficial and middle zone, compared to the negative control. Nevertheless, the middle zone pellet sections were witnessed to exhibit a higher degree of intensity than those of the superficial zone. Chondrocytes cultured following the micro-mass method and stained with Alcian blue showed positive staining for proteoglycans, confirming the validity of this staining method, which was reported in a study carried out by Tare *et al.*, (2005) on human chondrocytes and in another study by Agar *et al.* (2011) on human chondrocytes and MSCs.

Safranin O stain (0.1%) demonstrated the synthesis of the ECM by chondrocytes. Apigenin showed more intense staining at 5 μM and 50 μM concentrations in the superficial zone and more intense staining was observed at 5, 20 and 50 μM concentrations in the middle zone. Moreover, it is evident that more intense staining with Safranin O was observed in the middle zone than in the superficial zone. In light of this staining method, Safranin O staining in human chondrocytes exhibited positive staining for ECM in separate studies carried out by Tare *et al.* (2005) and by Grassel *et al.* (2010). The grading method on intensity of staining adopted from Sun *et al.* (2012), has aided in distinguishing the effective apigenin concentrations, and in this study we were able to prove that middle zone sections showed more staining, compared to superficial zone. The other grading methods include Bern score for staining of Safranin O, where the score accounts for uniformity intensity of matrix staining, cell density/extent of produced, and cellular morphologies. It also accounts for distance between cells/amount of matrix accumulated (Grogan *et al.*, 2005).

Collagen plays a role in providing AC with dynamic shear and tensile properties, thereby stabilising the matrix (Fox, Bedi & Rodeo, 2009). Among the different types of collagen, type II collagen is the principal component of macrofibril, accounting for over 90% of the AC collagen content, and is responsible for the stiffness and tensile strength of the AC (Responte, Natoli & Athanasiou, 2007; Bhosale & Richardson, 2008). In the present study, the researcher examined collagen type II immunolocalisation after 21 days of exposure of chondrocyte pellets to apigenin following the micromass culture method. Staining of collagen type II was detected extensively over all the pellet sections treated with the antibody. Specifically, more intense staining was highly evident in the middle zone compared to the superficial zone, with apigenin 5 μM, 20 μM and 50 μM being more intensely stained compared to the negative control and the other apigenin-treated sections. In a previous study conducted by Lim, Park & Kim (2011), apigenin successfully protected collagen by inhibiting the action of collagen degradation enzymes in cultured human chondrocytes at concentrations of 5–25 μM (Lim, Park & Kim, 2011).

ACKNOWLEDGEMENTS

The author would like to thank Tshwane University of Technology for full support and National Research Foundation for financial assistance.

REFERENCES

[1] Acharya, C., Yik, J.H.N., Kishore, A., Van Dinh, V., Di Cesare, P.E. and Haudenschild, D.R. (2014). Cartilage oligomeric matrix protein and its binding partners in the cartilage extracellular matrix: Interaction, regulation and role in chondrogenesis. *Matrix Biology*, 34: 102–111.

[2] Agar, G., Blumenstein, S., Bar-Ziv, Y., Kardosh, R., Schrift-Tzadok, M., Gal-Levy, R., Fischler, T., Goldschmid, R. and Yayon, A. 2011. The Chondrogenic Potential of Mesenchymal Cells and Chondrocytes from Osteoarthritic Subjects: A Comparative Analysis. *Cartilage*, 2(1): 40–49.

[3] Bhosale, A.M. and Richardson, J.B. (2008). Articular cartilage: Structure, injuries and review of management. *British Medical Bulletin*, 87: 77–95.

[4] Briggs, M.D., Hoffman, S.M.G., King, L.M., Olsen, A.S., Mohrenweiser, H., Leroy, J.G., Mortier, G.R., Rimoin, D.L., Lachman, R.S., Gaines, E.S., Cekleniak, J.A., Knowlton, R.G. and Cohn, D.H. (1995). Pseudoachondroplasia and multiple epiphyseal dysplasia due to mutations in the cartilage oligomeric matrix protein gene. *Nat. Genet*, 10: 330–336.

[5] Budde, B., Blumbach, K., Ylostalo, J., Zaucke, F., Ehlen, H.W.A., Wagener, R., Ala-Kokko, L., Paulsson, M., Bruckner, P. and Grassel, S. (2005). Altered integration of matrilin-3 into cartilage extracellular matrix in the absence of collagen IX. *Mol. Cell. Biol.* 25: 10465–10478.

[6] Chen, F.H., Herndon, M.E., Patel, N., Hecht, J.T., Tuan, R.S. and Lawler, J. (2007). Interaction of cartilage oligomeric matrix protein/thrombospondin 5 with aggrecan. *J Biol Chem*, 282(34): 24591–24598.

[7] Clouet, J., Vinatier, C., Merceron, C., Pot-Vaucel, M., Maugars, Y., Weiss, P., Grimandi, G. and Guicheux, J. (2009). Therapeutic strategies for effective management of OA and cartilage defects: From osteoarthritis treatments to future regenerative therapies for cartilage. *Drugs Discovery Today*, 14(19/20): 913–918.

[8] Dumond, H., Presle, N. and Pottie, P. (2004). "Site specific changes in gene expression and cartilage metabolism during early experimental osteoarthritis," *Osteoarthritis and Cartilage*, Vol. 12, No. 4, pp. 284–295.

[9] Durigova, M., Roughley, P.J. and Mort, J.S. (2008). Mechanism of proteoglycan aggregate degradation in cartilage stimulated with oncostatin M. *Osteoarthritis Cartilage*, 16: 98–104.

[10] Fernandes, J.C., Martel-Pelletier, J. and Lascau-Comanl, V. (1998). "Collagenaqse-1 and collagenase-3 synthesis in normal and early experimental osteoarthritic canine cartilage: an immunohistochemical study," *Journal of Rheumatology*, Vol. 25, No. 8, pp. 1585–1594, 1998.

[11] Fox, A.J.S., Bedi, A. and Rodeo, S.A. (2009). The basic science of articular cartilage: Structure, composition and function. *Sports Health*, 1(6): 461–468.

[12] Ickinger, C. and Tikly, M. (2011). Current approach to diagnosis and management of osteoarthritis. *South African Pharmaceutical Journal*, 78(8): 19–27.

[13] Iwamoto, M., Ohta, Y., Larmour, C. and Enomoto-Iwamoto, M. (2013). Towards regeneration of articular cartilage. *Birth Defects Res C Embryo Today*, 99(3): 192–202.

[14] Jalil, M.A.A., Shuid, A.N. and Muhammad, N. (2012). Role of medicinal plants and natural products on osteoporotic fracture healing. *Evidence-Based Complementary and Alternative Medicine*, 2012: 1–8.

[15] Kang, J.H., Kim, G.M. and Park, C.S. (2005). Composition for treatment of osteoarthritis containing apigenin as a chondroregenerative agent. (Patent WO2005034937A1).

[16] Kordich, J. and Kordich, L. (2013). *Jay Kordich the father of juicing* [online]. Available from: http://blog.jaykordich.com/?cat=306. [Accessed: 09/04/2015].

[17] Lee, J., Zhou, H.Y., Cho, S.Y., Kim, Y.S., Lee, Y.S. and Jeong, C.S. (2007). Anti-inflammatory mechanisms of apigenin: Inhibition of cyclooxygenase-2 expression, adhesion of monocytes to human umbilical vein endothelial cells, and expression of cellular adhesion molecules. *Archives of Pharmacal Research*, 30(10): 1318–1327.

[18] Lewis, J.R. and Carey-Smith, R.L. (2012). Osteoarthritis—Diagnosis, treatment and surgery. *Surgery for osteoarthritis of the knee* [online]. In Tech.com. Available from: http://www.intechopen.com/books/osteoarthritis-diagnosis-treatment-and-surgery / surgery-for-osteoarthritis-of-the-knee . [Accessed: 12/04/2015].

[19] Lim, H., Park, H. and Kim, H.P. (2011). Effects of flavonoids on matrix metalloproteinase-13 expression of interleukin-1β-treated articular chondrocytes and their cellular mechanisms: Inhibition of c-Fos/AP-1 and JAK/STAT signalling pathways. *Journal of Pharmacological Sciences*, 116: 221–231.

[20] Lotz, M.K., Otsuki, S., Grogan, S.P., Sah, R., Terkeltaub, R. and D'lima, D. (2010). Cartilage cell clusters. *Arthritis & Rheumatism*, 62(8): 2206–2218.

[21] Maepa, M., Razwinani, M. and Motaung, S. (2016). Effects of resveratrol on collagen type II protein in the superficial zone and middle zone chondrocytes of porcine articular cartilage. *Journal of Ethnopharmacology*, 178: 25–33.

[22] Makela, J.T.A., Huttu, M.R.J. and Korhonen. R.K. (2012). Structure-function relationships in osteoarthritic human hip joint articular cartilage. *Osteoarthritis and Cartilage*, 20:1268–1277.

[23] Mi, Z., Ghivizzani, S.C., Lechman, E., Glorioso, J.C., Evans, C.H. and Robbins, P.D. (2003). Adverse effects of adenovirus mediated gene transfer of human transforming growth factor beta into rabbit knees. *Arthritis Res Ther*, 5:132–139.

[24] Milner, P.I., Wilkins, R.J. and Gibson, J.S. (2012). Cellular physiology of articular cartilage in health and disease. *Principles of osteoarthritis – Its definition, character, derivation and modality-related recognition* [online]. In Tech.com. Available from: http://www.intechopen.com/books/principles-of-osteoarthritis-its-definition-character-derivation-and-modality-related-recognition/cellular-physiology-of-articular-cartilage-in-health-and-disease [Accessed: 09/04/2015].

[25] Moreira-Teixeira, L.S., Georgi, N., Leijten, J., Wu, L. and Karperien, M. (2011). Cartilage tissue engineering. *Cartilage and Bone Development and its Disorders*, 21: 102–115.

[26] Mobasheri, A., Kalamegam, G., Musumeci, G. and Batt, M.E. (2014). Chondrocyte and mesenchymal stem cell-based therapies for cartilage repair in osteoarthritis and related orthopaedic conditions. *Maturitas*, 78:188–198.

[27] Motaung, S.C.K.M., Di Cesare, P.E. and Reddi, H. (2011). Differential response of cartilage oligomeric matrix protein (COMP) to morphogens of bone morphogenetic protein/transforming growth factor-β family in the surface, middle and deep zones of the articular cartilage. *Journal of Tissue Engineering and Regenerative Medicine*, 5: e87–e96.

[28] Moulharat, N., Lesur, C., Thomas, M., Rolland-Valognes, G., Pastoureau, P., Anract, P., De Ceuninck, F. and Sabatini, M. (2004). Effects of transforming growth factor on aggrecanase production and proteoglycan degradation by human chondrocytes in vitro. *Osteoarthritis and Cartilage*, 12: 296–305.

[29] Muller, C., Khabut, A., Dudhia, J., Reinholt, F.P., Aspberg, A., Heinegard, D. and Onnerfjord, P. (2014). Quantitative proteomics at different depths in human articular cartilage reveals unique patterns of protein distribution. *Matrix Biology*, 40:34–45.

[30] Neogi, T. (2012). Clinical significance of bone changes in osteoarthritis. *Therapeutic Advance in Musculosckeletal Disease*, 4(4): 259–267.

[31] Pearle, A.D., Warren, R. F. and Rodeo, S.A. (2005). Basic science of articular cartilage and osteoarthritis. *Clin Sports Med*, 24 (2005): 1–12.

[32] Park, J.S., Kim, D.K., Shin, H., Lee, H.J., Jo, H.S., Jeong, J.H., Choi, Y. L., Lee, C.J. and Hwang, S. (2016). Apigenin regulates interleukin-1β-induced production of matrix metalloproteinase both in the knee joint of rat and in primary cultured articular chondrocytes. *Biomolecules and Therapeutics*, 24(2): 163–170.

[33] Pfander, D., Swoboda, B. and Kirsch, T. (2001). "Expression of early and late differentiation markers (proliferating cell nuclear antigen, syndecan-3,

annexin VI, and alkaline phosphatase) by human osteoarthritic chondrocytes," *American Journal of Pathology*, Vol. 159, No. 5, pp. 1777–1783.

[34] Responte, D.J., Natoli, R.M. and Athanasiou, K.A. (2007). Collagens of articular cartilage: Structure, function, and importance in tissue engineering. *Critical Reviews in Biomedical Engineering*, 35(5): 363–411.

[35] Roughley, P.J. (2006). The structure and function of cartilage proteoglycans. *European Cells and Materials*, 12:92–101.

[36] Sandell, L.J. and Aigner, T. (2001). Articular cartilage and changes in arthritis, an introduction: Cell biology of osteoarthritis. *Arthritis Research*, 3:107–113.

[37] Shen, Z., Heinegard, D. and Sommarin, Y. (1995). Distribution and expression of cartilage oligomeric matrix protein and bone sialoprotein show marked changes during rat femoral head development. *Matrix Biol*, 14: 773–781.

[38] Tare, R.S., Haward, D., Pound, J.C., Roach, H.I. and Oreffo, R.O.C. Tissue engineering strategies for cartilage generation – Micromass and three dimensional cultures using human chondrocytes and a continuous cell line. *Biochemical and Biophysical Research Communications*, 333(2005): 609–621.

[39] Tchetina, E.V., Kobayashi, M., Yasuda, T., Meijers, T., Pidoux, I and Poole, A.R. (2007). "Chondrocyte hypertrophy can be induced by a cryptic sequence of type II collagen and is accompanied by the induction of MMP-13 and collagenase activity: implications for development and arthritis," *Matrix Biology*, Vol. 26, No. 4, pp. 247–258.

[40] Tchetina, E.V. (2011). Developmental mechanisms in articular cartilage degradation in osteoarthritis. *Arthritis*, 2011:1–10.

[41] Temenoff, J.S. and Mikos, A.G. (2000). Review: Tissue engineering for regeneration of articular cartilage. *Biomaterials*, 21: 431–440.

[42] Thur, J., Rosenberg, K., Nitsche, D.P., Pihlajamaa, T., Ala-Kokko, L., Heinegard, D., Paulsson, M. and Maurer, P. (2001). Mutations in cartilage oligomeric matrix protein causing pseudoachondroplasia and multiple epiphyseal dysplasia affect binding of calcium and collagen I, II, and IX. *J. Biol. Chem.* 276: 6083–6092.

[43] Tiku, M.L. and Sabaawy, H.E. (2015). Cartilage regeneration for treatment of osteoarthritis: A paradigm for nonsurgical intervention. *Therapeutic Advances in Musculoskeletal Disease*, 1–12.

[44] Waittenauer, R., Smith, L. and Aden, K. (2013). Background Paper 6.12 Osteoarthritis. *Priority Medicines for Europe and the World "A Public Health Approach to Innovation*, 1–31.

[45] Wu, W., Billinghurst, R.C. and Pidoux, I. (2002). "Sites of collagenase cleavage and denaturation of type II collagen in aging and osteoarthritic

articular cartilage and their relationship to the distribution of matrix metalloproteinase 1 and matrix metalloproteinase 13," *Arthritis and Rheumatism*, Vol. 46, No. 8, pp. 2087–2094.

[46] Yoon, H.J., Kim, S.B., Somaiya, D., Noh, M.J., Choi, K., Lim, C., Lee, H., Lee, Y., Yi, Y. and Lee, K.W. (2015). Collagen type II and aggrecan expression induction in primary human chondrocyte by TGF-β1. *BMC Musculoskeletal Disorders*, 16(141): 1–15.

The Effects of Standardized *Ficus deltoidea* var. *kunstleri* Aqueous Extract on Prenatal Development in Rats

M. Hussin[1*], O. Maizatul Hasyima[2], Elda Nurafnie[1] and A. Norizah[1]

[1]Toxicology & Pharmacology Unit, Herbal Medicine Research Centre, Institute for Medical Research, Kuala Lumpur-50588, Malaysia

[2]Phytochemistry Unit, Herbal Medicine Research Centre, Institute for Medical Research, Kuala Lumpur-50588, Malaysia

*E-mail: hussin@imr.gov.my

ABSTRACT: In Malaysia, Ficus deltoidea is traditionally used for various consumptions; however, no safety data is available of this plant on pregnancy and its effects on fetal development. The present study was conducted to evaluate the toxicity of Ficus deltoidea var. kunstleri aqueous extract (FDAE) in the development of fetuses in female rats (n = 20). The FDAE at 0, 250, 500, 1000 and 2000 mg/kg body weight/day was orally treated on gestation day 6–20. Clinical signs of maternal toxicity, body weight gain and food and water intake were recorded. The pregnant rats were sacrificed and caesarean sections were performed on day 21. Vital organs were collected and examined for any abnormal morphology. Numbers of resorptions, live and dead fetuses were counted. All the fetuses from each litter were cleared and stained with Alizarin red S for skeletal examination. FDAE did not affect the body weight gain and the consumption of food and water and produced sign of maternal toxicity throughout the study. No external malformation, growth retardation and embryo lethality on fetuses were observed in all groups. The no-observed adverse effect level (NOAEL) of FDAE for prenatal developmental toxicity in rats was determined to be > 2000 mg/kg body weight/day via the oral route.

Keywords: *Ficus deltoidea*, Prenatal Development, Toxicity, Rats.

1. INTRODUCTION

Medicinal plants have a long history of use and their application is widespread in both developing and developed countries.

However, herbal toxicity has become an issue of concern due to wide use and easy availability of herbal medicines (Martins 2014). Although, herbal medicinal products are widely considered to be of lower risk compared with synthetic drugs, they are not completely free from the possibility of toxicity or other adverse effects (De Smet, 2004).

In National Pharmaceutical Regulatory Agency, Malaysia guideline, the safety data on reproductive system should be provided prior to register a new drug even though they are originated from natural resources. Therefore, more detailed and systemic toxicological studies should be performed to control the potential toxicities even if they have been used as traditional folk medicine (Kim *et al.*, 2012).

Ficus deltoidea is an epiphytic shrub, which is commonly known as Mas cotek, serapat angina, telingaberuk by Malaysian communities. It has been traditionally used for headache, cold, rheumatism and to strengthen the uterus after birth (Sulaiman *et al.*, 2008). Most of the benefits are due to flavonoids presents in the plants. Various studies have demonstrated that vitexin, quercetin and catechin play roles in producing the anticarcinogenic, antiviral, antioxidant, anti-inflammatory activities and other pharmacological activities (Harborne and Williams, 2000; Havsteen, 2002). Despite the prevalent use of *F.deltoidea* as medicine, the toxicity effects of this plant have not been fully investigated (Hamidun *et al.*, 2014). Previous study by Fazliana *et al.* (2008) showed that aqueous extract of *F. deltoidea* leaves did not cause any hematological and biochemical changes in rats when administered orally at 100 and 300 mg/kg body weight. Further findings on acute toxicity of the methanol extract of *F. deltoidea* leaves also demonstrated LD_{50} higher than 5000 mg/kg body weight (Farsi *et al.*, 2013) which indicates low toxicity effect of the extracts. Despite the widespread use of *F. deltoidea* plant in traditional medicine, no prenatal developmental toxicity profile is available; therefore, the present study was carried out to evaluate the potential toxicity effect of *F. deltoidea* aqueous extract treated in Sprague Dawley rats during organogenesis period.

2. MATERIALS AND METHODS

2.1 Plant Materials and Extract Preparation

F. deltoidea dried leaves were purchased locally from Pahang, Malaysia. Leaves were dried in oven (Mammert, Germany) at 45°C for 2 days and ground to a powdered form prior to extraction with water by boiling it for 1 hour before passing through filter paper (Whatman, No. 1). Filtrates collected were sprayed dried (Buchi, Switzerland) to form a powder that was further used in the experiments.

2.2 Phytochemical Analysis

One hundred milligram of the powdered aqueous extract of *F. deltoidea* was dissolved in 10 ml of methanol-water (50%) (10 mg/ml) and centrifuged at 10000 g for 5 min at 4°C and subsequently filtered by 0.4 µm filter (Whatman, No. 1). Samples were then analyzed by HPLC with absorbance, fluorescence and mass spectrometric detection.

2.3 Instrumentation and Chromatographic Conditions

The HPLC system employed consisted of Surveyor gradient (Thermo-Finnigan, USA), comprising of a pumping system, autosampler, and degasser coupled with photodiode array absorbance (PDA) detector scanning from 200 to 700 nm controlled by Xcalibur software version 1.3. Separation was carried out using MAX-RP 4 µm, 250 mm × 4.6 mm C12 reverse phase column (Phenomenex, Torrance, CA) maintained at 40°C and eluted at a flow rate of 1.0 ml/min with 60 min gradient from 15 to 50% methanol in water containing 0.1% formic acid. After passing through the flow cell of the photodiode array and fluorescence detectors, the column eluate was split and 20% directed to an LCQ Duo mass spectrometer (Thermo-Finnigan) with an electrospray interface operating in full scan data dependent MS/MS mode from 150 to 1000 amu. (+)-Catechin and (–)-epicatechin were identified by fluorescence (FL) detector (Jasco FP-920) at the wavelengths (XM-excretion/EM-emission) 280/315 nm.

2.4 Prenatal Developmental Toxicity

2.4.1 *Chemicals*

Glycerol, methanol, ammonium sulphide and potassium hydroxide were purchased from Merck, Chemical Germany. Acetic acid and 95% ethanol were from Hamburg. Diethyl ether was purchased from Fisher. Bouin's solution and Alizarin Red S were from Sigma Aldrich, UK.

2.4.2 *Animals*

Virgin females (n = 105; 180–200 g) and fertile males (n = 55; 200–250 g) Sprague-Dawley (SD) rats, supplied by the Animal Resource Unit (Medical Resource Centre, Institute for Medical Research, Malaysia) were used. Upon arrival at the lab, animals were individually housed in the Individual Ventilated Cage, lined with wood shavings and kept at controlled temperature (20 ± 2°C), air relative humidity (40–60%) and photoperiod (12 h of light and 12 h of dark cycle). All rats were acclimatized for one week prior to the start of the study. A commercial rat diet (Specialty Feeds, Australia) and water were available *ad libitum*. Approval for this study was obtained from the Animal Care and Ethics Committee, Ministry of Health Malaysia (ACUC No: ACUC/KKM/02 (2/2017).

2.4.3 *Experimental Design*

Female rats in the pro-oestrous phase (oestrous cycle phase was determined by vaginal smear cytology) were placed into the cage of males (on a one-to-one basis) in the late morning and removed in the following morning (24 h). The day on which overnight mating was confirmed by the presence of sperm in the vaginal smear was designated as gestation day 0 (GD0).

2.4.4 *Treatment*

The FDAE (0, 250, 500, 1000 or 2000 mg/kg/day), dissolved in distilled water, was administered (volume: 10mL/kg) orally (gavage) to pregnant rats on GD 6–20. FDAE aqueous solutions were prepared daily. Once a day, after treatment, rats were observed in their cages for 60 min, and behavioral changes and clinical signs of toxicity were recorded. Maternal body weight (on a daily basis) and food and water intake (on a weekly basis) were measured and recorded.

2.4.5 *Caesarean Section and Fetal Examination*

On GD21 rats were euthanized by ethyl ether inhalation and caesarean section was performed. Gravid uterus was removed and weighed with its contents. The number of corpora lutea in both ovaries was then counted. Implantation sites were determined by the method of Salewski (1964). Resorptions and living and dead fetuses were counted. Placentas were examined and weighed. Fetuses were removed by cutting the umbilical cord close to their bodies, examined for externally visible abnormalities under a stereomicroscope, sexed and numbered. The fetuses of each litter, selected at random, were macerated in potassium hydroxide, cleared with glycerin KOH solutions and stained with Alizarin Red S for skeleton evaluation (Staples & Schnell, 1964). Maternal organs were examined for gross pathology abnormalities and liver, kidneys, lungs, heart, adrenals and ovaries were removed and weighed.

2.4.6 *Statistical Analysis*

Data on maternal body weight, weight gain during pregnancy, food and water consumption, fetal body weight, placenta weight, maternal organ weights (absolute and relative weights) were analyzed by one-way analysis of variance (ANOVA) and Dunnett's post hoc test. Number (per litter) of corpora lutea graviditatis, implantations, live and dead fetuses, and resorptions were evaluated by the Kruskal-Wallis test followed by the Mann-Whitney U test. Proportions of fetuses and litters showing a given abnormality were compared by the chi-square. In any case, a difference was significant when $p < 0.05$.

3. RESULTS

3.1 Phytochemical Analysis

HPLC-absorbance profiles of the extract at 280 and 365 nm are shown in Figure 1. Chemical structures of the identified compounds are shown in Table 1.

3.2 Pregnancy Weight Gain and Clinical Signs of Maternal Toxicity

During the treatment period, no maternal death was registered. There were no significant changes in behavior, piloerections or alterations in locomotor activity. All animals appeared healthy at sacrifice. No gross pathology alterations were found in FDAE treated rats. The effect of FDAE on maternal body weight and weight gain on animals during pregnancy period are shown in Table 2.

The body weight of animals increased proportionally with the days of pregnancy and no significant changes were observed in all groups. In relation to maternal body weight gain, no significant difference was detected prior to, during and after 15 days treatment among the five groups of animals ($p < 0.05$). Food and water intake was about similar in all treated groups throughout pregnancy. There was no morphology changes found in any maternal organs. No significant difference were noted in both maternal relative and absolute weight of kidneys, liver, gravid uterus, lung, heart or ovaries between the control and FDAE-treated groups as shown in Table 3.

Table 1: Mass spectral characteristics and identity of phenolics present in FDAE analyzed by HPLC coupled to tandem mass spectrometry. (Reproduced with permission from Omar *et al.* 2011)

Peak	t_R *(min)*	λ_{max}	*Compound*
1	6.6	270	Gallocatechin
2	11.4	275	Epigallocatechin
3	12.5	280	(+)- Catechin
4	12.7	280	(+)- Catechin-(Epi)Afz
5	14.2	280	(+)- Catechin-(Epi)Afz
6	15.1	275	(+)- Catechin-(Epi)Afz-(Epi)Afz
7	15.9	280	(+)- Catechin-(Epi)Afz
8	18.5	275	(+)- Catechin-(Epi)Afz-(Epi)Afz
9	19.4	280	(–)- Epicatechin
10	21.8	350	Luteolin-6-8-*C*-diglu (Lucenin-2)
11	25.7	340	Apigenin-6, 8-*C*-diglu (Vicenin-2)
12	27.0	345	Luteolin-6-*C*-hex-8-*C*-pent
13	27.8	345	Luteolin-6-*C*-glu-8-*C*-ara
14	29.6	335	Apigenin-6-*C*-ara-8-*C*-glu (Isoschaftoside)
15	30.4	345	Luteolin-6-*C*-ara-8-*C*-glu
16	30.7	335	Apigenin-6-*C*-glu-8-*C*-ara (Schaftoside)
17	31.4	335	Luteolin-8-*C*-glu (Orientin)
18	31.9	320	Apigenin-6-*C*-pent-8-*C*-glu
19	33.0	310	4-ρ-coumaroylquinic acid
20	35.5	335	Apigenin-8-*C*-glu (Vitexin)
21	36.5	335	Apigenin-6-*C*-glu-8-*C*-pent
22	37.5	335	Apigenin-6-*C*-pent-8-*C*-pent
23	38.5	335	Apigenin-6-*C*-pent-8-*C*-pent
24	39.6	335	Apigenin-6-*C*-glu (Isovitexin)
25	42.1	335	Apigenin-6-*C*-pent-8-*C*-pent
26	44.7	335	Apigenin-6-*C*-pent-8-*C*-pent

Table 2: Maternal weight gain of rats orally treated with FDAE at 0, 250, 500, 1000 and 2000 mg/kg body weight/day on gestation day 6–20

Parameters	*FDAE (mg/kg body weight)*				
	Control	*250*	*500*	*1000*	*2000*
Treated females (n)	20	20	20	20	20
Pregnant females (n)	20	20	20	19	20
Pregnant/treated females (%)	100	100	100	95	100
Maternal weight (g)					
GD6	237.01 ± 50.08	235.88 ± 49.37	225.32 ± 48.57	243.67 ± 50.02	228.07 ± 43.91
GD21	340.44 ± 44.15	345.38 ± 41.43	338.62 ± 46.85	345.84 ± 43.75	330.34 ± 42.86
Maternal weight gain (n)					
GD6-9	13.69 ± 8.64	16.31 ± 13.16	16.71 ± 9.24	13.53 ± 10.25	9.53 ± 12.64
GD9-12	13.22 ± 8.86	14.40 ± 5.35	13.10 ± 4.70	13.59 ± 4.70	12.38 ± 6.47
GD12-15	13.66 ± 10.47	14.96 ± 5.42	14.91 ± 8.09	13.67 ± 9.68	17.48 ± 7.96
GD15-18	31.35 ± 9.16	29.03 ± 5.99	31.59 ± 5.72	31.34 ± 6.75	30.63 ± 7.34
GD18-21	31.50 ± 9.67	34.80 ± 10.39	36.99 ± 9.66	30.32 ± 21.98	32.25 ± 5.65
GD6-21	103.43 ± 22.98	109.52 ± 22.50	113.31 ± 19.23	102.17 ± 23.25	102.27 ± 15.45

Data shown as mean ± SD were analyzed by ANOVA and no difference ($p > 0.05$) among dose groups was observed.

Table 3: The absolute and relative maternal organ weights of rats orally treated with FDAE at 0, 250, 500, 1000 and 2000 mg/kg body weight/day on gestation day 6–20

Absolute Organ Weight	*FDAE (mg/kg body weight)*				
	Control	*250*	*500*	*1000*	*2000*
Liver	11.37 ± 1.32	12.04 ± 1.44	12.00 ± 1.47	12.02 ± 1.30	11.47 ± 1.60
Right Kidney	0.75 ± 0.09	0.76 ± 0.11	0.75 ± 0.11	0.79 ± 0.10	0.72 ± 0.21
Left Kidney	0.73 ± 0.08	0.74 ± 0.10	0.72 ± 0.11	0.76 ± 0.11	0.69 ± 0.19
Heart	0.78 ± 0.12	0.84 ± 0.15	0.79 ± 0.16	0.81 ± .10	0.77 ± 0.07
Lung	1.24 ± 2.16	1.22 ± 0.20	1.27 ± 0.22	1.21 ± 0.19	1.17 ± 0.19
Right Ovary	0.06 ± 0.02	0.06 ± 0.22	0.06 ± 0.02	0.06 ± 0.02	0.06 ± 0.01
Left Ovary	0.06 ± 0.01	0.06 ± 0.03	0.06 ± 0.03	0.05 ± 0.02	0.05 ± 0.02
Right Adrenal	0.03 ± 0.01	0.03 ± 0.01	0.03 ± 0.01	0.03 ± 0.01	0.02 ± 0.01
Left Adrenal	0.03 ± 0.01	0.03 ± 0.01	0.03 ± 0.01	0.03 ± 0.01	0.03 ± .01

Relative Organ Weight (%)	*FDAE (mg/kg body weight)*				
	Control	*250*	*500*	*1000*	*2000*
Liver	3.38 ± 0.36	3.55 ± 0.48	3.60 ± 0.38	3.46 ± 0.38	0.32 ± 0.49
Right Kidney	0.22 ± 0.02	0.22 ± 0.02	0.22 ± 0.02	0.23 ± 0.02	0.22 ± 0.06
Left Kidney	0.22 ± 0.02	0.22 ± 0.03	0.22 ± 0.02	0.22 ± 0.02	0.21 ± 0.05
Heart	0.23 ± 0.03	0.25 ± 0.03	0.23 ± 0.03	0.23 ± 0.02	0.24 ± 0.03
Lung	0.37 ± 0.04	0.36 ± 0.05	0.38 ± 0.07	0.35 ± 0.04	0.36 ± 0.05
Right Ovary	0.02 ± 0.007	0.02 ± 0.004	0.02 ± 0.005	0.02 ± 0.005	0.02 ± 0.004
Left Ovary	0.02 ± 0.003	0.02 ± 0.007	0.02 ± 0.005	0.01 ± 0.005	0.02 ± 0.003
Right Adrenal	0.007 ± 0.003	0.007 ± 0.002	0.008 ± 0.002	0.008 ± 0.002	0.007 ± 0.001
Left Adrenal	0.008 ± 0.001	0.008 ± 0.002	0.009 ± 0.002	0.009 ± 0.002	0.008 ± 0.002

Data shown as mean ± SD were analyzed by ANOVA and no difference ($p > 0.05$) among dose groups was observed.

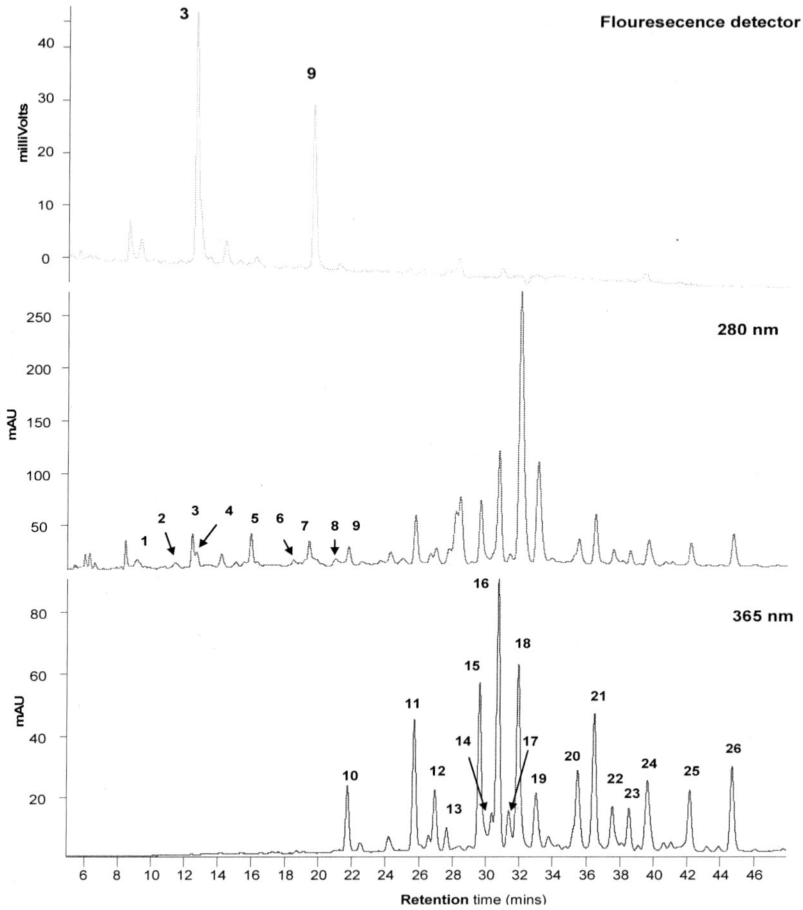

Fig. 1: HPLC–ESI/MS spectra of FDAE by reverse-phase chromatography. The chromatograms were recorded at UV 365 nm and 280 nm. The numbering of their peaks indicates their subsequent identification by MS (Figure reproduced with permission from Omar *et al.* 2011).

3.3 Effects on the Incidence of Embryo-Fetal Death

Pregnancy was confirmed for all sperm positive females with the presence of implantation sites in their uteri. The data obtained at the caesarean section is shown in Table 4. Mean numbers of corpora lutea and implantation sites per litter did not differ between FDAE-treated and control groups. The exposure of FDAE from GD6 onwards did not induce peri-implantation losses. The occurrence of early and late resorptions was low in all groups and the percentage of resorption per litter (median) was not altered by the administration of

Table 4: Caesarean section data of rats orally treated with FDAE at 0, 250, 500, 1000 and 2000 mg/kg body weight/day on gestation day 6–20

Parameters	*FDAE (mg/kg body weight)*				
	Control	*250*	*500*	*1000*	*2000*
Implantations					
Total (n)	236	246	250	223	228
Per litter (n)[a]	11.80 ± 2.69	12.30 ± 2.08	12.50 ± 2.16	11.74 ± 3.03	11.40 ± 2.44
Resorptions					
Total (n)	19	21	16	7	14
Per litter (n) for Early[b]	1(1)	0(1)	0.5(1)	0(0)*	0(1)
Late[b]	0(0)	0(0)	0(0)	0(0)	0(0)
No. of fetuses					
Male	117	112	119	112	109
Female	100	111	115	104	105
No. of dead fetuses/litter	0	0	0	0	0
No. of live[a] fetuses/litter	10.60 ± 3.42	11.25 ± 2.49	11.70 ± 2.18	11.37 ± 3.04	10.70 ± 2.83
Fetal body weight (g)					
Male[a]	5.82 ± 0.50	5.81 ± 0.57	5.80 ± 0.42	5.96 ± 0.42	5.87 ± 0.54
Female[a]	5.54 ± 0.49	5.64 ± 0.54	5.48 ± 0.50	5.55 ± 0.40	5.61 ± 0.52
No of fetuses with external malformation	0	1	1	1	0
Placenta weight (g)	0.517 ± 0.07	0.527 ± 0.07	0.527 ± 0.02	0.524 ± 0.07	0.508 ± 0.05

[a] Data shown as mean ± SD were analyzed by ANOVA and no differences ($p > 0.05$) among groups was detected.
[b] Data shown as median and interquartile range (IQR) were analysed by the Kruskal-Wallis and Mann-Whitney U test and differences ($p < 0.05$) are indicated by an asterisk (*).

FDAE. The average number of live fetuses and the mean number of males and females per litter was similar in control and FDAE treated groups.

3.4 Effects on Placenta and Fetal Body Weight

The mean weight of placentas in FDAE-treated groups was comparable to that of the control group (Table 4). The mean fetal body weight for both male and female in treated groups did not differ from that in the control group either.

4. DISCUSSION

The phytochemical analysis of FDAE revealed the presence of flavornoids. Flavonoids belong to a group of natural substances with variable phenolic structures which are found in a variety of vegetables and plant-derived products such as fruits, grains, bark, roots, stems, flowers, tea and wine (Middleton, 1998). Our findings are consistent with results from previous studies suggesting that flavonoids like (–)-Epicatechin, catechins and Apigenin-8-*C*-glu (Vitexin) are the marker compounds that commonly presence in *F.deltoidea.* Farsi E *et al.* (2013) demonstrated that high level of vitexin and isovitexin found in a standardized methanolic extract of *F.deltoidea* leaves with amounts of 18.76% and 9.68% of the dry weight of the extract respectively.

The presence of phenolic and flavonoid compounds has received a great attention on their free radical scavenging activities as a cellular defense mechanism to suppress the toxicity and genotoxicity of various mutagens in life organism. However, besides to their beneficial effects, various studies have been reported about the cellular toxicity effects of flavonoids as a result of their pro-oxidant activities (Hippeli and Elstner, 1999).

Our study demonstrated that doses of FDAE up to 2000 mg/kg body weight/day did not caused maternal toxicity in GD6-20. This is parallel with the previous reports by Farsi *et al.* (2013) which indicated that (Lethal dose) LD_{50} of methanol extract of *F. deltoidea* > 5000 mg/kg body weight do not lead to acute and sub-chronic toxicities. In fact, the resorption rates and number of live fetuses per litter remained unaltered indicated that FDAE did not cause embryo and fetal death.

Congenital anomalies may results from genetic or chromosomal disorders caused by certain chemicals or drugs during pregnancy. Our previous studies on the genotoxicity testing of FDAE have demonstrated that the extract did not cause gene/chromosomal mutation when tested using *Salmonella typhimurium* and *in vitro* micronucleus assays (unpublished data). The absence of effects on placenta and fetal body weight showed that FDAE administered to pregnant rats throughout embryogenesis (GD6-15) and fetal maturation (GD15-20) periods did no retard prenatal growth of fetuses. In addition, the administration of FDAE did not cause external anomalies in the exposed fetuses.

Data provided by this study showed that FDAE, tested in oral doses up to 2000 mg/kg body weight/day to Sprague Dawley rats on gestation day 6 until 20, was not maternally toxic or caused embryo-fetal deaths, prenatal growth retardation or malformation in the exposed fetuses. Further study on human clinical trials is needed to confirm this finding.

ACKNOWLEDGMENT

The authors gratefully acknowledge the Director General of Health, Malaysia and Director of the Institute for Medical Research, Kuala Lumpur, for permission to publish this paper. This research was funded by the Ministry of Health, Malaysia grant (JPP-IMR 14-023). The authors declare no conflict of interest. The research has received an approval from the Animal Care and Ethics Committee, Ministry of Health Malaysia (ACUC No: ACUC/KKM/02 (2/2017).

REFERENCES

[1] De Smet, P.A. (2004). Health risks of herbal remedies: an update. *Clinical Pharmacology & Therapeutics* 76(1):1–17.

[2] Farsi, E., Shafaei, A., Yee, H.S., Khadeer, A.M.B., Yam, M.F., Asmawi, M. and Ismail, Z. (2013). Safety evaluation of *Ficusdeltoidea*. Clinics, 68(6):865–875.

[3] Fazliana, M.S., Muhajir, H., Hazilawati, H., Shafii, K. and Mazleha, M. (2008). Effects of Ficusdeltoidea aqueous extract on hematological and biochemical parameters in rats. Med J Malaysia. 63 (Supplement A): 103–104.

[4] Hamidun, B., Noriha, M.A., Siti, N.B., Syarul, N.B. and Normah, M.N. (2014). *Ficusdeltoidea* Jack: A Review on its Phytochemical and

Pharmacological Importance. *Evidence-Based Complementary and Alternative Medicine,* 2014.

[5] Harborne, J.B. and Williams, C.A. (2000). Advances in Flavonoid Research since 1992. *Phytochemistry,* 55, 481–504.

[6] Havsteen, B.H. (2002). The biochemistry and medical significance of the flavonoids. *Pharmacology & Therapeutics,* 2002, 96(2–3): 67–202.

[7] Hippeli, S. and Elstner, E.F. (1999). Transition metal ion-catalyzed oxygen activation during pathogenic processes. FEBS letters, 443(1):1–7.

[8] Kim, K.-H., Gam, C.-O., Choi1, S.-Hand Ku S.-K. (2012). Mouse Single Oral Dose Toxicity Test of *Bupleuri Radix* Aqueous Extracts. *Toxicological Research,* 28(1):11–18.

[9] Martins, E. (2014). The growing use of herbal medicines: issues relating toadverse reactions and challenges in monitoring safety. *Frontier in Pharmacology,* 4(177):1–10.

[10] Middleton E. Jr (1998). Effect of plant flavonoids on immune and inflammatory cell function. *Advances in Experimental Medicine and Biology,* 439:175–82.

[11] Omar, M.H., Mullen, W. and Crozier, A. (2011). Identification of proanthocyanidin dimers and trimers, Flavone C-Glycosides, and antioxidants in *Ficus deltoidea,* a Malaysian herbal tea. *Journal of Agricultural and Food Chemistry,* 59(4):1363-1369. ISSN 0021-8561 (doi:10.1021/jf1032729).

[12] Salewski, E. (1964). Farbemethodezummarkroskopishennachweisvon implant at consstellen an uterus der ratter naunynschmuderbergs. *Archives of Pharmacology,* 247, 367.

[13] Staples, R.E. and Schnell, Y.L. (1964). Refinements in rapid clearing technic in the KOH-Alizarin Red A method for fetal bone. *Stain Technology,* 39:61–3.

[14] Sulaiman, M.R., Hussain, M.K., Zakaria, Z.A., Somchit, M.N., Moin, S., Mohamad, A.S. and Israf, D.A. (2008). Evaluation of the antinociceptive activity of *Ficusdeltoidea* aqueous extract. Fitoterapia, 2008, Dec.; 79(7–8): 557–61.

SECTION 2

Medicinal Plants Research in Egypt, Vietnam, Nepal and Nigeria

Antimicrobial Properties of the Essential Oils of Some Plants Growing in Egypt: A Review

Mai M. Ahmed
Desert Research Centre, Cairo, Egypt
E-mail: dr.maimohamed87@gmail.com

ABSTRACT: Medicinal plants are known since ancient civilizations to exhibit many therapeutic properties. The Egyptian medicine dates from about 2900 BC. Historic medicine in Egypt is full of recipes for curing various diseases and the use of plants as medicines well documented on the walls of temples and the best known Egyptian pharmaceutical record is the "Ebers papyrus" dating from 1500 BC which documents over 700 drugs (mostly plants). A large number of Egyptian plants are reported to possess many activities like anti-oxidant, anti-inflammatory, anti-insecticidal, anti-parasitic, antibiotic, anti-hemolytic properties. A wide range of Medicinal and Aromatic Plants (MAPs) have been explored for their essential oils in the past few decades. Essential oils are complex volatile compounds, synthesized naturally in different plant parts during the process of secondary metabolism. Essential oils have a great potential in the field of biomedicine as they effectively destroy several bacterial, fungal, and viral pathogens. Thus, the present study aimed to explore the potential of essential oils of some Egyptian plants in the development of novel broad-spectrum key molecules against a broad range of pathogenic microbes.

Keywords: Traditional Medicine, Medicinal Plants, Phytochemistry, Antimicrobial Activity, Essential Oils.

1. INTRODUCTION

Medicinal plants are the richest bio-resource of drugs for traditional systems of medicine, folk medicines, modern medicines, food supplements, pharmaceutical intermediates and chemical entities for synthetic drugs (Saranraj, 2016). Ethnopharmacologists, botanists, microbiologists, and natural-products chemists are combing the Earth for phytochemicals and "leads" which could be developed for treatment of infectious diseases. According to World Health Organization (WHO) data, about 80% of world population is using products based on medicinal herbs (Newman *et al.*, 2000). Now-a-days, the natural products are used to treat many diseases including hypertension, heart diseases and cancer for better prevention as well as therapeutic actions. The research on natural products explores a variety of major structures used for the evolution of new drugs by the pharmaceutical industry. Traditional folk remedies from plants have always guided scientists to search for new medications in order to maintain and promote healthy life for human and animals (Hosseinzadeh *et al.*, 2015).

In Egypt, like in other developing countries, medicinal plants still represent one of the main therapeutic tools in traditional medicine. The Egyptian flora offers great possibilities for the discovery of new compounds with various medicinal activities.

Essential oils obtained from Medicinal and Aromatic Plants (MAPs) are aromatic in nature because of a mixture of multifarious chemical substances that belong to different chemical families, including terpenes, aldehydes, alcohols, esters, phenolic, ethers and ketones. An important role of essential oils in nature is protection of plants by acting as antifungal, antibacterial, antiviral, and insecticidal agents and also protection against herbivores by reducing appetite of herbivores for plants with such properties. Essential oils have tremendous business potential on the global market owing to their unique flavor and fragrance properties and also biological activities. Essential oils are employed in aromatherapy and for the treatment of several diseases including cardiovascular disease, diabetes, Alzheimer's, cancer (Ali *et al.*, 2015). The antimicrobial impacts of essential oils and their chemical components have been recognized by several researchers because of the current problems associated with the antibiotics resistance. Therefore, there has been an increased interest in anti-microbial agents from essential oils, which have been used in folk medicine (Stefanakis *et al.*, 2013).

2. MATERIALS AND METHODS

Ethnobotanical data was collected by in Egypt and relevant literature was reviewed by probing scientific databases (PubMed, Scopus, Google Scholar, b-on, Web of knowledge) and other web sources such as records from WCSP, IUCN, APG and the Missouri Botanical Garden database. Various keywords were used during the bibliographic research including: Traditional medicine, Medicinal plants, Phytochemistry, Antimicrobial activity, Essential oils, Egypt. Information was gathered and summarized in table form where appropriate.

3. RESULTS AND DISCUSSION

Table 1: Chemical Composition of Essential Oils and their Antibacterial Activity against Human Pathogens

MAPs	*Part Used*	*Extractant Used*	*Major Chemical Compounds*	*Inhibited Microorganisms*	*References*
Achillea clavennae	Leaves	Water	Camphor, Myrcene	*Klebsiella pneumonia, Streptococcus pneumonia, Haemophilus influenzae, Pseudomonas aeruginosa*	(Skocibusic *et al.*, 2004)
Artemisia judaica	*Leaves*	Water	*β-Thujone*	*Pseudomonas aeruginosa*	(Elansary *et al.*, 2018)
Cuminum cyminum	*Seeds*	Water	*γ-Terpinene, γ-Pinene*	*Salmonella typhimurium, Escherichia coli*	(Bisht *et al.*, 2014)
Cymbopogon citratus	*Stems*	Water	*γ-Cadinene*	*Salmonella typhimurium, Escherichia coli*	(Grohs and Kunz, 2000)
Cyperus longus	*Arial parts*	Water	*β-Himachalene, α-Humulene, γ-Himachalene*	*Staphylococcus aureus, Escherichia coli Pseudomonas aeruginosa*	(Ait-Ouazzou *et al.*, 2012)
Eremanthus erythropapps	*Leaves*	Water	*Caryophyllene, p-Cymene, γ-Terpinene*	*Staphylococcus epidermidis*	(Dos Santos *et al.*, 2015)
Eugenia caryophyllata	*Leaves*	Water	*Eugenol*	*Bacillus subtilis*	(Chaieb *et al.*, 2007)
Foeniculum vulgare	*Leaves*	Water	*Trans-anethole, Methylchavicol, Limonene*	*Salmonella typhimurium Escherichia coli*	(Bisht *et al.*, 2014)
Lavandula angustifolia	*Arial parts*	Water	*Camphor, Linalool, β-Pinene, α-Pinene*	*Mycobacterium smegmatis Escherichia coli*	(Flores *et al.*, 2014)

(Table contd...)

(Table 1 contd...)

MAPs	*Part Used*	*Extractant Used*	*Major Chemical Compounds*	*Inhibited Microorganisms*	*References*
Mentha pulegium	*Arial parts*	Water	*Piperitone, Piperitenone, α-Terpineol, Pulegone*	*Staphylococcus aureus, Bacillus cereus, Staphylococcus epidermidis, Salmonella typhimurium, Escherichia coli*	(Ait-Ouazzou *et al.*, 2012)
Ocimum basilicum.	*Seeds*	Water	*α-Linolenic acid*	*Staphylococcus aureus, Bacillus cereus*	(Runyoro *et al.*, 2010)
Origanum vulgare	*Leaves*	Water	*Pulegone*	*Escherichia coli*	(Santoyo *et al.*, 2006)
Pimpinella anisum	Seeds	Water	*Trans-anethole*	*Salmonella typhimurium Escherichia coli*	(Elgayyar *et al.*, 2001)
Rosmarinus officinalis	Flowers	Water	*Camphor, Limonene, Myrcene, Linalool*	*Staphylococcus aureus, Bacillus cereus Staphylococcus epidermidis, Salmonella typhimurium, Escherichia coli*	(Teixeira *et al.*, 2013)

Table 2: Chemical Composition of Essential Oils and their Antifungal Activity against Human Pathogens

MAPs	*Part Used*	*Extractant Used*	*Major Chemical Compounds*	*Inhibited Microorganisms*	*References*
Aegle marmelos	Leaves	Water	γ-Cadinene, δ-Carene, α-Pinene	*Candida albicans, Aspergillus niger, Fusarium oxysporum*	(Ibrahim *et al.*, 2015a)
Artemisia judaica	Aerial parts	Water	β-Thujone	*Fusarium oxysporum*	(Lopes-Lutz *et al.*, 2008)
Coriandrum sativum	Leaves	Water	2E-Decenal, Decanal, 2E-decen-1-ol, n-Decanol	*Candida albicans*	(Begnami *et al.*, 2010)

(Table contd...)

(Table 2 contd...)

MAPs	*Part Used*	*Extractant Used*	*Major Chemical Compounds*	*Inhibited Microorganisms*	*References*
Eremanthus erythropappus	Leaves	Water	(Z)-Caryophyllene, germacrene D, Viridiflorol, p-Cymene, γ-Terpinene	*Candida albicans, Candida gattii, Candida neoformans, Saccharomyces cerevisiae*	(Dos Santos *et al.*, 2015)
Feoniculum vulgare	Seeds	Water	Trans-anethole, Methylchavicol, Limonene	*Alternaria alternata, Fusarium oxysporum, Aspergillus flavus*	(Bisht *et al.*, 2014)
Mentha pulegium	Arial parts	Water	Piperitone, Piperitenone, α-Terpineol pulegone	*Aspergillus niger, Candida albicans, Candida zemplinina, Kloeckera apiculata*	(Ait-Ouazzou *et al.*, 2012)
Momordica charantia	Seeds	Water	Trans-nerolidol, Apiole, cis-dihydrocarveo, Germacrene D	*Candida albicans*	(Braca *et al.*, 2008)
Myrtus communis	Leaves	Water	Eugenol, α-Terpineol, γ-Terpinene, α-Caryophyllene	*Candida albicans, Aspergillus flavus*	(Aleksic and Knezevic, 2014)
Ocimum basilicum	Leaves, flowers	Water	Eugenol, Methyl eugenol, cis-ocimene, trans-ocimene, α-Pinene Camphor	*Candida albicans, Candida tropicalis, Candida glabrata, Penicillium notatum, Rizopus stolonifer*	(Beatovic *et al.*, 2015)
Pelargonium graveolens	Leaves	Water	Citronellol, Citronellyl formate, Geraniol	*Candida tropicalis*	(Souza *et al.*, 2016)

(Table contd...)

(Table 2 contd...)

MAPs	*Part Used*	*Extractant Used*	*Major Chemical Compounds*	*Inhibited Microorganisms*	*References*
Rosmarinus officinalis	Leaves	Water	Cineole, Camphor, Camphene, Limonene, α-Pinene, α-Terpinolene	*Aspergillus flavus, Candida albicans*	(Papajani *et al.*, 2015)
Salvia sclarea	Arial parts	Water	Linalool, Linalyl acetate, Geranyl acetate, β-ocimene acetate, Caryophyllene oxide	*Candida albicans, Candida tropicalis, Candida krusei, Candida glabrata, Candida parapsilosis*	(Hristova *et al.*, 2013)
Syzygium aromaticum	Leaves	Water	Eugenol, Eugenylacetate	*Aspergillus fumigatus, Candida albicans*	(Andrade *et al.*, 2014)
Teucrium leucocladum	Whole plant	Water	α-Cadinol	*Pseudomonas aeruginosa, Bacillus subtilis*	(El-shazly and Hussein, 2004)

3.1 Chemical Composition of Essential Oils

Essential oils have the ability to hamper the growth of a diverse range of pathogens because of the presence of natural compounds produced by the organs of plants. Importantly, the unique aroma and other bioactive properties of an essential oil depend on its chemical constituents. In MAPs, essential oils generally accumulate in the secretary canals or cavities and glandular trichomes and sometimes in the epidermal cells (Arumugam *et al.*, 2016). Essential oils and their chemical constituents exhibit more bioactivity when present in the oxygenated or active form (Morsy, 2017). In general, the chemical composition of essential oils is relatively complex, and about 20 to 60 different bioactive components are observed in many of these essential oils. Many of these compounds are pharmaceutically appreciated for their numerous culinary properties. Usually, the chemical characterization of many essential oils reveals the presence of only 2–3 major components at a fairly high concentration (20–70%) compared to other components present in trace amounts (Degenhardt *et al.*, 2009; Lang and Buchbauer, 2012).

Table 3: Chemical Composition of Essential Oils and their Antiviral Activity against Human Pathogens

MAPs	*Part Used*	*Extractant Used*	*Major Chemical Compounds*	*Inhibited Microorganisms*	*References*
Achillea fragrantissima	Aerial parts	Water	Trans-2,7-Dimethyl 4, 6 octadien-2-ol	*ORF virus (a parapox virus)*	(Zeedan *et al.*, 2014)
Artemisia arborescens	Aerial parts	Water	β-Thujone, Linalool, Myrcene, Carvacrol	*Herpes simplex virus type 1 (HSV-1)*	(Sinico *et al.*, 2005)
Fortunella margarita	Leaves	Water	Gurjunene, Eudesmol, Muurolene-capillene	*Avian influenza A virus (H5N1), Alternaria alternata*	(Ibrahim *et al.*, 2015b)
Jasonia montana	Aerial parts	Water	Camphor, Endoborneol, 1-α-Terpineol, and α-Pinene	*poliomyelitis-1 virus (POLIO)*	(Soltan, and Zaki, 2009)
Melissa officinalis	Leaves	Water	Myrcene, Linalool, Camphor, Citronellal, β-Caryophyllene, Caryophyllene oxide, Citral	*avian influenza virus (AIV) subtype H9N2*	(Allahverdiyev *et al.*, 2004)
Moringa peregrina	Seeds	Water	Δ-Tocopherols, Methylene-cholesterol, Campesterol, Stigmasterol	*simplex-1 virus (HSV)*	(Tsaknis, 1998)
Trachyspermum ammi	Leaves	Water	Thymol, α-Pinene, p-Cymene, Limonene	*Japanese encephalitis virus (JEV)*	(Roy *et al.*, 2015)

3.2 Mechanism of Antimicrobial Action of Essential Oils against Human Pathogens

The antimicrobial effects of essential oils derived from MAPs are the basis of copious applications, in various revenue generating sectors such as pharmaceutical, nutraceutical, cosmetic, perfume, agronomy, and sanitary industries. In the following section, we have broadly discussed the antibacterial, antifungal, and antiviral effects of essential oils obtained from MAPs (Akhtar *et al.*, 2014).

MAPs contain several types of chemical constituents that have antimicrobial properties. These are synthesized to protect the plants from microbial pathogens. The antimicrobial properties of essential oils mainly depend on their chemical constituents and the quantity of the major single compounds (Nazzaro *et al.*, 2013). These chemical compounds are secreted through a series of molecular interactions under specific biotic/abiotic stress conditions. Each compound may exhibit a different mechanism of action against microbes (Holley and Patel, 2005). In the following sections, the mechanism of antimicrobial activities of essential oils is described with reference to the available literature. The possible antimicrobial actions of essential oils are illustrated in Figure 1.

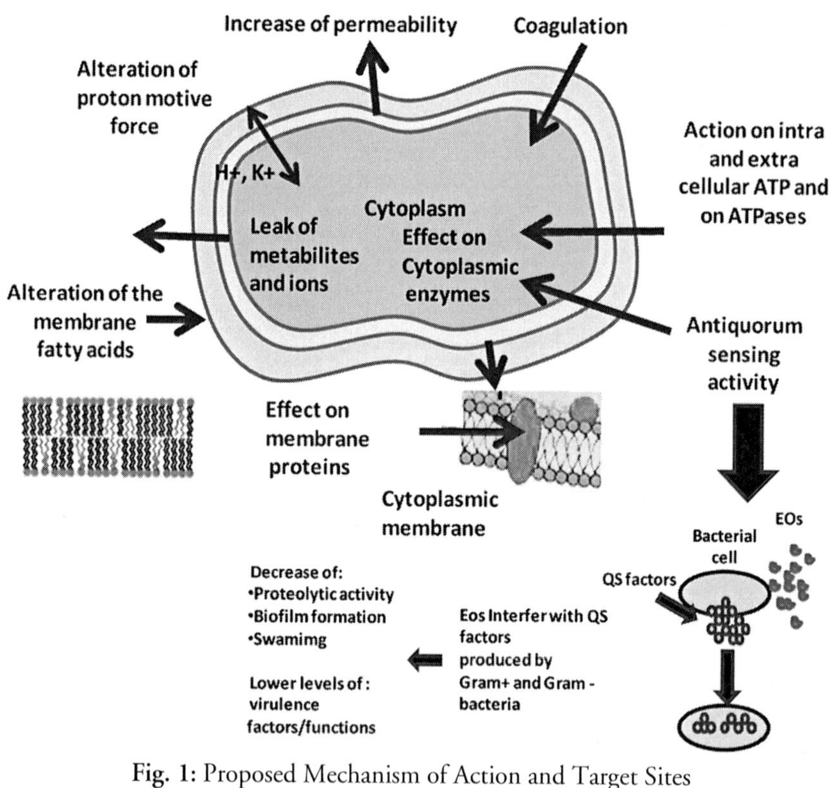

Fig. 1: Proposed Mechanism of Action and Target Sites of Secondary Plant Metabolites on Microbial Cells

QS: Quorum sensing; EOs: Essential oils

Various mechanisms of antibacterial activity of essential oils have been proposed. Essential oils primarily destabilize the cellular architecture, leading to the breakdown of membrane integrity and increased permeability, which disrupts many cellular activities, including energy production (membrane-coupled), membrane transport, and other metabolic regulatory functions. The disruption of the cell membrane by essential oils may assist various vital processes such as energy conversion processes, nutrient processing, the synthesis of structural macromolecules, and the secretion of growth regulators. The essential oils may affect both the external envelope of the cell and the cytoplasm (Nazzaro *et al.*, 2013). Owing to their lipophilic nature, essential oils are easily penetrable through the bacterial cell membranes. Essential oils of various MAPs were reported to cause increased bacterial cell membrane permeability leading to the leakage of cellular components and loss of ions (Oussalah *et al.*, 2006).

The antibacterial effect of essential oils is also linked to reduced membrane potentials, the disruption of proton pumps, and the depletion of the ATP. This alteration in the cell organization may cause a cascade effect, resulting in other cell organelles being affected. Likewise, Cox *et al.* (Cox *et al.*, 1998) have demonstrated that tea tree oil inhibits the growth of *Staphylococcus aureus* and *Escherichia coli* by altering cell permeability, increasing the leakage of intracellular K^+ ions and disturbing cell respiration. The essential oils pass through the cell wall and cytoplasmic membrane, which may disrupt the arrangement of dissimilar fatty acids, phospholipids bilayers, and polysaccharides molecules (Raut and Karuppayil, 2014).

All these events may be responsible for the coagulation of inner cellular components in the cytoplasm and break down of the bonds between the lipid and protein layers. In some cases, the pure compounds of essential oils exhibit higher antibacterial activity compared to the essential oil (Burt, 2004).

Another effect of essential oils on cell membranes is the inhibition of toxin secretion. Ultee and Smid (Ultee and Smid, 2001) reported that exposure of *Bacillus* cereus to carvacrol resulted in the inhibition of toxin production, and application of oregano essential oil completely abolished the enterotoxin production of S. aureus. Thus, the secretion of toxins may be prevented by modifications in the bacterial membrane due to the influence of the essential oil compounds on the transmembrane transport process in the plasma membrane, which limits the release of toxins to the external environment. Another mechanism of action is by trans-cinnamaldehyde, which enters the periplasm of the cell and disrupts cellular functions. Moreover, p-cymene has a greater affinity towards bacterial cell membranes and thus may disturb the membrane integrity (Rudramurthy *et al.*, 2016).

The outer membrane proteins are also affected by essential oil components. For example, carvacrol can disturb the insertion and folding of proteins such as DnaK and GroEL (Rudramurthy *et al.*, 2016). Carvacrol can also inhibit the synthesis of flagellin, a microbial protein required for bacterial motility. The phenylpropene, eugenol, also exhibits activity by modifying the fatty acid outline to alter the cytoplasmic membrane of different bacteria. In addition, it can destroy various bacterial enzymes such as ATPase, amylase, histidine carboxylase, and proteases. Likewise, cinnamaldehyde was reported to inhibit ATPase enzymes and disrupt the outer cell membrane (Wendakoon and Sakaguchi, 1995). Other studies have found that vanillin exhibited antimicrobial activity by obstructing the pathways of bacterial respiration and disrupting the flux of K^+ ions and pH gradient. Similarly carveol, citronellal, and carvone essential oils were shown to modify hydrophobicity and disrupt membrane integrity, leading to the leakage of K^+ ions.

Some essential oils can inhibit the cell-cell communication quorum sensing network mediated by various bacterial signal molecules. The efficacy of the antibacterial effect of essential oils or their individual compounds may differ from one microbe to another. Hence, elucidation on the exact mechanisms of action of each essential oil and their components is required, including further study on the numerous microbial strains/species. Furthermore, detailed study on the components of essential oils would be helpful to improve our understanding of their mechanism of antimicrobial activity (Szabo *et al.*, 2010).

Action against the Fungal Pathogens: The antifungal actions of essential oils are similar to that of previously explained antibacterial mechanisms. Generally, exposure of essential oils leads to the coagulation of the cellular components because of irreversible cell membrane damage. In yeast cells, essential oils establish a membrane potential across the cell membrane and disrupt the production of ATP, which leads to cell membrane damage. The essential oils have the ability to penetrate and disrupt the fungal cell wall and cytoplasmic membranes through a permeabilization process, which leads to the disintegration of mitochondrial membranes. This is caused by alterations in the flow of electrons inside the electron transport system (ETS) pathway. This may also damage the lipids, proteins, and nucleic acid contents of cells infected by the fungal pathogens (Arnal-Schnebelen *et al.*, 2004).

The essential oils could also disrupt the depolarization of the mitochondrial membranes by affecting ions channels, especially Ca^{2+} ions, proton pumps, and ATP pools, and therefore decreases the membrane potential. This change in the fluidity of membranes may cause electrolyte leakage and hinder cytochrome C pathways, proteins metabolism, and calcium ion concentrations. Therefore, the permeabilization of inner and outer mitochondrial membranes may result in the cell apoptosis or necrosis leading to cell death (Yoon *et al.*, 2000).

Actions against the Viruses: At present, various essential oils may be a promising alternative against viral infections. However, the detailed understanding on the antiviral action of essential oils still requires more research. Some of the reported mechanisms of action of essential oils are reported in this section. Essential oils might interfere with virion envelopment, designed for entry into host cells. For instance, the sesquiterpene triptofordin C-2 was reported to suppress the synthesis of viral proteins and inhibit the early gene expression process of the HSV-1 virus (Hayashi *et al.*, 2001). The antiviral activity of star anise essential oil is investigated as well as compounds such as eugenol, trans-anethole, farnesol, *β*-eudesmol, *β*-caryophyllene, and *β*-caryophyllene oxide against *Herpes simplex virus type 1 (HSV-1).* They found the direct inactivation of HSV-1 particles, which is also reported in another study where eugenol was used. Moreover, eugenol directly inactivates the growth of the herpes virus, whereas isoborneol (monoterpene) affected the glycosylation process of viral proteins, which inhibited the growth of HSV-1 (Armaka *et al.*, 1999). Similarly, essential oils of ginger, thyme, hyssop, and sandalwood were able to inhibit acyclovir-resistant HSV-1 (Schnitzler *et al.*, 2001). Possible mechanisms of action include the inhibition of virus replication by hindering cellular DNA polymerase and alteration in phenylpropanoid pathways. Furthermore, sesquiterpenes are known to inhibit cytomegalovirus (CMV) early gene expression. According to Pourghanbari *et al.* (Pourghanbari *et al.*, 2016), the essential oil of lemon balm inhibits influenza virus replication at different replication cycles by directly interacting with the virus particles.

4. CONCLUSION

Medicinal plants can be used as alternative antimicrobial drugs. The medicinal value of these plants lies in some bio-active natural chemicals (phytochemicals) as possible sources of non-phytotoxic and easily biodegradable alternative antibiotics. The essential oils extracted from various MAPs possess strong antimicrobial activity against various bacterial, fungal, and viral pathogens. The reactivity of essential oils depends upon the nature of their functional groups and orientation. Essential oils are considered to be potent against a diverse range of pathogens. Essential oils may disrupt the cell membrane of the targeted pathogens by increasing the membrane permeability, inducing leakage of vital intracellular constituents, and interrupting the cellular metabolism and enzyme kinetics of the targeted pathogens.

As this review reveals many EOs possess strong antimicrobial activity against various microorganisms. Nevertheless, some disadvantages have to be considered as it can cause contact dermatitis, burns, and skin irritation. In most cases, their activity is a result of the additive, synergistic or antagonistic effects of the individual constituents. Therefore, the main compound generally exerts the strongest activity, but can be influenced by the other molecules. Moreover, the composition of the EO is dependent on the growing place, the time of harvest and the individual chemotype. Therefore, further tests are needed to learn more about the interactions between the individual compounds of these complex multicomponent mixtures. A further interesting aspect is the use of individual EO compounds as starting material to generate stronger antimicrobial molecules. Also, interesting possible applications of EOs as antimicrobials have been discussed, such as the chemical modification of EO constituents to increase their antimicrobial activity or using EOs to treat infections by drug resistant bacterium strains but, of course, further studies in this field are recommended.

REFERENCES

[1] Ait-Ouazzou, A., Loran, S. and Arakrak, A. (2012). Evaluation of the chemical composition and antimicrobial activity of *Mentha pulegium, Juniperus phoenicea* and *Cyperus longus* essential oils from Morocco. Food Res Int, 45(1): 313–319.

[2] Akhtar, M.S., Degaga, B. and Azam, T. (2014). Antimicrobial activity of essential oils extracted from medicinal plants against the pathogenic microorganisms: A review. IBSPR, 2(1): 1–7.

[3] Aleksic, V. and Knezevic, P. (2014). Antimicrobial and antioxidative activity of extracts and essential oils of *Myrtus communis* L. MICROBIOL RES, 169(4): 240–254.

[4] Ali, B., Al-Wabel, N.A., Shams, S., Ahamad, A., Khan, S.A. and Anwar, F. (2015). Essential oils used in aromatherapy: a systemic review. Asian Pacific Journal of Tropical Biomedicine, 5(8): 601–611.

[5] Allahverdiyev, A., Duran, N., Ozguven, M. and Koltas, S. (2004). Antiviral activity of the volatile oils of *Melissa officinalis* L. against *Herpes simplex* virus type-2. Phytomedicine, 11(7– 8): 657–661.

[6] Andrade, B.F.M.T., Barbosa, L.N., Probst, I.S., and Junior, A.F. (2014). Antimicrobial activity of essential oils. J. Essent. Oil Res., 26(1): 34–40.

[7] Armaka, M., Papanikolaou, E., Sivropoulou, A., and Arsenakis, M. (1999). Antiviral properties of isoborneol, a potent inhibitor of *herpes simplex* virus type 1. Antivir. Res., 43(2): 79–92.

[8] Arnal-Schnebelen, B., Hadji-Minaglou, F., Peroteau, J.-F., Ribeyre, F., and De Billerbeck, V.G. (2004). Essential oils in infectious gynaecological disease: a statistical study of 658 cases. Int. J. Aromather., 14(4): 192–197.

[9] Arumugam G., Swamy M.K. and Sinniah U.R. (2016). *Plectranthus amboinicus* (Lour.) Spreng: botanical, phytochemical, pharmacological and nutritional significance. *Molecules.*, 21(4): p. 369.

[10] Beatovic, D., Krstic-Milosevic, D. and Trifunovic, S. (2015). Chemical composition, antioxidant and antimicrobial activities of the essential oils of twelve *Ocimum basilicum* L. cultivars grown in Serbia. REC NAT PROD, 9(1): 62–75.

[11] Begnami, A.F., Duarte, M.C.T., Furletti, V. and Rehder, V.L.G. (2010). Antimicrobial potential of *Coriandrum sativum* L. against different Candida species in vitro. Food Chem, 118(1):. 74–77.

[12] Bisht, D.S., Menon, K.R.K. and Singhal, M.K. (2014). Comparative antimicrobial activity of essential oils of *Cuminum cyminum L.* and *Foeniculum vulgare* Mill. seeds against *Salmonella typhimurium* and Escherichia coli. J ESSENT OIL BEAR PL. 17(4): 617–622.

[13] Braca, A., Siciliano, T., D'Arrigo, M., and Germano, M. P. (2008). Chemical composition and antimicrobial activity of *Momordica charantia* seed essential oil. Fitoterapia, 79(2): 123–125.

[14] Burt, S. (2004). *Essential* oils: Their antibacterial properties and potential applications in foods—a review. Int J Food Microbiol, 94(3): 223–253.

[15] Chaieb, K., Hajlaoui, H. and Zmantar T. (2007). The chemical composition and biological activity of clove essential oil, *Eugenia caryophyllata* (*Syzigium aromaticum* L. Myrtaceae): a short review. Phytother Res, 21(6): 501–506.

[16] Cox, S.D., Gustafson, J.E. and Mann, C.M. (1998). Tea tree oil causes K+ leakage and inhibits respiration in *Escherichia coli. LETT APPL MICROBIOL*, 26(5): 355–358.

[17] Degenhardt, J., Kollner, T.G. and Gershenzon, J. (2009). Monoterpene and sesquiterpene synthases and the origin of terpene skeletal diversity in plants. Phytochemistry, 70(15– 16): 1621– 163.

[18] Dos Santos, N. O., Mariane, B. and Lago, J.H.G. (2015). Assessing the chemical composition and antimicrobial activity of essential oils from Brazilian plants—*Eremanthus erythropappus* (Asteraceae), *Plectrantuns barbatus*, and *P. amboinicus* (Lamiaceae). Molecules, 20(5): 8440–8452.

[19] Elansary, H.O., Abdelgaleil, S.A.M., Mahmoud, E.A., Yessoufou, K., Elhindi, K. and El-Hendawy, S. (2018). Effective antioxidant, antimicrobial and anticancer activities of essential oils of horticultural aromatic crops in northern Egypt. *BMC COMPLEM ALTERN M*, 18(1): 1–10.

[20] Elgayyar, M., Draughon, F.A., Golden, D.A. and Mount, J.R. (2001). Antimicrobial activity of essential oils from plants against selected pathogenic and saprophytic microorganisms. *J Food Prot*, 64(7): 1019–1024.

[21] El-Shazly, A.M. and Hussein, K.T. (2004). Chemical analysis and biological activities of the essential oil of *Teucrium leucocladum Boiss.* (Lamiaceae). *BIOCHEM SYST ECOL*, 32: 665–674.

[22] Flores, C.R., Pennec, A., Nugier-Chauvin, C., Daniellou, R., Herrera-Estrella, L. and Chauvin, A.L. (2014). Chemical composition and antibacterial activity of essential oils extracted from plants cultivated in Mexico. *J MEX CHEM SOC*, 58(4): 452–455.

[23] Grohs, B.M. and Kunz, B. (2000). Use of spice mixtures for the stabilisation of fresh portioned pork. *Food Control*, 11(6): 433–436.

[24] Hayashi, K., Hayashi, T., Ujita, K., and Takaish, Y.i. (2001). Characterization of antiviral activity of a sesquiterpene, triptofordin C-2. *J Antimicrob Chemother*, 37(4): 759– 768.

[25] Holley, R.A. and Patel, D. (2005). Improvement in shelf-life and safety of perishable foods by plant essential oils and smoke antimicrobials. *Food Microbiology*, 22(4):273–292.

[26] Hosseinzadeh, S., Jafarikukhdan, A., Hosseini, A. and Armand, R. (2015). The Application of Medicinal Plants in Traditional and Modern Medicine: A Review of Thymus vulgaris. *Int J Clin Exp Med*, 6: 635–642.

[27] Hristova, Y., Gochev, V. and Wanner, J. (2013). Chemical composition and antifungal activity of essential oil of *Salvia sclarea* L. from Bulgaria against clinical isolates of *Candida* species. *J. BioSci. Biotechnol*, 2(1): 39–44.

[28] Ibrahim, N.A., El-Sakhawy, F.S., Mohammed, M.M.D., Farid, M.A., Abdel-Wahed, N.A.M. and Deabes, D.A.H. (2015). Chemical composition, antimicrobial and antifungal activities of essential oils of the leaves of *Aegle marmelos* (L.) Correa growing in Egypt. *J Appl Pharm Sci*, 5(2): 1–5.

[29] Ibrahim, N.A., El-Hawary, S.S. and Mohammed, M.M.D. (2015)b. Chemical composition, antiviral against *avian influenza* (H5N1) virus and antimicrobial activities of the essential oils of the leaves and fruits of *Fortunella margarita*, lour. swingle, growing in Egypt. *J Appl Pharm Sci,* 5(1): 6–12.

[30] Lang, G. and Buchbauer, G. (2012). A review on recent research results (2008–2010) on essential oils as antimicrobials and antifungals. A review. *Flavour Fragr. J.,* 27(1): 13–39.

[31] Lopes-Lutz, D., Alviano, D.S., Alviano, C.S. and Kolodziejczyk, P.P. (2008). Screening of chemical composition, antimicrobial and antioxidant activities of *Artemisia* essential oils. *Phytochemistry,* 69(8): 1732–1738.

[32] Morsy, N.F.S. (2017). Chemical Structure, Quality Indices and Bioactivity of Essential Oil Constituents. In: El-Shemy, HA., ed. Active Ingredients from Aromatic and Medicinal Plants. *UK: IntechOpen*; 175–208.

[33] Nazzaro, F., Fratianni, F., De Martino, L., Coppola, R. and De Feo, V. (2013). Effect of essential oils on pathogenic bacteria. *Pharmaceuticals,* 6(12): 1451–1474.

[34] Newman, D.J., Cragg, G.M. and Snader, K.M. (2000). The influence of natural products upon drug discovery. *Natural Product Reports,* 17(3): 215–234.

[35] Oussalah, M., Caillet, S. and Lacroix, M. (2006). Mechanism of action of Spanish oregano, Chinese cinnamon, and savory essential oils against cell membranes and walls of *Escherichia coli* O157:H7 and *Listeria monocytogenes.* J Food Prot, 69(5): 1046–1055.

[36] Papajani, V., Haloci, E., Goci, E., Shkreli, R. and Manfredini, S. (2015). Evaluation of antifungal activity of *Origanum vulgare* and *Rosmarinus officinalis* essential oil before and after inclusion in β-cyclodextrine. *J Pharm Pharm Sci.,* 7(5): 270–273.

[37] Pourghanbari, G., Nili, H., Moattari, A., Mohammadi, A. and Iraji, A. (2016). Antiviral activity of the *oseltamivir* and *Melissa officinalis* L. essential oil against *avian influenza* A virus (H9N2). Virusdisease, 27(2): 170–178.

[38] Raut, J.S. and Karuppayil, S.M. (2014). A status review on the medicinal properties of essential oils. *IND CROP PROD,* 62: 250–264.

[39] Roy, S., Chaurvedi, P. and Chowdhary, A. (2015). Evaluation of antiviral activity of essential oil of *Trachyspermum Ammi* against *Japanese encephalitis virus.* Pharmacogn. Res, 7(3): 263–267.

[40] Rudramurthy, G.R., Swamy, M.K., Sinniah, U.R., and Ghasemzadeh, A. (2016). Nanoparticles: alternatives against drug-resistant pathogenic microbes. *Molecules,* 21(7): 836.

[41] Runyoro, D., *N*gassapa, O., Vagionas, K., Aligiannis, N., Graikou, K. and Chinou, I. (2010). Chemical composition and antimicrobial activity of the essential oils of four *Ocimum* species growing in Tanzania. *Food Chem,* 119(1): 311–316.

[42] Santoyo, S., Cavero, S., Jaime, L., Ibanez, E., Senorans, F.J. and Reglero, G. (2006). Supercritical carbon dioxide extraction of compounds with

antimicrobial activity from *Origanum vulgare* L.: determination of optimal extraction parameters. *J Food Prot,* 69(2): 369–375.

[43] Saranraj, P., Sivasakthi, S. and Deepa, M.S. (2016). Phytochemistry of pharmacologically important medicinal plants—A Review. *International Journal of Current Research in Chemistry and Pharmaceutical Sciences,* 3(11): 56–66.

[44] Schnitzler, P.P., Schon, K. and Reichling, J. (2001). Antiviral activity of Australian tea tree oil and eucalyptus oil against *herpes simplex* virus in cell culture. *Pharmazie,* 56(4): 343–347.

[45] Sinico, C., De Logu, A. and Lai, F. (2005). Liposomal incorporation of *Artemisia arborescens* L. essential oil and *in vitro* antiviral activity. *Eur. J. Pharm. Biopharm,* 59(1): 161–168.

[46] Skocibusic, M., Bezic, N., Dunkic, V. and Radoni, C.A. (2004). Antibacterial activity of *Achillea clavennae* essential oil against respiratory tract pathogens, *Fitoterapia,* 75: 733–736.

[47] Soltan, M.M., and Zaki, A.K. (2009). Antiviral screening of forty-two Egyptian medicinal plants. *J Ethnopharmacol,* 126(1):102–107.

[48] Souza, C.M.C., Pereira Junior, S.A. and da Silva Moraes, T. (2016). Antifungal activity of plant-derived essential oils on *Candida tropicalis* planktonic and biofilms cells. *Med Mycol,* 54(5): 515–523.

[49] Stefanakis, M.K., Touloupakis, E., Anastasopoulos, E., Ghanotakis D., Katerinopoulos, H.E. and Makridis, P. (2013). Antibacterial activity of essential oils from plants of the genus Origanum. *Food Control,* 34(2): 539–546.

[50] Szabo, M.A., Varga, G.Z. and Hohmann, J. (2010). Inhibition of quorum-sensing signals by essential oils. *Phytother Res,* 24(5): 782–786.

[51] Teixeira, B., Marques, A. and Ramos C. (2013). Chemical composition and antibacterial and antioxidant properties of commercial essential oils. *Ind Crop Prod,* 43(1): 587–595.

[52] Tsaknis, J. (1998). Characterisation of Moringa peregrine Arabia seed oil. *Grasas Aceites,* 49(2): 170–176.

[53] Ultee, A. and Smid, E.J. (2001). Influence of carvacrol on growth and toxin production by *Bacillus cereus. Int J Food Microbiol,* 64(3): 373–378.

[54] Wendakoon, C.N. and Sakaguchi, M. (1995). Inhibition of amino acid decarboxylase activity of *Enterobacter aerogenes* by active components in spices. *J Food Prot,* 58: 280–283.

[55] Yoon, H.S., Moon, S.C., Kim, N.D., Park, B.S., Jeong, M.H. and Yoo, Y.H. (2000). Genistein induces apoptosis of RPE-J cells by opening mitochondrial PTP. *Biochem. Biophys. Res. Commun.,* 276(1): 151–156.

[56] Zeedan, G.S.G.; Abdalhamed, A.M., Ottai, M.E., Abdelshafy, S. and Abdeen, E. (2014). Antimicrobial, Antiviral Activity and GC-MS Analysis of Essential Oil Extracted *from Achillea fragrantissima* Plant Growing In Sinai Peninsula, Egypt. *J. Microb Biochem Technol,* 8(1): 1–7.

Antimicrobial Potential of Vietnam Marine-Derived Actinomycetes

Duc Tuan Cao[1], Thi Hong Lien Hoang[2], Thi Hong Minh Le[3], Huong Doan Thi Mai[4] and Van Cuong Pham[5]

[1]Hai Phong University of Medicine and Pharmacy, Hai Phong, Vietnam

[2]Department of Scientific Management, Hai Phong University, Hai Phong, Vietnam

[3-5]Institute of Marine Biochemistry, Vietnam Academy of Science and Technology, Ha Noi, Vietnam

E-mail: [1]cdtuan@hpmu.edu.vn; [2]lienhth@dhhp.edu.vn; [3]lhminhbk@gmail.com; [4]doanhuong7@yahoo.com; [5]phamvc@yahoo.com

ABSTRACT: The East Sea of Vietnam covers an area of approximately three-million km^2 with more than 3,000 km coastline that encompasses a widerange of microenvironments covering depths up to 5,000 m. The marine biodiversity of the Vietnam's East Sea is considered to be among the most extensive in the world, but remains poorly understood and minimally explored. In the course of our screening program, 46 strains of actinomycetes were isolated from 55 marine samples collected from three coastal provincesinthe middle of Vietnam. Seven strains,with the highest antimicrobial activity against a panel of clinically significant microorganisms (MIC values from 2 μg/mL to 256 μg/mL), were chosen and identified by morphological studies as well as phylogenetic analysis based on their 16S rRNA gene sequences. It has been shown that six strainsbelonged to the genus Streptomyces and onestrain to the genus Micromonospora. Analysis of extract prepared from culture broth of the actinomycete Streptomyces sp. G278, one of the strongest antimicrobial strains, led to the isolation of ten compounds, 1–10. Two compounds, 2,5-Bis(5-tert-butyl-2-benzoxazolyl)thiophene (1), and 3-hydroxyl-2-methylpyridine (2) were isolated from a natural source for the first time. The structures of the isolated compounds were established by their spectral data analysis, including mass spectrometry, 1D-NMR, 2D-NMR, and X-ray crystallographic analysis in case of compound 3. All isolated compounds were also evaluated for their antimicrobial activity. Compounds 1 and 3 selectively inhibited Enterococcus faecalis (MIC: 256 μg/mL). Compound 2 was found to have antibacterial and anti-fungal activity against Escherichia coli (MIC: 64 μg/mL), Salmonella *enterica (MIC: 256 μg/mL), Staphylococcus aureus (MIC: 256 μg/mL), Enterococcus faecalis (MIC: 256 μg/mL), and Candida albicans (MIC: 64 μg/mL). Except for compounds 9 and 10, the other known metabolites (4-8) also exhibited antimicrobial activity. Obtained results indicated that marine actinomycetes isolated from the East Sea of Vietnam promise to be a rich source of materials for secondary bioactive compounds, especially antimicrobials.*

Keywords: East Sea of Vietnam, Actinomycetes, Antimicrobial, Streptomyces sp. G278, Benzoxazole, *2-methyl-3-pyridinol.*

1. INTRODUCTION

Emerging infectious diseases and multidrug-resistant microorganisms has been recognised as a global health issue (Khan, 2016). Resistant microorganisms exist in humans, animals, food and the environment, and there are no barriers to the transmission of resistance genes across bacterial species and compartments. They can be naturally resistant; however, exposure to antibiotics is one of the main drivers for the emergence and spread of resistance genes (Founou, 2016). Vietnam is one of the most antibiotic resistance prevalence country in the world, therefore, there is an urgent need for new antibiotics to fight evolving microbial infections (World Health Organization, 2018).

Over the years, the number of reported marine natural products has grown gradually. Recently, many researchers directed their attention toward marine microorganisms, resulted in the rapid increase of the number of new metabolites published (Blunt, 2018). Marine Actinobacteria are yet one of the richest sources of secondary metabolites, of which, up to 80% of these compounds are derived from the single genus *Streptomyces*, a biosynthetic capacity that remains without rival in the microbial world (Manivasagan, 2014). These metabolites are known to display a wide array of biological activities (Yasuzawa, 1995, Dharmaraj, 2010) and most of the clinically relevant antibiotics, to date, are from actinomycetes (Baltz, 2007). Marine actinomycetes is projected to be the future source of novel antimicrobials (Fenical, 1993).

Though, the recent search for novel antibiotics has established an approach of target based discovery using bacterial genomics, combinatorial chemistry; these powerful tools have not yet yielded any antibiotics approved for clinical use, and the prospects for their success are not encouraging (Baltz, 2007). Alternatively, programs aimed at the discovery of antibiotics from microbial sources have yielded an impressive number of compounds over the past 50 years, many of which have application in human medicine and agriculture (Busti, 2006). Therefore, the traditional method of screening antibiotics from microorganisms is still very effective (Baltz, 2007).

In search for antimicrobial metabolites from marine-derived actionmycetes, 46 strains of actinomycetes were isolated from 55 marine samples collected from three coastal provinces at the middle of Vietnam (Hue, Da Nang and Quang Nam). Seven strains of actinomycetes that have the highest biological activity were chosen to be identified by morphological and phylogenetic based on their 16S rRNA gene sequences. The *Streptomyces* strain (coded: G278), isolated from echinoderm *Holothuria edulis* (Lesson, 1830) from the sea of Cu Lao Cham–Quang Nam, showing strongest antimicrobial activities, was analyzed further for its chemical profile. Isolation and structural characterization of ten compounds from the fermentation broth of strain G278 was achieved. Two compounds 1 and 2, were reported for the first time from a nature source and all compounds, except 9 and 10, exhibited antimicrobial activity against a panel of clinically significant microorganisms (Cao, 2018).

2. MATERIALS AND METHODS

2.1 Materials

2.1.1 *Chemicals*

The genomic DNA isolation kits were purchased from Promega (Madison, WI, USA). The mini-prep and DNA gel extraction kits were purchased from Qiagen (Mannheim, Germany). PCR master mix was purchased from Bioneer. Glucose and all other chemicals (for media) were obtained from Himedia (India), Duc Giang (Vietnam) and Sigma-Aldrich (St. Louis, MO, USA). Thin-layer chromategraphy (TLC) used TLC silica gel Mecrk 60 F_{254}. Column chromategraphy (CC) was carried out on silica gel 40–63 µm or Sephadex LH-20.

2.1.2 *Reference Microorganisms*

Seven standard reference microorganisms were acquired from ATCC Bacteriology Collection, USA including: Three Gram negative bacteria (*Escherichia coli* ATCC25922, *Pseudomonas aeraginosa* ATCC27853, *Salmonella enterica* ATCC13076), three Gram positive bacteria (*Enterococcus faecalis* ATCC29212, *Stapphylococus aureus* ATCC25923, *Bacillus cereus* ATCC13245) and one yeast strain (*Candida albicans* ATCC10231).

2.1.3 *Marine Materials*

The samples of echinoderm *Holothuria edulis* (Lesson, 1830) were collected in Cu Lao Cham – Quang Nam in October 2016, and were identified by Prof. Do Cong Thung, Institute of Marine Environment and Resources, Vietnam Academy of Science and Technology (VAST). Voucher specimens were deposited at the Institute of Marine Biochemistry and Institute of Marine Environment and Resources, VAST.

2.2 Methods

2.2.1 *Sample Collections*

The marine samples were collected using Ponar and Scuba-diving from three locations at 4 m–24 m in depth with different geographic coordinates (Appendix Table A.1); the temperature of water in three coastal provinces of north-middle of Vietnam was 26–29°C (Figure 1).

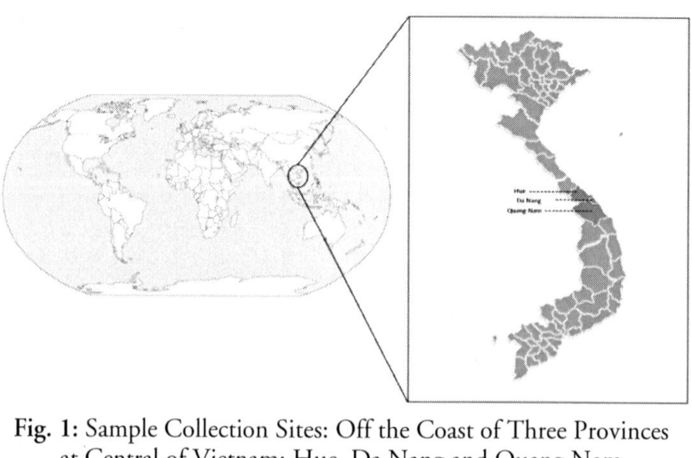

Fig. 1: Sample Collection Sites: Off the Coast of Three Provinces at Central of Vietnam: Hue, Da Nang and Quang Nam

The samples were collected into 15 mL or 50 mL sterile Falcon tubes and preserved in ice-box and processed onsite within 24 hours.

2.2.2 *Isolation of Actinomycetes*

First, 0.5 g of sample was suspended in 4.5 mL of sterile distilled water, homogenized by vortexing for 1 min, and the suspension was treated using a wet-heat technique (60°C for 6 min). Next, 0.5 mL of this suspension was transferred to 4.5 mL sterile distilled water and this step was repeated to set up a tenfold dilution series to 10^{-3}. At the final dilution step, aliquots of 50 μL were spread on eight different solid culture media: A1 (soluble starch: 10 g/L; yeast extract: 4 g/L; peptone: 2 g/L; instant ocean: 30 g/L; agar: 15 g/L), M1 (soluble starch: 5 g/L; yeast extract: 2 g/L; peptone: 1 g/L; instant ocean: 30 g/L; agar: 15 g/L), SWA (instant ocean: 30 g/L; agar: 15 g/L), A+ (soluble starch: 10 g/L; yeast extract: 4 g/L; peptone: 2 g/L; instant ocean: 30 g/L; $CaCO_3$: 1 g/L; agar: 15 g/L), SCA (soluble starch: 10 g/L; K_2HPO_4: 2 g/L; KNO_3: 2 g/L; casitone: 300 mg/L; $MgSO_4 \cdot 7H_2O$: 50 mg/L; $FeSO_4 \cdot 7H_2O$: 10 mg/L; instant ocean: 30 g/L; $CaCO_3$: 2 mg/L; agar: 15 g/L), NZSG (soluble starch: 20 g/L; yeast extract: 5 g/L; glucose: 10 g/L; NZ amine A: 5 g/L; Instant ocean: 30 g/L; agar: 15 g/L); ISP1 (soluble starch: 5 g/L; yeast extract: 2 g/L; casitone: 5 g/L; instant ocean: 30 g/L; Agar: 15 g/L), ISP2 (soluble starch: 5 g/L; yeast extract: 2 g/L; malt extract: 10 g/L; glucose: 10 g/L; instant ocean: 30 g/L; agar: 15 g/L). These media were supplemented with 50 μg/mL polymycin B and cycloheximide to inhibit Gram-negative bacterial and fungal contamination. After 21 days of aerobic incubation at 30°C, the colonies of actinomycete strains were transferred onto A1 agarmedium (Williams, 1965, T., 1971).

2.2.3 *Antimicrobial Assay*

Antibacterial assays were carried out using *E. coli* (ATCC25922), *P. aeruginosa* (ATCC27853), *S. enterica* (ATCC13076), *E. faecalis* (ATCC29212), *S. aureus* (ATCC25923), *B. cereus* (ATCC13245), and anti-yeast activity was performed against *C. albicans* (ATCC10231). Stock solutions of samples were prepared in DMSO, and the antimicrobial assays were carried out in 96 well microtiter plates against the microbial strains (5×10^5 CFU/mL) using a modification of the published method (Andrews, 2001). After incubation for 24 h at 37°C, the absorbance at 650 nm was measured using a microplate reader. Streptomycin, Nystatin and Cycloheximide were used as reference compounds while the vehicle banks were prepared by adding the similar volume of DMSO to the growth medium to achieve the same DMSO concentration in all tested wells.

2.2.4 *Identification of Actinomycetes*

Morphological studies: The actinomycete strains were grown for 14 days at 28°C on starch casein agar (SCA) and examined using scanning electron microscopy (model JSM-5410 LV; JEOL). Samples for scanning electron microscopy (SEM) were prepared as described by Itoh (Itoh, 1989).

Identification based on the 16S rRNA gene sequences: PCR amplifications were performed in a 25.0 μL mixture containing: 16.3 μL of sdH_2O, 2.5 μL of 10× PCR buffer, 1.5 μL of 25 mM $MgCl_2$, 0.5 μL of 10 mM dNTP's, 0.2 μL of Taq polymerase, 1.0 μl for both 0.05 mM of 9F (5'-GAGTTTGATCCTGGCTCAG3') and 0.05 mM of 1541R (5'-AAGGAGGTGATCCAACC3') primers (Muthu, 2013) and 2.0 μL of genomic DNA. The reaction tube was then put into MJ Thermal Cycler, which had been programmed to preheat at 94°C for 3 min, followed by 30 cycles of denaturation at 94°C for 1 min, annealing at 60°C for 30 s and elongation at 72°C for 45 s before a final extension of 72°C for 10 min. The estimated PCR product size was about 1,500 bp. PCR products were purified by DNA purification kit (Invitrogen) then sequenced by DNA Analyzer (ABI PRISM 3100, Applied Bioscience). Gene sequences were handled by BioEdit v.2.7.5. and compared with bacterial 16S rRNA sequences in GeneBank database by NBCI Blast program. The alignment was manually verified and adjusted prior to the construction of a phylogenetic tree. The phylogenetic tree was constructed by using the neighbor-joining the MEGA program, version 7 (Saitou, 1987).

2.2.5 *Extraction and Isolation*

Production of crude extracts

Small scale extracts preparation for antimicrobials screening: The isolated actinomyces strains were cultivated at 28°C in sterile 1000 mL flasks containing 500 ml of culture media A+ with glucose 1%, pH 7.0, at 200 rpm and 30°C. After 7 days of cultivation, the fermentation broths were filtered and then extracted with EtOAC (5 × 0.25 L). The extracts were evaporated under reduced pressure to yield crude extracts (Orelle, 2013).

Large scale extracts preparation for chemical analysis: The strain G287 was isolated from above-mentioned marine sample. Strain G278 was activated and inoculated into 1 L of A1 medium pH 7.0. After 7 days of incubation at 28°C with agitation, the culture broth was used to inoculate the fermentation in 50 L of high-nutrient medium A^+, pH 7.0. The fermentation was incubated at 28°C with agitation of 200 rpm and harvested on the seventh day. Culture broth (50 L) of Streptomyces strains was then filtered and extracted. The solvent was concentrated under reduced pressure to afford 8.4 g crude extracts.

2.2.5 *Secondary Metabolite Isolations and Structure Elucidations*

The crude extract was isolated by Column Chromatography and Preparative Thin Layer Chromatography with suitable organic solvent systems. The structure of pure isolated compounds was determined by analysis of their spectroscopic data (Infrared spectroscopy, Mass spectroscopy, 1D and 2D Nuclear Magnetic Resonance Spectroscopy), X-ray crystallographic data and compare with literature.

HR-ESI-MS were recorded on a FT-ICR 910-MS TQFTMS-7T and a VARIAN 910 mass spectrometers. X-ray diffraction analysis was achieved with a STOE IPDS 2T instrument. IR spectra were recorded on a Nicolet Impact 410 FT-IR spectrometer, UV spectra measured on a UV-1601 spectrometer, and NMR spectra were recorded on a Bruker AM500 MHz spectrometer operating at 125.76 MHz for 13C NMR, and at 500.13 MHz for 1H-NMR. The HMBC measurements were optimized to 7.0 Hz long-range couplings.

2.2.6 *X-ray Crystallographic Analysis*

The intensities for the X-ray determination were collected at 100 K with Mo Kα X-rays from a Bruker D8 Quest diffractometer equipped with TRIUMPH monochromator and a CMOS detector. Standard procedures were applied for data reduction and absorption correction. Using Olex2 (Dolomanov, 2009), the structure was solved with the ShelXT (Sheldrick, 2015b) structure solution program using Intrinsic

Phasing method and refined with the ShelXL 2016/6 (Sheldrick, 2015a) refinement package using Least Squares minimization. Non-H atoms were refined with anisotropic displacement parameters. Hydrogen atoms were constrained to parent sites, using a riding model.

3. RESULTS AND DISCUSSION

3.1 Isolation and Screening the Antimicrobial Activity of Actinomycetes

From 55 marine samples collected in Hue, Da Nang and Quang Nam, 46 actinomycete strains were isolated. These strains then were cultured and extracted to determine their antimicrobial activity. From the results of screening, seven strains of actinomycetes that have the highest biological activity (Coded: G244, G246, G261, G266, G278, G280 and G290) were chosen to identify based on their morphology and 16S rRNA gene sequence (Table 1).

Table 1: Antimicrobial Activity of Crude Ethyl Acetate Extracts from 7 Strains

No.	Strain	*MIC (µg/mL)*						
		Gram-positive			*Gram-negative*			*Yeast*
		E. faecalis ATCC 29212	*S. aureus ATCC 25923*	*B. cereus ATCC 13245*	*E. coli ATCC 25922*	*P. aeruginosa ATCC 27853*	*S. enterica ATCC 13076*	*C. albicans ATCC 10231*
1	G244	64	–	256	128	–	32	32
2	G246	64	–	128	–	–	–	32
3	G261	64	–	256	–	16	–	16
4	G266	–	16	256	–	32	16	–
5	**G278**	**256**	**32**	–	**16**	–	**16**	**2**
6	G280	256	–	256	16	32	–	2
7	G290	–	–	32	–	16	8	16
Streptomycin		256	256	128	32	256	128	–
Nystatin		–	–	–	–	–	–	8

The result reveals that most of the isolates were active against both Gram positive and Gram negative bacteria. Strains G244, G278, G280 were active against 5/7 strains of micro-organisms test, with the MIC values from 2 µg/mL to 256 µg/mL; and three strains G261, G266, G290 showed the inhibitory effect towards 4/7 strains of micro-organisms test, with respective value of MIC from 2 µg/mL to 256 µg/mL. In addition, six of the seven strains selected were highly resistant to *C. albicans* ATCC10231 with MIC value from 2 μg/mL to 256 μg/mL. Comparison of antimicrobial activity among screening strains in Hue, Quang Nam and Da Nang with isolated strains in the North-East Coast of Vietnam showed that 7 strains of actinomycetes selected above have potent activity against both Gram-positive and Gram-negative bacteria. Of the 15 strains screened in the North-East Coast of Vietnam, only four strains of G057, G115, G119, and G120 were resistant to *P. auruginosa* ATCC27853 with a MIC value of 64–32 μg/mL (Le, 2016). This result shows that the biological activity of the strains depends very much on its original geographic location.

3.2 Identification of Actinomycetes by Morphological Characteristic

The spore morphology is considered as one of the important characteristics in the identification of Streptomyces and it greatly varies among the species. It has been found that the majority of the marine isolates produced aerial coiled mycelia and the spores arranged in chains as already reported by Mukherjee and Sen (Mukherjee, 2004). *Micromonospora* species produced well-developed and branched substrate hyphae on yeast extract-malt extract medium, but no aerial hyphae. Spores were borne singly on the substrate hyphae having an approximate diameter of 0.5–1 μm. The spores were nodular and smooth on the surface and non-motile (Figure 2).

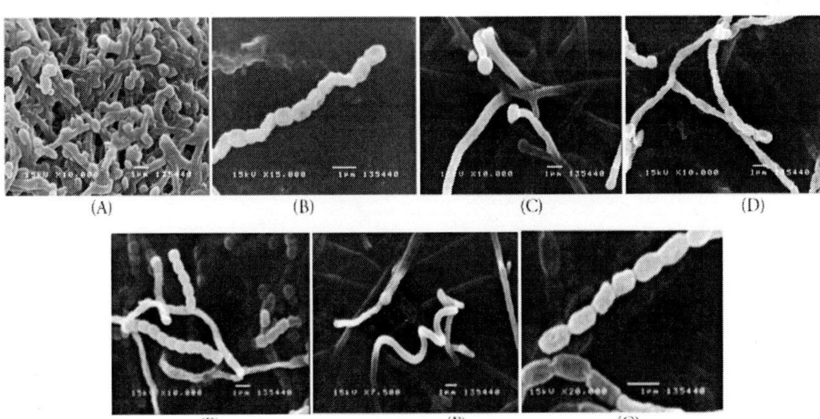

Fig. 2: Scanning Electron Micrographs of the Selected Strains Grown on SCA Agar for 2 Weeks at 30°C. **A**: G244; **B**: G246; **C**: G266; **D**: G290; **E**: G261; **F**: G278; **G**: G280

The colors of the substrate mycelium were yellowish white to vivid orange and turned to brownish black to black after sporulation (Figure 3). The morphological characteristics of these isolates were consistent with their classification in the genus (Kawamoto I, 1989).

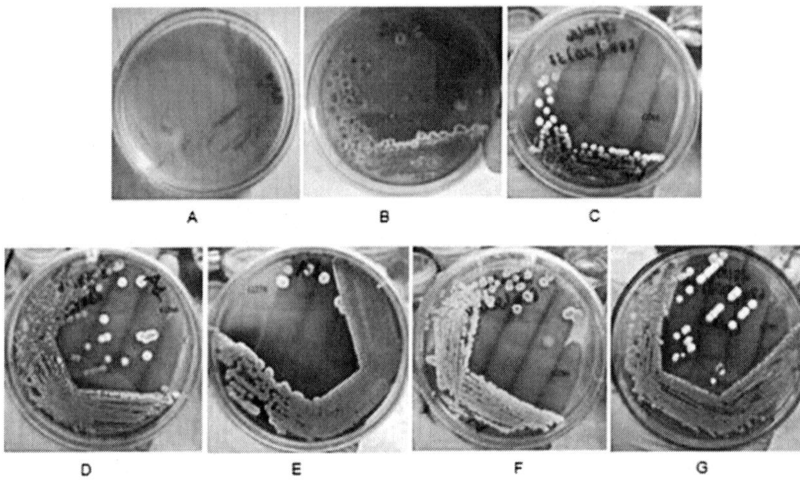

Fig. 3: Morphological Appearance of Isolates. The Colors of the Substrate Mycelium were Vivid Orange **A**(G244) and from white Turned to Brownish after Sporulation **B**(G246), **C**(G261), **D**(G266), **E**(G278), **F**(G280) and **G**(G290)

3.3 Identification of Actinomycetes by Phylogenetic based on 16S rRNA Gene Sequences

Seven potential isolates were selected for identification by 16S rRNA gene sequencing. The obtained sequences were analyzed by Bioedit program and compared with GenBank database. The obtained results showed that 16S rRNA sequences of G246, G261, G266, G278, G280 and G290 strains exhibited high similarity (99%) with genus *Stretomyces* spp; The strain G244 was identified (99% similarity) of 16S rRNA gene sequence with genus *Micromonospora* in Gen Bank (Figure 4).

Streptomyces is a genus of Gram-positive bacteria that grows in various environments, with a filamentous form similar to fungi. The morphological differentiation of *Streptomyces* involves the formation of a layer of hyphae that can differentiate into a chain of spores. The most interesting property of *Streptomyces* is the ability to produce bioactive secondary metabolites such as antifungals, antivirals, antitumor, antihypertensive, and mainly antibiotics and immune suppressive (Khan, 2011, Patzer, 2010). Another characteristic of the genus is complex multicellular development, in which their germinating spores form hyphae. Then, multinuclear aerial mycelium forms septa at regular intervals, creating a chain of spores (Ohnishi, 2008).

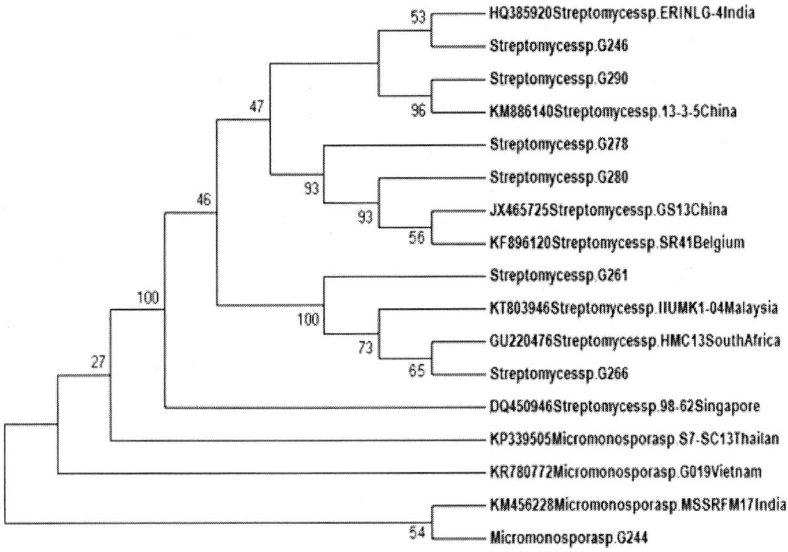

Fig. 4: Neighbor-joining tree based on almost-complete 16S rRNA gene sequences showing relationships between the strains in groups and representative members of the genera *Streptomyces* and *Micromonospora* were used as an outgroup. The numbers on the branches indicate the percentage bootstrap values of 1,000 replicates; Bar, 0.01 substitutions per nucleotide position

Marine environment contains a wide range of distinct *Streptomyces* that are not present in the terrestrial environment. Though, some reports are available on antibiotic and enzyme production by marine actionmycetes, the marine environment is still a potential source for isolating new actinomycetes, which can yield novel bioactive compounds and industrially important enzymes (Cai, 2007).

In addition, *Micromonospora* species, one of the dominant actionmycetes, are possible to be isolated from aquatic habitats such as streams, lake mud, river sediments, beach sands, sponge and marine sediments (Eccleston, 2008, Rifaat, 2003). *Micromonospora* species, together with *Streptomyces* species are best known for synthesizing antibiotics, especially aminoglycoside, enediyne and oligosaccharide antibiotics. Thus, their clinical impact is considerable. Of common antibiotics used in clinical setting, gentamicin and netamicin belong to the aminoglycoside antibiotics yielded by *Micromonospora* (Berdy, 2005).

Research focused on marine environment has been gaining importance in recent years. However, still it has not been fully explored and there is tremendous potential to identify novel organisms with various biological properties. The present investigation showed that action-mycetes tentatively identified as Streptomyces species have strong antimicrobial activities against pathogenic bacteria, similar to reports in literature (Ramesh, 2009, Sujatha, 2005).

3.4 Chemical Analysis of the *Streptomyce s*sp. G278 Strains

3.4.1 *Isolation*

Ten compounds (**1–10**) were isolated from the 8.4 g crude extract of strain G278 following procedure in Appendix Figure A.2. Firstly, the crude extract was subjected to column chromatography (CC) on silica gel, eluted with a continuous gradient mixture CH_2Cl_2/MeOH(10 to 60% of MeOH in CH_2Cl_2) to give 5 fractions (F1–F5). Fraction F1 (635 mg) was separated by CC on silica gel (0 to 30% EtOAc in *n*-hexane) furnishing 4 sub-fractions (F1.1–F1.4). Subfraction F1.2 (37 mg) was purified by preparative TLC (*n*-hexane/acetone: 95/5) to provide compound **3** (3.5 mg). Fraction F2 (535 mg) was subjected to a CC on silica gel (0% to 50% of acetone in *n*-hexane) to afford 5 subfractions (F2.1-F2.5). Subfraction F2.2 (132 mg) was separated on a Sephadex LH-20 column (MeOH/CH_2Cl_2: 9/1), followed by recrystallization in a solvent mixture *n*-hexane/ethyl acetate (8/2, v/v), yielding compound **1** (12 mg). Subfraction F2.3 (110 mg) was purified on silica gel CC (5 to 50% EtOAc in *n*-hexane) to give compound 4 (9 mg). Fraction F3 (735 mg) was separated by CC on Sephadex LH-20 (MeOH/CH_2Cl_2: 9/1), leading to 4 sub-fractions (F3.1-F3.4). Sub-fraction F3.2 (156 mg) was purified by CC on Sephadex LH-20 (MeOH/CH_2Cl_2: 9/1), followed by preparative TLC (*n*-hexane/ acetone: 7/3) giving compounds, **9** (4 mg) and **6** (5 mg). Sub-fraction F3.3 (230 mg) was subjected to a CC on silica gel, eluted with a gradient mixture of dichloromethane/acetone to provide compound **5**

(9 mg). Fraction F4 (366 mg) was purified by Sephadex LH-20 column ($MeOH/CH_2Cl_2$: 9/1), furnishing 4 sub-fractions. Subfraction F4.3 (135 mg) was separated by CC on silica gel (CH_2Cl_2/EtOAc gradient) to give compounds, **8** (8 mg) and **10** (5 mg). Subfraction F4.4 (105 mg) was subjected to a CC on Sephadex LH-20 (MeOH/ CH_2Cl_2: 9/1), followed by preparative TLC (CH_2Cl_2/ MeOH: 9/1) to yield compound 7 (13 mg). Fraction F5 (220 mg) was separated by CC on Sephadex LH-20 ($MeOH/CH_2Cl_2$: 8/2), providing 3 sub-fractions F5.1-F5.3. Subfraction F5.3 (35 mg) was purified by preparative TLC (CH_2Cl_2/MeOH: 85/15) to give compound **2** (4.5 mg).

3.4.2 *Spectroscopic Data*

2,5-Bis (5-tert-butyl-2-benzoxazolyl)thiophene (**1**): White solid; mp. 202-203°C; FT-IR (KBr) ν_{max}: 3442, 2959, 2867, 1635, 1581, 1504, 1478, 1362, 1348, 1266, 1195, 1027, 935, 810, 715 cm^{-1}; UV (MeOH) λ_{max} (log ε): 209 (1.08), 247 (0.38), 264 (0.37), 370 (1.77), 3.73 (1.78) nm; ^{1}H-NMR (500 MHz, DMSO): δ_H (ppm) 1.37 (9H, s, 3 × CH_3), 7.54 (1H, dd, *J* = 2.0, 8.0 Hz, H-5), 7.72 (1H, d, *J* = 8.0 Hz, H-4), 7.81 (1H, d, *J* = 2.0 Hz, H-7), 8.06 (1H, s, H-3'); ^{13}C-NMR (125 MHz, DMSO): δ_C (ppm) 31.5 (3 × CH_3), 34.8 (C-8), 110.3 (C-4), 116.3 (C-7), 123.9 (C-5), 131.3 (C-3′), 132.4 (C-2′), 141.3 (C-3a), 148.3 (C-6), 148.6 (C-7a), 157.5 (C-2); HR-ESI-MS: m/z 431.1785$[M+H]^+$(calcd. for $C_{26}H_{27}N_2O_2S$, 431.1793).

3-Hydroxyl-2-methylpyridine (**2**): White solid; FT-IR (KBr) ν_{max}: 3398, 3311, 3060, 2920, 1889, 1730, 1697, 1615, 1455, 1419, 1337, 1220, 1097, 1008, 874, 741 cm^{-1}; UV (MeOH) λ_{max} (log ε): 224 (1.56), 283 (0.30) nm; ^{1}H-NMR (500 MHz, CD_3OD): δ_H (ppm) 2.30 (3H, s, CH_3), 7.01 (1H, dd, J = 5.0, 8.0 Hz, H-5), 7.09 (1H, d, J = 8.0 Hz, H-4), 7.86 (1H, d, J = 5.0 Hz, H-6). ^{13}C-NMR (125 MHz, CD_3OD): δ_C (ppm) 18.4 (CH_3), 123.2 (C-5), 122.6 (C-4), 139.3 (C-6), 147.7 (C-2), 154.0 (C-3); HR-ESI-MS: m/z 110.0609 $[M+H]^+$ (calcd. for C_6H_8NO, 110.0606).

Ethylene terephthalate cyclic trimer (**3**): White, microcrystalline solid; mp. 195–196°C; FT-IR (KBr) ν_{max}: 2963, 1729, 1629, 1578, 1457, 1408, 1367, 1288, 1264, 1133, 1098, 1015, 874, 729 cm^{-1}; UV (MeOH) λ_{max} (log ε): 242 (1.89), 288 (0.17) nm; ^{1}H-NMR (500 MHz,

$CDCl_3$): δ_H (ppm) 4.69 (s, H-4), 8.10 (s, H-3); ^{13}C-NMR (125MHz, $CDCl_3$): δ_C (ppm) 62.7 (C-4), 129.7 (C-3), 133.8 (C-2), 165.3(C-1); HR-ESI-MS: m/z 385.2738 $[M+H]^+$ (calcd. for $C_{25}H_{37}O_3$, 385.2743).

X-ray crystallographic analysis of compound 3: *Crystal data:* $C_{30}H_{24}O_{12}$, M = 576.49, monoclinic, a = 16.7653(8), b = 19.6477(9), c = 8.2705(4) Å, β = 95.632(2)°, V = 1136.77(11) $Å^3$, space group C2/c, Z = 4, Z' = 0.5, μ = 0.111 mm^{-1}, D_{calcd} = 1.412 g cm^{-3}, θ range 5.69–56.66°, 36359 reflections measured, 3376 unique (R_{int}= 0.0389, R_{sigma} = 0.0186) which were used in all calculations. The final $wR_2(F^2)$ was 0.1054 and the S (goodness-of-fit) value 1.040 (all data). The R_1(F) was 0.0377 [I > 2σ (I)]. Crystallographic data (including structure factors) for compound **3** have been deposited with the Cambridge Crystallographic Data Center as supplementary publication number CCDC 1575272. Copies of the data can be obtained, free of charge, on application to CCDC, 12 Union Road, Cambridge CB2 1EZ, UK (fax: +44 0 1223 336033 or deposit@ccdc.cam.ac.uk).

Benzyl salicylate (4): White solid;^{1}H-NMR (500MHz, $CDCl_3$): *δ*(ppm) 5,39 (2H, s, CH_2-9), 6,87 (1H, dt, *J* = 1,0, 7,5 Hz, H-5), 6,98 (1H, d, *J* = 8,5 Hz, H-6), 7,36-7,47 (5H, m, Ph), 7,46 (1H, td, *J* = 1,5, 7,5 Hz, H-4), 7,88 (1H, dd, *J* = 2,0, 8,0 Hz, H-6), 10,73 (1H, s, OH); ^{13}C-NMR (125 MHz,$CDCl_3$): δ_C (ppm) 66,9 (C-9), 112,0 (C-1), 117,6 (C-3), 119,2 (C-5); 128,3 (C-2', C-6'), 128,6 (C-4'), 128,7 (C-3', C-5'), 130,0 (C-6),135,3 (C-1'), 135,8 (C-4), 161,8 (C-2), 169,9 (C-7).

N-phenylnaphthalen-2-amine (5): Light yellow, microcrystalline solid; ESI-MS: *m/z* 220 $[M+H]^+$; ^{1}H-NMR (500MHz, $CDCl_3$): *δ*(ppm) 6,98 (1H, t, *J* = 8,5 Hz, H-4'), 7,16 (2H, d, *J* = 8,0 Hz, H-2', H-6'), 7,23 (1H, dd, *J* = 1,0, 8,5 Hz, H-2), 7,28 (1H, t, *J* = 8,0 Hz, H-5), 7,29 (2H, t, *J* = 8,0 Hz, H-3', H-5'), 7,40 (1H, t, *J* = 7,5 Hz, H-6), 7,44 (1H, br s, H-8), 7,64 (1H, d, *J* = 8,0 Hz, H-7), 7,74 (2H, br d, *J* = 8,0 Hz, H-3, H-4), ^{13}C-NMR (125 MHz,$CDCl_3$): δ_C (ppm) 111,6 (C-8), 118,3 (C-2', C-6'), 120,1 (C-2), 121,4 (C-3), 123,5 (C-5), 126,5 (C-7), 126,5 (C-6), 127,7 (C-4), 129,1 (C-3a), 129,2 (C-3), 129,4 (C-3', C-5'), 134,5 (C-7a), 141,2 (C-1), 143,0 (C-1').

Scopoletin (6): ^{1}H-NMR (500 MHz, $CDCl_3$): δ_H (ppm) 3,96 (3H, s, O-CH_3); 6,27 (1H, d, *J* = 9,5 Hz, H-3); 6,85 (1H, s, H-5); 6,92 (1H, s, H-8); 7,60 (1H, d, *J* = 9,5 Hz, H-4). ^{13}C-NMR (125 MHz, $CDCl_3$):

δ_C (ppm) 56,4 (O-CH_3); 103,2 (C-8); 107,5 (C-5); 111,5 (C-4a); 113,5 (C-3); 143,2 (C-4); 144,0 (C-6); 149,7 (C-7); 150,3 (C-8a); 161,4 (C-2).

Cyclo-(Pro-Tryp) (7): ^{1}H-NMR (500 MHz, $CDCl_3$): δ_H (ppm) 1,86 (1H, m, H_a-4), 2,0 (2H, m, H_b-4, H_a-5); 2,32 (1H, m, H_b-5); 2,98 (1H, dd, *J* = 10,5; 15,0 Hz; H_a-10); 3,55-3,68 (2H, m, H-3); 3,74 (1H, dd, *J* = 3,0; 15,0 Hz; H_b-10); 4,07 (1H, m, H-6), 4,38 (1H, br d, *J* = 9,5 Hz, H-9); 7,09 (1H, s, H-2'), 7,10-7,60 (4H, H-aromatic); ^{13}C-NMR (125 MHz, $CDCl_3$): δ_C (ppm) 22,6 (C-4), 26,9 (C-10), 28,3 (C-5), 45,4 (C-3), 54,6 (C-9), 59,8 (C-6), 109,5-136,7 (C-Phe), 123,4 (C-2'), 167,4 (C=O); 170,3 (C=O).

1H-indole-3-ethanol (**8**): White solid; ^{1}H- NMR (500 MHz, $CDCl_3$): δ_H (ppm) 3,05 (2H, t, *J* = 6,5 Hz, CH_2-1'), 3,92 (2H, t, *J* = 6,5 Hz, CH_2-2'), 7,05 (1H, s, H-2), 7,15 (1H, dt, *J* = 1,0, 8,0 Hz, H-5), 7,23 (1H, dt, *J* = 1,0, 8,0 Hz, H-6), 7,36 (1H, d, *J* = 8,0 Hz, H-7), 7,64 (1H, *J* = 8,0 Hz, H-4); ^{13}C- NMR (125 MHz, CD_3OD): δ_C (ppm) 28,7 (C-1'), 62,6 (C-2'), 111,3 (C-7), 112,2 (C-3), 118,8 (C-4), 119,4 (C-5), 122,2 (C-6), 122,6 (C-2), 127,5 (C-3a), 136,5 (C-7a).

3-indolecarbadehyde (**9**): ^{1}H-NMR (500 MHz, $CDCl_3$): δ_H (ppm) 7,32 (1H, m, H-5); 7,33 (1H, m, H-6); 7,45 (1H, m, H-7); 7,85 (1H, d, *J* = 3,0 Hz, H-2); 8,32 (1H, m, H-4); 10,1 (-CHO). ^{13}C-NMR (125 MHz, $CDCl_3$): δ_C (ppm) 111,4 (C-7); 120,1 (C-7a); 122,0 (C-4); 123,1 (C-5); 124,0 (C-3); 124,5 (C-6); 135,1 (C-2); 136,9 (C-3a); 185,1 (CHO).

Indole-3-carboxylic acid (**10**): Light brown powder; mp.231-232°C; ESI-MS: *m/z* 162 $[M+H]^+$; ^{1}H- NMR (500 MHz, CD_3OD): 7,17 (1H, dd, *J* = 1,5, 7,0 Hz, H-5), 7,22 (1H, dd, *J* = 1,5; 7,0 Hz, H-6), 7,45 (1H, dd, *J* = 1,0, 7,0 Hz, H-7), 7,96 (1H, s, H-2), 8,08 (1H, dd, *J* = 1,5; 7,0 Hz, H-4). ^{13}C- NMR (125 MHz, CD_3OD): 108,6 (C-3a), 112,9 (C-7), 122,0 (C-4), 122,4 (C-5), 123,6 (C-6), 127,5 (C-3a), 133,4 (C-2),138,2 (C-7a), 169,2 (COOH).

3.4.3 *Structure Elucidations*

Structure of Compound **1–3** wasdetermined by Cao *et al.*, 2018 (Cao, 2018) and presented in Figure 5. Compound **1** previously synthesized and used as a fluorescent brightening agent (Li, 2008) and compound **2** has been also previously synthesized (Jida, 2008), however, these compounds were reported for the first time from a natural source (Strain G278). The structure of **3** was confirmed by X-ray diffraction analysis (Appendix Figure A.3). Therefore, compound **3** was identified as ethylene terephthalate cyclic trimer. This compound was previously reported as a synthetic derivative (Kint, 2003). Since recent reports described that the phthalates were found to contaminate natural environments or migrate from plasticized films into foods (Bianco, 2014, Castle, 1988, Parveen, 2008), the compound **3** was a contaminant.

Structures of other compounds, also presented in Figure 5, including: benzyl salicylate (**4**) (Talzi, 2006), *N*-phenylnaphthalen-2-amine (**5**) (Cazorla, 2011), scopoletin (**6**) (Darmawan, 2012), cyclo-(L-Pro-L-Trp) (**7**) (Ying, 2013), tryptophol (**8**) (Guzmán-López, 2007), indole-3-carbaldehyde (**9**) (Ashour, 2007), indole-3-carboxylic acid (10) (Tan, 2004), were determined by spectral data analysis and comparison with reported data in the literature.

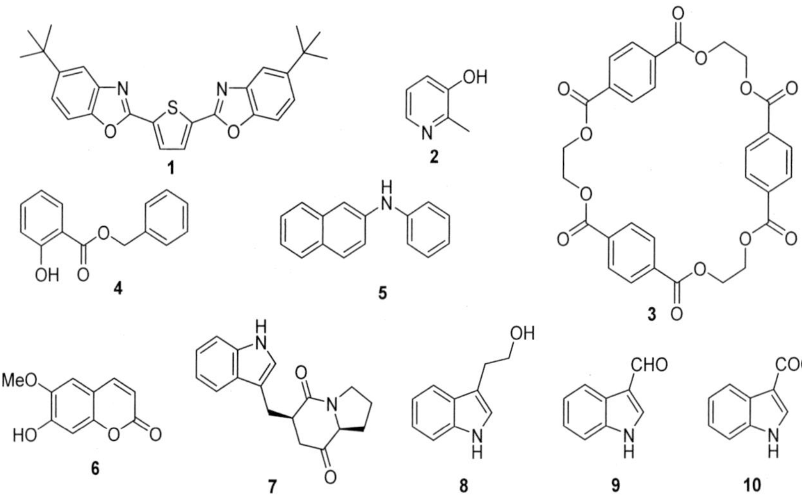

Fig. 5: Secondary Metabolites **1–10** isolated from *Streptomyces* sp. G278

3.5 Biological Activities of Pure Isolated Compounds from Two *Streptomyces* Strains

Compounds **1–10** were evaluated for their antibacterial and anti-yeast activity (Table 2). Compounds **1** and **3** selectively inhibited *E. faecalis* (MIC: 256 μg/mL). Whereas, compound **2** was found to have broad-spectrum antimicrobial activity against *E. coli* (MIC: 64 µg/mL), *S. enterica* (MIC: 256 µg/ml), *S. aureus* (MIC: 256 µg/mL), *E. faecalis* (MIC: 256 µg/mL), and *C. albicans* (MIC: 64 µg/mL). Except for compounds **9** and **10**, the other known metabolites (**4–8**) also exhibited antimicrobial activity. Moreover, compounds **6**, 7 and **8** selectively inhibited *E. coli* with MIC values of 64, 64 and 8 µg/mL, respectively. Compound **4** selectively inhibited *E. faecalis* with MIC value of 64 µg/mL. Finally, compound **5** inhibited *E. faecalis, S. aureus, B. cereus, E. coli* and *C. albicans* with MIC values of 128, 256, 256, 128 and 128 µg/mL, respectively. Scopoletin (**6**) has been mainly isolated from plants, and rarely from bacterial broth culture. Whereas, cyclo-(L-Pro-L-Trp) (7) has been found to be produced by various bacteria strains (Huayue, 2008, Li, 2006, Wattana-Amorn, 2016). Previous reports showed that **6** possessed antibacterial and antifungal properties (Gnonlonfin, 2012), while 7 had antibacterial and antifouling activities.

Table 2: Antibacterial and Antifungal Activities of Compounds **1–10** (MIC: µg/mL)

Compd.	*Gram-Positive*			*Gram-Negative*			*Yeast*
	E. faecalis	*S. aureus*	*B. cereus*	*E. coli*	*P. aeruginosa*	*S. enterica*	*C. albicans*
1	256	>256	>256	>256	>256	>256	>256
2	256	256	>256	64	>256	256	64
3	256	>256	>256	>256	>256	>256	>256
4	64	>256	>256	>256	>256	>256	>256
5	128	256	256	128	>256	>256	128
6	>256	>256	>256	64	>256	>256	>256
7	256	>256	>256	64	>256	>256	>256
8	>256	>256	>256	8	>256	>256	>256
9	>256	>256	>256	>256	>256	>256	>256
10	>256	>256	>256	>256	>256	>256	>256
Streptomycin	256	256	128	32	256	128	
Cycloheximide							32

4. CONCLUSIONS

From 56 samples including sediments, sponges, soft corals, echinoderms and starfish collected from three sea areas of Vietnam: Hue, Da Nang, and Quang Nam, 46 strains of actinomycetes were isolated. Most of the isolates exhibited antimicrobial activity, seven strains of actinomycetes that have the highest biological activity (MICs from 2 μg/mL to 256 μg/mL) were chosen to be identified by morphological and phylogenetic investigations based on 16S rRNA gene sequences. The strains G246, G261, G266, G278, G280, and G290 belonged to genus *Stretomyces*; strain G244 were identified as genus *Micromonospora*. In addition, six of the seven strains selected were highly resistant to yeast *C. Albicans* ATCC10231 with MIC values from 2 μg/mL to 256 μg/mL. Analysis of the crude extract of the echinoderm-derived actinomycete *Streptomyces* sp. G278, led to the isolation and structural characterization of ten compounds **1–10**. Two compounds **1** and **2** have not been reported previously to occur in nature. This was also the first discovery of antimicrobial activity for compounds **1–3**. The results indicated that the marine actinomycetes isolated from the East Sea of Vietnam, promise to be a rich source of materials for secondary bioactive compounds, especially antimicrobials.

ACKNOWLEDGEMENTS

The Vietnam Academy of Science and Technology (VAST) are gratefully acknowledged for financial support (Grant No: VAST. TĐ.DLB.04/16-18).

REFERENCES

[1] Andrews, J.M. (2001). Determination of minimum inhibitory concentrations. *Journal of antimicrobial Chemotherapy,* 48, 5–16.

[2] Ashour, M.A. (2007). Indole alkaloid from the Red Sea sponge *Hyrtios erectus. Arkivoc,* 15, 225–231.

[3] Baltz, R. (2007). Antimicrobials from Actinomycetes: Back to the Future. *Microbe,* 2, 125–131.

[4] Berdy, J. (2005). Bioactive microbial metabolites. *J Antibiot (Tokyo),* 58, 1–26.

[5] Bianco, A. (2014). A new problem. Contamination of botanicals by phthalates. Rapid detection tests. *Nat Prod Res,* 28, 134–7.

[6] Blunt, J.W. (2018). Marine natural products. *Nat Prod Rep,* 35, 8–53.

[7] Busti, E. (2006). Antibiotic-producing ability by representatives of a newly discovered lineage of actinomycetes. *Microbiology,* 152, 675–83.

[8] Cai, P. (2007). Polyene antibiotics from Streptomyces mediocidicus. *J Nat Prod,* 70, 215–9.

[9] Cao, D.T. (2018). Antimicrobial metabolites from a marine-derived Actinomycete Streptomyces sp. G278. *Nat Prod Res,* 1–8.

[10] Castle, L. (1988). Migration from plasticized films into foods. 3. Migration of phthalate, sebacate, citrate and phosphate esters from films used for retail food packaging. *Food Addit Contam,* 5, 9–20.

[11] Cazorla, C. (2011). O-Alkylation of phenol derivatives via a nucleophilic substitution. *Green Chemistry,* 13, 2482–2488.

[12] Darmawan, A. (2012). Scopoletin, a coumarin derivative compound isolated from *Macaranga gigantifolia* Merr. *Journal of Applied Pharmaceutical Science,* 2, 175–177.

[13] Dharmaraj, S. (2010). Marine *Streptomyces* as a novel source of bioactive substances. *World Journal of Microbiology and Biotechnology,* 26, 2123–2139.

[14] Dolomanov, O.V. (2009). OLEX2: A complete structure solution, refinement and analysis program. *Journal of Applied Crystallography,* 42, 339–341.

[15] Eccleston, G.P. (2008). The occurrence of bioactive micromonosporae in aquatic habitats of the Sunshine Coast in Australia. *Mar Drugs,* 6, 243–61.

[16] Fenical, W. (1993). Chemical studies of marine bacteria: developing a new resource. *Chemical Reviews,* 93, 1673–683.

[17] Founou, L.L. (2016). Antibiotic Resistance in the Food Chain: A Developing Country-Perspective. *Front Microbiol,* 7, 1881.

[18] Gnonlonfin, G.J.B. (2012). Review Scopoletin—A Coumarin Phytoalexin with Medicinal Properties. *Critical Reviews in Plant Sciences,* 31, 47–56.

[19] Guzmán-López, O. (2007). Tyrosol and tryptophol produced by *Ceratocystis adiposa. World Journal of Microbiology and Biotechnology,* 23, 1473–1477.

[20] Huayue, L.I. (2008). Bioactive Cyclic Dipeptides from a Marine Sponge-Associated Bacterium, Psychrobacter sp. *Biomolecules & Therapeutics,* 16, 356–363.

[21] Itoh, T. (1989). Amended Description of the Genus Kineosporia, Based on Chemotaxonomic and Morphological Studies. *Int J Syst Bacteriol,* 39, 168–173.

[22] Jida, M. (2008). Convergent and Selective Synthesis of Pyrrolidinones, Piperidinones, Dihydropyridinones and Pyridinols from a Common Intermediate–Potential Precursors of Bioactive Products. *European Journal of Organic Chemistry,* 2008, 4041–4049.

[23] Kawamoto, I., W.S.T., Sharpe, M.E. and Holt J.G. (1989). Genus *Micromonospora. Bergey's Manual of Systematic Bacteriology.*

[24] Khan, S.N. (2016). Breaking the Spell: Combating Multidrug Resistant 'Superbugs'. *Front Microbiol,* 7, 174.

[25] Khan, S.T. (2011). Streptomyces associated with a marine sponge Haliclona sp.; biosynthetic genes for secondary metabolites and products. *Environ Microbiol,* 13, 391–403.

[26] Kint, D.P. (2003). Synthesis, characterization, and properties of poly (ethylene terephthalate)/poly (1, 4-butylene succinate) block copolymers. *Polymer,* 44, 1321–1330.

[27] Le, T.H.M. (2016). Isolation, screening and identification of micro-organisms having antimicrobial activity isolated from samples collected on seabed of Northeast Vietnam. *Vietnam Journal of Biotechnology,* 14, 539–547.

[28] Li, X. (2006). Antifouling diketopiperazines produced by a deep-sea bacterium, Streptomyces fungicidicus. *Biofouling,* 22, 201–8.

[29] Li, Y. (2008). 5-tert-Butyl-2-[5-(5-tert-butyl-1, 3-benzoxazol-2-yl)-2-thienyl]-1, 3-benzoxazole. *Acta Crystallographica Section E: Structure Reports Online,* 64, o2410-o2410.

[30] Manivasagan, P. (2014). Pharmaceutically active secondary metabolites of marine actinobacteria. *Microbiol Res,* 169, 262–78.

[31] Mukherjee, G. (2004). Characterization and identification of chitinase producing Streptomyces venezuelae P10. *Indian J Exp Biol,* 42, 541–4.

[32] Muthu, M.R. (2013). Isolation and Identification of Actinomycetes Isoptericola variabilis From Cauvery River Soil Sample. *International journal of current Microbiology and Applied sciences,* 2, 236–245.

[33] Ohnishi, Y. (2008). Genome sequence of the streptomycin-producing microorganism Streptomyces griseus IFO 13350. *J Bacteriol,* 190, 4050–60.

[34] Orelle, C. (2013). Tools for characterizing bacterial protein synthesis inhibitors. *Antimicrob Agents Chemother,* 57, 5994–6004.

[35] Parveen, M. (2008). Evaluation of estrogenic activity of phthalate esters by gene expression profiling using a focused microarray (EstrArray). *Environ Toxicol Chem,* 27, 1416–25.

[36] Patzer, S.I. (2010). Gene cluster involved in the biosynthesis of griseobactin, a catechol-peptide siderophore of Streptomyces sp. ATCC 700974. *J Bacteriol,* 192, 426–35.

[37] Ramesh, S. (2009). Characterization of a thermostable alkaline protease produced by marine Streptomyces fungicidicus MML1614. *Bioprocess Biosyst Eng,* 32, 791–800.

[38] Rifaat, H.M. (2003). The biodiversity of *Actinomycetes* in the River Nile exhibiting antifungal activity. *Journal of Mediterranean Ecology Journal of Mediterranean E,* 4, 5–7.

[39] Saitou, N. (1987). The neighbor-joining method: a new method for reconstructing phylogenetic trees. *Mol Biol Evol,* 4, 406–25.

[40] Sheldrick, G.M. (2015a). Crystal structure refinement with SHELXL. *Acta Crystallographica Section C: Structural Chemistry,* 71, 3–8.

[41] Sheldrick, G.M. (2015b). SHELXT–Integrated space-group and crystal-structure determination. *Acta Crystallographica Section A: Foundations and Advances,* 71, 3–8.

[42] Sujatha, P. (2005). Studies on a new marine streptomycete BT-408 producing polyketide antibiotic SBR-22 effective against methicillin resistant Staphylococcus aureus. *Microbiol Res,* 160, 119–26.

[43] T., W.S. (1971). *Actinomycetes in: Methods in Microbiology,* Academic Press (London).

[44] Talzi, V. (2006). A 13C and 1H NMR analysis of perfumes. *Russian journal of applied chemistry,* 79, 107–116.

[45] Tan, J. (2004). Universally occurring phenylpropanoid and species-specific indolic metabolites in infected and uninfected *Arabidopsis thaliana* roots and leaves. *Phytochemistry,* 65, 691–699.

[46] Wattana-Amorn, P. (2016). Antibacterial activity of cyclo(L-Pro-L-Tyr) and cyclo(D-Pro-L-Tyr) from Streptomyces sp. strain 22–4 against phytopathogenic bacteria. *Nat Prod Res,* 30, 1980–3.

[47] Williams, S.T. (1965). Use of Antibiotics for Selective Isolation and Enumeration of Actinomycetes in Soil. *J Gen Microbiol,* 38, 251–61.

[48] World Health Organization (2018). *Fact Sheet: Antibiotic resistance* [Online]. WHO. Available: https://www.who.int/news-room/fact-sheets/detail/antibiotic-resistance [Accessed November 19, 2018].

[49] Yasuzawa, T. (1995). Duocarmycins, potent antitumor antibiotics produced by *Streptomyces* sp. structures and chemistry. *Chemical and pharmaceutical bulletin,* 43, 378–391.

[50] Ying, Y.M. (2013). Alkaloids and nucleoside derivatives from a fungal endophyte of *Huperzia serrata. Chemistry of Natural Compounds,* 49, 184–186.

APPENDIX

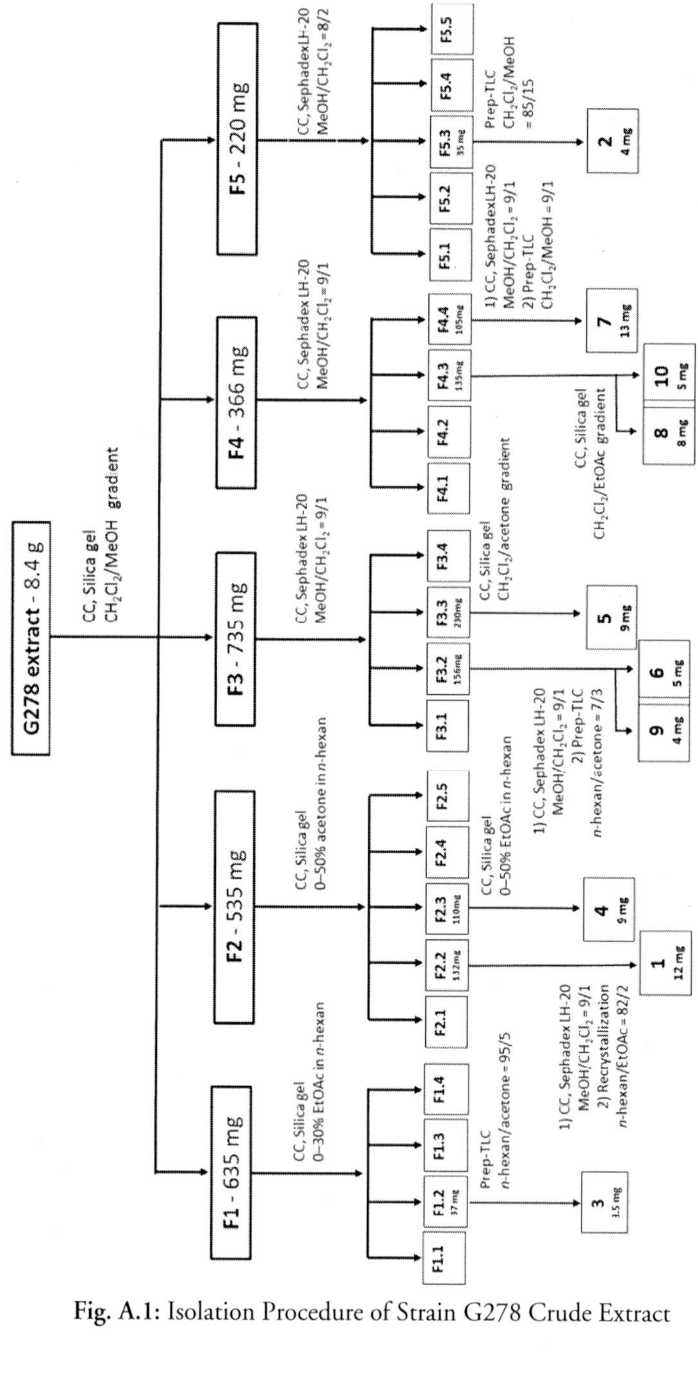

Fig. A.1: Isolation Procedure of Strain G278 Crude Extract

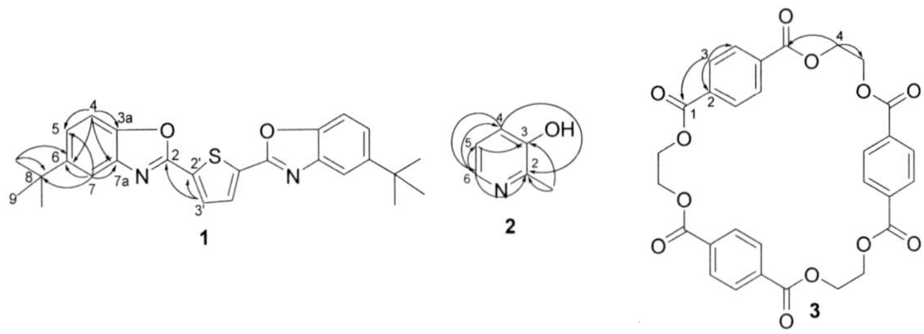

Fig. A.2: Selected HMBC Correlations of Compound **1–3**

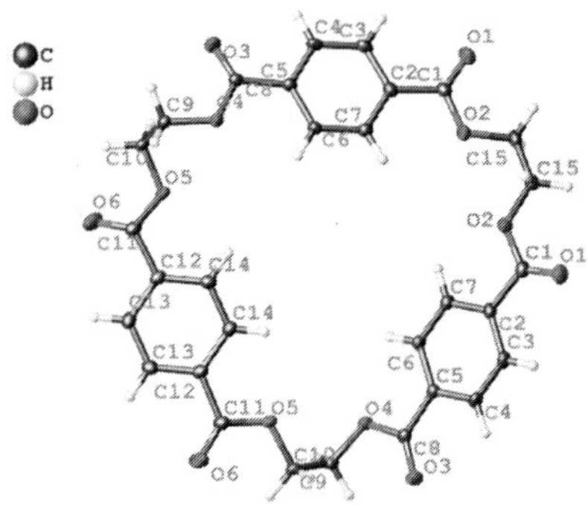

Fig. A.3: X-ray Crystal Structure of Compound **3**

Table A.1: Detail of the Samples Collected Off the Coast of There Middle Provinces of Vietnam: Hue, Da Nang and Quang Nam

Locations	*Geographic Coordinates*	*No of Samples*	*Water Depth (m)*
Hue (MuiTho Lo in Hai Van)	16°13′3″–108°7′57″	3	5–24
Hue (Bai Chuoi, Son Cha in Hai Van)	16°13′1″–108°8′37″	2	6
Hue (BanhTranh, Son Cha in Hai Van)	16°12′58″–108°7′59″	2	5
Đa Nang (Northeast of the Son Tra)	16°09′1 –108°13′50	12	10
Đa Nang (Northeast of the Son Tra)	16°34′50 – 108°11′4	7	7
Quang Nam (Hon Tai in Cu Lao Cham)	15°54′13″–108 °31′54″	6	3–5
Quang Nam (Hon Mo in Cu Lao Cham)	15°55′50″–108°28′30″	8	3–7
Quang Nam (Hon Dai in Cu Lao Cham)	15°56′24″–108 °28′56″	15	4–90

Preliminary Results of Survey on Medicinal Plant Resources in the Northeast Frontier Limestone Mountain Areas of Vietnam

Pham Thanh Huyen[1]*, Nguyen Quynh Nga[1], Phan Van Truong[1], Hoang Van Toan[1], Nguyen Minh Khoi[1], Vu Anh Tai[2], Hoang Thi Hong Lien[3] and Pham Thi Ngoc[1]

[1]National Institute of Medicinal Materials, Ministry of Health, Vietnam

[2]Institute of Geography, Vietnam Academy of Science and Technology, Vietnam

[3]Hai Phong University, Vietnam

*E-mail: huyenptnimm@gmail.com

ABSTRACT: *Along with the unique characteristics of topography, geology and climate, the Northeast frontier limestone mountain areas of Vietnam have abundant and diverse natural vegetation, including valuable medicinal plants. Through survey on medicinal plant resources in 17 districts, we have recorded 1865 species of 892 genera, 209 families, 62 orders of 6 divisions of the vascular plants and five species of the fungi. Ten species of medicinal plants have been newly recorded for the study areas; and 113 medicinal plant species are listed in the Decree No. 06/2019/ND-CP, Vietnam's Red Data Book, Red List of Vietnamese Medicinal Plants for the purpose of national conservation target. Results of this study will contribute to a master plan for development of medicinal plants in the Northeast frontier limestone mountain areas in Vietnam.*

Keywords: Medicinal Plant Resources, Lang Son, Ha Giang, Northeast Frontier Limestone Mountain Areas, New Medicinal Plants.

1. INTRODUCTION

The Northeast of Vietnam includes 5 administrative provinces as Quang Ninh, Lang Son, Cao Bang, Ha Giang and Lao Cai, which are on the national boundary to the China (Figure 1) and cover an area of 35,688 km^2. Most area of these provinces is limestone mountains. Topography of this region is composed of high mountains, low mountains and hills with an average altitude of 350 m above the sea level. The lowest point is at 20 m above the sea level and the highest point is Chieu Lau Thi mountain peak (Ho Thau commune, Hoang Su Phi district) with an elevation of 2,402 m. The Northeast mountainous area average rainfall is low, about 1,400–1,450 mm/year. Soil is mostly reddish-brown or yellow feral soil developed on limestone and alluvial soil.[1, 2] The ecological system on limestone mountain in these areas become more and more sensitive because of the continually illegal trading of medicinal plants across the borders to China.

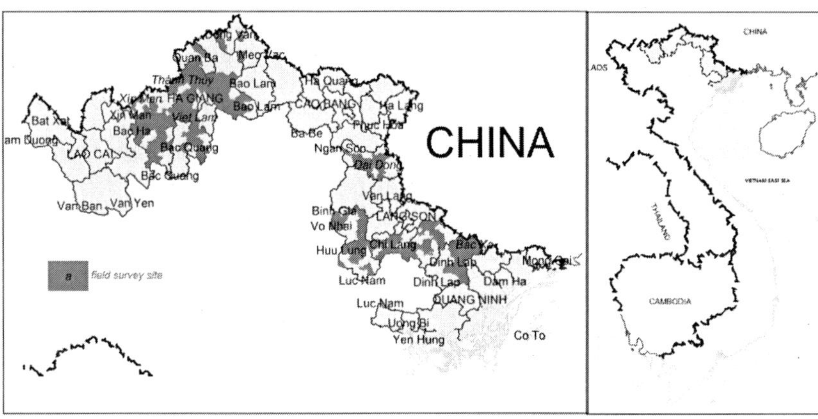

Fig. 1: Survey Sites of Medical Plants Resources of the Northeast Frontier Limestone Mountain Area

The field survey focused the investigation of medicinal plant resources in 06 districts of Lang Son province and 11 districts of Ha Giang province. The preliminary results presented in this paper would contribute additional data on medicinal plant resources of Northeast frontier limestone mountain areas in Vietnam.

2. MATERIALS AND METHODS

2.1 Investigated Method

The general method for investigating medicinal plants followed the "Process of medicinal investigation" approved in 1973 and revised in 2006 by Ministry of Health.

Interviewing the traditional healers: Local healers were interviewed for recording species which are used as medicine in the local community.

Route-based research: Is applied on the field to identify and collect the most complete existing species of medicinal plants in the study area. At each survey site, the routes for specific topography types and ecological forms to collect data on species was established using maps and GPS to determine the surveyed routes and sites.

Medicinal plants were collected for specimens. The voucher specimens were deposited in the Herbarium of Department of Medicinal Plant Resources, National Institute of Medicinal Materials. The scientific name of medicinal plant species was identified by using morphology comparison method and the classification keys.

2.2 Survey Sites

During the period from 2012 to 2015, the study area focused on 65 communes of 6 districts in Lang Son province and 84 communes of 11 districts in Ha Giang province: 65 communes of 6 districts of Lang Son province including Trang Dinh (12 communes: Cao Minh, Tan Tien, Bac Ai 1, Bac Ai 2, Kim Dong, Chi Lang, De Tham, Hung Viet, Khang Chien, Dai Dong, Tri Phuong and Doi Can), Loc Binh (14 communes: Huu Lan, Nam Quan, Dong Quan, Xuan Tinh, Nhu Khue, Bang Khanh, Xuan Le, Xuan Man, Dong Buc, Huu Khanh, Mau Son, Tu Doan, Khuat Xa and San Vien), Dinh Lap (06 commune: Bac Lang, Chau Son, Cuong Loi, Binh Xa, Kien Moc and Bac Xa), Chi Lang (11 communes: Bac Thuy, Bang Mac, Chi Lang, Hoa Binh, Huu Kien, Mai Sao, Nhan Ly, Quang Lang, Quan Son, Thuong Cuong and Van Linh), Huu Lung (12 communes: Dong Tan, Son Ha, Ho Son, Tan Thanh, Hoa Binh, Huu Lien, Nhat Tien, Minh Tien, Quyet Thang, Yen Binh, Yen Vuong and Yen Thinh), Bac Son (10 communes: Long Dong, Quynh Son, Bac Son, Hung Vu, Tran Yen, Vu Son, Vu Le, Tan Tri, Chien Thang and Dong Y) and 84 communes and towns of 11 districts of Ha Giang province including Xin Man (10 communes and a town: Nam Dan, Khuon Lung, Quang Nguyen, Na Chi, Chi Ca, Thu Ta, Xin Man, Che La, Ban Ngo, Ngan Chien, and Coc Bai town), Hoang Su Phi (11 communes and a town: Nang Don, Po Ly Ngai, San Xa Ho, Ho Thau, Nam Ty, Thong Nguyen, Nam Dich, Nam Khoa, Nam Ty, Nam Son, Ta Su Choong, and Vinh Quang town)

Quang Binh (7 communes and 1 town: Tien Nguyen, Na Khuong, Bang Lang, Xuan Giang, Ban Ria, Tan Trinh, Tan Bac, and Yen Binh town), Bac Quang (7 communes and 1 town: Quang Minh, Lien Hiep, Duc Xuan, Kim Ngoc, Bang Hanh, Dong Tam, Dong Tien, and Tan Quang town), Vi Xuyen (15 communes and 2 town: Thuong Son, Cao Bo, Quang Ngan, Trung Thanh, Viet Lam, Thanh Thuy, Thanh Duc, Lao Chai, Xin Chai, Quang Ngan, Cao Bo, Phong Quang, Thuan Hoa, Minh Tan, Tung Ba, Vi Xuyen town and Viet Lam town), Bac Me (8 communes and 1 town: Lac Nong, Minh Ngoc, Phieng Luong, Thuong Tan; Minh Son, Yen Dinh, Yen Cuong, Yen Phong; Yen Phu town), Ha Giang city (4 communes: Phuong Thien, Phuong Do, Ngoc Duong, Phong Quang), Quan Ba (5 communes: Bat Dai Son, Can Ty, Quyet Tien, Tam Son, and Quan Ba), Yen Minh (2 communes: Du Gia, Du Tien), Dong Van (5 communes: Pho Bang, Lung Thau, Pho Cao, Pho La, and Van Chai), Meo Vac (Meo Vac town and 2 communes: Ta Lung, Nam Ban).

3. RESULTS AND DISCUSSION

3.1 Taxonomy Records on Medicinal Plants and Fungi

Results have shown that shown that 1865 species of medicinal plants, belonging to 892 genera, 213 families, 62 orders, 6 divisions and 5 species of medicinal fungi, belonging to 4 genera, 4 families, 4 orders, 1 divisions were recognized (Table 1).

Table 1: Survey Results of Species of Medicinal Plants and Fungi in some of the Northeast Frontier Limestone Mountain Areas of Vietnam

No.	*Taxon*	*Families*	*Genera*	*Species*
I	**Fungi Kingdom**	4	4	5
1	Basidiomycota	4	4	5
II	**Plantae Kingdom**	**209**	**892**	**1865**
1	Lycopodiophyta	2	5	14
2	Equisetophyta	1	1	3
3	Polypodiophyta	17	25	43
4	Gnetophyta	1	1	3
5	Pinophyta	7	16	23
6	Magnoliophyta	181	844	1780
6.1	Magnoliopsida/ Dicotyledonae	*146*	*708*	*1493*
6.2	Liliopsida/ Monocotyledonae	*35*	*136*	*286*
	Total	**213**	**896**	**1870**

Diversity of life forms: Except Fungi, Polypodiophyta and Equisetophyta, the rest are 1820 species classified into 5 life forms based on the general appearance, includes Herbaceous plant (709 species as 38.96%), Shrub and subshrub (449 species as 24.67%), Vine/lianas/non-woody vines (262 species as 14.40%), Tree (379 species as 20.82%) and Palm-like form (11 species as 1.15%, mostly belong to Arecaceae family). Among that, Northeast frontier limestone mountain areas are medicinal plants are mainly herbs (38.96%) and shrubs (24.67%). Medicinal plants including vine, tree and palm-like ones account for a small proportion. Along with species of Fungi, Polypodiophyta, Equisetophyta, have been showed that study area' medicinal plants is diverse in natural life forms.

Biodiversity of phyto-medicinal sources: As mentioned above, there are a total of 1870 species of medicinal plants and fungi recorded, belonging to 213 families, of which 18 families have 27–125 species. The detailed information is shown in Table 2.

Table 2: Plant Families which are Rich in Species

No.	*Family*	*Genera*	*Species*	*No.*	*Family*	*Genera*	*Species*
1.	Asteraceae	68	125	10.	Rosaceae	15	35
2.	Euphorbiaceae	41	85	11.	Verbenaceae	11	33
3.	Rubiaceae	31	77	12.	Apocynaceae	20	32
4.	Fabaceae	31	63	13.	Cucurbitaceae	16	31
5.	Lamiaceae	26	48	14.	Poaceae	23	30
6.	Orchidaceae	29	48	15.	Araceae	14	29
7.	Moraceae	8	40	16.	Lauraceae	9	28
8.	Rutaceae	14	40	17.	Solanaceae	10	28
9.	Zingiberaceae	8	36	18.	Acanthaceae	16	27

Each of 195 remaining families has only 1–25 species of medicinal plants recorded. Among them, some families have only 1 genus in Vietnam. However, the species known in Northeast frontier limestone mountain areas have significances in terms of biodiversity as well as use value such as Taccaceae has only 1 genus of *Tacca* with 4 species: Rau hum hoa tia (*Tacca chantrieri*), Ngai rom (*T. integrifolia*), Hoi dau (*T. plantaginea*) and Pha lua (*T. subflabellata*); Costaceae have only a genus of *Costus* with 2 species: Mia do (*Costus speciosus*) and Mia do hoa goc (*C. tonkinensis*) or Dioscoreaceae with only 1 genus of *Dioscorea* with 8 species of medicinal plants.

At genus level, genera with many known medicinal plant species include: *Ficus* (Moraceae) with 28 species; *Solanum* (Solanaceae) and *Smilax* (Smilacaceae) with 15 species; *Ardisia* (Myrsinaceae), *Clematis* (Ranunculaceae) and *Alpinia* (Zingiberaceae) with 13 species; *Piper* (Piperaceae) and *Polygonum* with 12 species; *Desmodium* (Fabaceae) and *Callicarpa, Clerodendrum* (Verbenaceae) with 11 species.; *Uncaria* (Rubiaceae) and *Cinnamomum* (Lauraceae) with 10 species. *Dendrobium* (Orchidaceae), *Litsea* (Lauraceae), *Elsholtzia* (Lamiaceae), *Clausena, Citrus* (Rutaceae), Jasminum (Oleaceae), *Asarum* (Aristolochiaceae), *Blumea, Artemisia* (Asteraceae), *Begonia* (Begoniaceae), *Hypericum* (Hypericaceae), *Illicium* (Illiciaceae) have 7–9 species/ genus. Besides, some genera have only few species but most of them are valuable for medicinal use as well as genetic diversity, for example: *Gynostemma* (Cucurbitaceae) with 4 species of medicinal plants such as: Giao co lam (*Gynostemma pentaphyllum, G. cochinchinense, G. laxum, Gynostemma* sp.), *Aristolochia* (Aristolochiaceae) with 7 species used for medicinal purposes with the name "Phong ky".

Some new findings for the flora of Northeast frontier limestone mountain areas: In comparison with previous documents and other previously surveyed data,[4, 6–9] previously surveyed data, 10 species that were newly recorded for the study area, included Ba gac vong (van nam) (*Rauvolfia verticillata* (Lour.) Baill.) in Dinh Lap and Bac Son, recorded in the Red Data Book and Red List of medicinal plants of Vietnam;[6, 9] San rung (*Vaccinium bullatum* (Dop.) Sleum) in Mau Son, recorded in Red List of medicinal plants of Vietnam;[9] Hoang duong voi to (*Buxus latistyla* Gagnep.) in Hoa Binh commune, Huu Lung district; Hoang lien o ro (*Mahonia japonica* DC.) in Mau Son, recorded in the Red Data Book and Red List of medicinal plants of Vietnam;[6, 9] Phong ky la to (*Aristolochia kwangsiensis* Chun et How ex Liang) in Khau Luong commune, Trang Dinh, recorded in the Red Data Book and Red List of medicinal plants of Vietnam[6, 9] and Re gio (*Aristolochia contorta* Bunge) in Mau Son, Loc Binh, recorded in the Red Data Book and Red List of medicinal plants of Vietnam.[6, 9] It is noteworthy that 5 out of 10 of the above medicinal plant species are considered as priority for conservation in Vietnam; through this survey, Northeast frontier limestone mountain areas is founded as an additional distribution location.

3.2 Abundance of Valuable Genetic Resources for Conservation and Use

Among the above families, Asteraceae including many species such as Hy thiem (*Sigesbeckia orientalis*), Ngai cuu dai (*Artemisia vulgaris* var. *indica*), Co cut lon (*Ageratum conyzoides*), which are common medicinal plants with abundant resources. Among 36 known species of Gung family (Zingiberaceae), Dau khau genus (*Alpinia*) has 13 species and Sa nhan genus (*Amomum*) has 7 species, Nghe genus (*Cucurma*) has 5 species. These species are evenly distributed in Northeast frontier limestone mountain areas and can be collected for annual export with high economic value.

Besides, Phong lan family (Orchidaceae) has 15 species/29 known as priority for conservation. There are 4 species of *Anoectochilus* genus (Lan kim tuyen); 9 species of *Dendrobium* genus (Hoang thao/Thach hoc) and 2 species of *Nervilia fordii* (Lan mot la). Tiet de (Menispermaceae) family have species of Binh voi (*Stephania* spp.), Hoang dang (*Fibraurea tinctoria*), Day dau xuong (*Tinospora sinensis*) both of them are high value medicinal plants and priority for conservation.

Among 1870 species of medicinal plants and fungi recorded in 17 districts of Northeast frontier limestone mountain areas, there are 113 species of conservation concern in Vietnam (listed in the Decree No. 06/2019/ND-CP,[10] Vietnam's Red Data Book,[6] Red List of Vietnamese Medicinal Plants[9] belonging to 73 genera and 50 families. Among these 113 species, Polypodiophyta has 2 species, belonging to 1 genus and 1 family; Pinophyta has 12 species, belonging to 10 genera and 5 families; Magnoliophyta has 99 species, belonging to 62 genera and 44 families. Remarkably, some very rare species are critically endangered (CR), namely Sam vu diep (*Panax bipinnatifidus*), Tam that hoang (*Panax stipuleanatus*), Bach vang (*Cupressus vietnamensis*), Hoang dan huu lien (*Cupressus tonkinensis*), Re huong (*Cinnamomum parthenoxylon*), Hoang lien (*Coptis chinensis*); some rare species are endangered (EN), namely Tam (*Altingia chinensis*), Ngu gia bi huong (*Acanthopanax gracilistylus*), Ngu gia bi gai (*Acanthopanax trifoliatus*), Ba gac vong (*Rauvolfia verticillata*), Bat giac lien (*Podophyllum tonkinense*), Bay la mot hoa (*Paris* spp.), Lan mot la (*Nervilia fordii*), Lan kim tuyen (*Anoectochilus setaceus*), Hoang tinh cach

(*Disporopsis longifolia*), Thach hoc (*Dendrobium nobile*), Tram huong (*Aquilaria crassna*), Sen mat (*Madhuca pasquieri*), Cot toai bo (*Drynaria fortunei*), Bach hop (*Lilium brownii var. viridulum*).

3.3 Other Related Information

In comparison with previous surveys 30 years ago (1975, 1999–2000) with about 1000 recorded species, this survey had recorded 1870 species in 17 districts. However, this number does not fully reflect the current state of medicinal plant resources in Northeast frontier limestone mountain areas. In fact, due to increasing demand for using medicinal plants, many medicinal plants have been over-exploited, leading to a serious decline in natural resources.

Nearly 41 species/group species have been and being exploited for local use and sale at markets: Binh voi (*Stephania* spp.), Den toong/ Giao co lam (*Gynostemma pentaphyllum* (Thunb.) Makino), Dang sam (*Codonopsis javanica* (Blume) Hook.f. & Thomson), Ha thu o do (*Fallopia multiflora* (Thunb.) Haraldson), Hoang dang (*Fibraurea tinctoria* Lour.), Hoang tinh cach (*Disporopsis longifolia* Craib), Hoai son (*Dioscorea* spp.), Hoang lien o ro (*Mahonia* spp.), La khoi (*Ardisia gigantifolia* Stapf.), Ngu gia bi gai (*Acanthopanax trifoliatus* (L.) Merr.), Tac ke da (*Drynaria* spp.). Among them there are 15 species/group species of rare medicinal plants named in the Decree No. 06/2019/ND-CP[10] and the Vietnam's Red Data Book[6] which have been sold in local market and illegally exported to China: Bay la mot hoa (*Paris* spp.), Binh voi (*Stephania* spp.), Hoang dang (*Fibraurea tinctoria* Lour.), Lan mot la (*Nervilia fordii* (Hance) Schltr.), Lan kim tuyen (*Anoectochilus roxburghii* (Wall.) Lindl. and *Anoectochilus calcareus* Aver.), Lan thach hoc (*Dendrobium nobile* Lindl.), Hoang thao (*Dendrobium* spp.), Sam vu diep and Tam that hoang (*Panax* spp.). Some rare species may have previously been exploited for timber: Kim giao (*Nageia wallichiana* (C.Presl.) Kuntze), Thong tre (*Podocarpus neriifolius* D.Don), Nghien (*Excentrodendron tonkinense* (Gagnep.) Chang & Miau.

Some species, according to local people, have no longer been exploited: Ba gac van nam (*Rauvolfia yunnaensis* Tsiang), Bat giac lien (*Podophyllum tonkinense* Gagnep.), Hoi da voi (*Illicium difengpi* B.N.Chang), Phong ky (*Aristolochia kwangsiensis* Chun et How ex Liang), Tho sam (*Talinum paniculatum* (Jacq.) Gaertn.).

Consequently, most medicinal plants of conservation concern have been exploited. Most serious matter is looking for some species in Orchidaceae (Mot la, Kim tuyen, Hoang thao, Thach hoc, etc.) for smuggling into China.

113 species of conservation concern recorded in Northeast frontier limestone mountain areas account for 78.47% of total species of conservation concern (144 species) in Vietnam. Notably, Phong ky la to (*Aristolochia kwangsiensis* Chun et How ex Liang) and Re gio (*Aristolochia contorta* Bunge) are rare species in Vietnam and Northeast frontier limestone mountain areas is one of the 3 locations of them in the territory of Vietnam.

4. CONCLUSIONS

Based on the preliminary results of surveys on medicinal plant and fungi resources at the Northeast frontier limestone mountain areas, we have concluded that biodiversity of this medicinal resources is very high with 1865 species of 892 genera, 209 families, 62 orders of 6 divisions of the vascular plants and five species of the fungi; 10 species of medicinal plants have been newly recorded for the study areas; 113 medicinal plant species are listed in the Decree No. 06/2019/ND-CP, Vietnam's Red Data Book, Red List of Vietnamese Medicinal Plants in the purpose of the national conservation target. This study results will contribute to a master plan for the development of medicinal plants in the Northeast frontier limestone mountain areas in Vietnam.

REFERENCES

[1] Lang Son Province People's Committee (1999). Geography Book of Lang Son. National Politics publishing house, Hanoi, Vietnam.

[2] Lang Son Province People's Committee – Department of Statistics, 2010. Statistical Yearbook (2010). Statistical publishing house, Lang Son, Vietnam.

[3] The Social Republic of Vietnam, Central Government (2013). Decision No.1976/2013/QD-TTg of the Prime Minister on approving the master plan for medicinal material development by 2020 and vision to 2030. Hanoi, Vietnam.

[4] Institute of Medicinal Materials (2019). List of wild medicinal plants being exploited and widely used in Vietnam (Annually updated and internally circulated documents). Hanoi, Vietnam.

[5] Institute of Medicinal Materials (2019). Survey Data of Medicinal Materials in Vietnam - Annually updated (since 1961). Hanoi, Vietnam.

[6] Nguyen Tien Ban (Chief Editor) (2007). Vietnam's Red Data Book, Part II: Plant. Science and Technology Publishing House, Ha Noi, Vietnam.

[7] Nguyen Tien Ban (Chief Editor) (2003–2005). A Checklist of plant species in Vietnam, Vol. 2 & 3. Agriculture Publishing House, Ha Noi, Vietnam

[8] Do Huy Bich (Chief Editor) (2013). Medicinal Plants and Medicinal Animals in Vietnam. Science and Techniques Publishing House. Hanoi, Vietnam.

[9] Nguyen Tap (2006). Red List of Vietnamese Medicinal Plants, Journal of Medicine No. 3 (11):97–105.

[10] The Social Republic of Vietnam, Central Government (2019). Decree No. 06/2019/ND-CP of the Prime Minister on Management of precious and rare plant and Animal Species in Vietnam. Hanoi, Vietnam.

Records of Recent Surveys on Medicinal Plant Resources in Ha Giang Province, Vietnam

Pham Thanh Huyen[1]*, Nguyen Quynh Nga[1], Phan Van Truong[1], Hoang Van Toan[1], Bui Van Thanh[2], Vu Anh Tai[3], Hoang Thi Hong Lien[4] and Pham Thi Ngoc[1]

[1]National Institute of Medicinal Materials, Ministry of Health, Vietnam

[2]Institute of Ecology and Biological Resources, Vietnam

[3]Institute of Geography, Vietnam Academy of Science and Technology, Vietnam

[4]Hai Phong University, Vietnam

*E-mail: huyenptnimm@gmail.com

ABSTRACT: Ha Giang is a province in Northeast of Vietnam. Along with the unique characteristics of topography, geology and climate. Ha Giang province has abundant and diverse natural vegetation, including valuable plants. For the period of 2013–2015, the research team conducted many surveys on 84 communes of 11 districts and a city in Ha Giang province. As a result, 1565 species of medicinal plants and fungi, belonging to 824 genera, 202 families, 5 divisions of vascular plants and 1 division of fungi were recorded. At the same time, 4 new species of medicinal plants were recorded for the flora of Vietnam including: Paris cronquistii, Paris xichouensis, Loniceracalcarata and Trichosanthestruncata. Besides, this survey recorded 97 medicinal plant species of conservation concern at national level. Medicinal plant resources of Ha Giang province are not only diverse in terms of life forms, richness of taxa but also have a great value in terms of conservation.

Keywords: Medicinal Plant, Resources, Ha Giang.

1. INTRODUCTION

Ha Giang is mountain province, located at the northeast of Vietnam where the nature condition and the climate are very diverse, making advance conditions for a typical fauna and flora forming, as well as abundant medicinal resources. Ha Giang has up to 22 communities of different ethnic groups residing and living.

Therefore, the indigenous knowledge about the use of medicinal plant for curing diseases is extremely plentiful.[1-4]

The investigation of medicinal resources potential and assessment of medicinal plants at Ha Giang had been recorded within 4 mountain districts as Dong Van, MeoVac, Quan Ba and Yen Minh in 1970s.[5, 6] However, the medicinal resources had not been investigated or assessed for the whole province until this decade. Therefore, in recent years, some surveys of medicinal plants and fungi were conducted in all areas of the province, mostly in a project funded by the provincial people committee of Ha Giang titled "Study, investigation, planning for medicinal plants development of Ha Giang province" with a purpose of finding the general potential and situation of provincial medicinal resources, suggesting a suitable management and utilization solution of medicinal plant resources of the province.

2. MATERIALS AND METHODS

2.1 Survey Sites

Recently, new surveys were conducted at 7 districts of the province, including Xin Man, Hoang Su Phi, Quang Binh, Bac Quang, Vi Xuyen, Bac Me and Ha Giang city. In addition, surveys were also conducted at Quan Ba, Yen Minh, Dong Van and MeoVac districts. The surveys were covered for total of 84 communes belonging to 11 district level units (see the map).

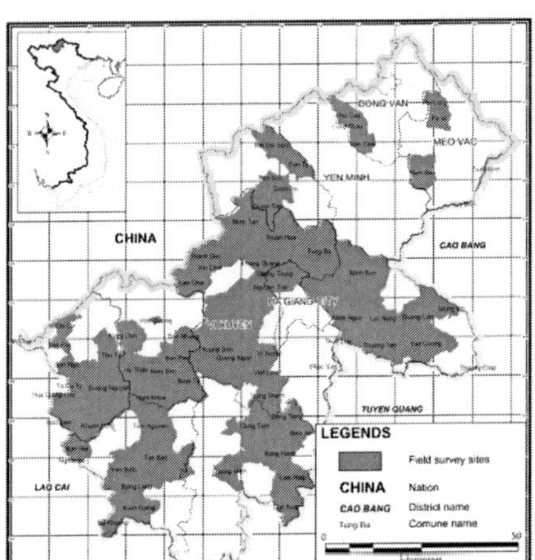

Fig. 1: Survey Sites of Medicinal Plants and Fungi at Ha Giang Province in Recent Years

2.2 Investigated Method

The general method for investigating medicinal plants followed the "Process of medicinal investigation" approved in 1973 and revised in 2006 by Ministry of Health.

Interviewing the traditional healers: local healers were interviewed for recording species which are used as medicine in local community.

Route-based research: is applied on the field to identify and collect the most complete existing species of medicinal plants in the study area. At each survey site, the routes for specific topography types and ecological forms to collect data on species were established using maps and GPS to determine the surveyed routes and sites.

Medicinal plants were collected for specimens. The voucher specimens were deposited in the Herbarium of Department of Medicinal Plant Resources, National Institute of Medicinal Materials. The scientific name of medicinal plant species was identified by using morphology comparison method and the classification keys.

3. RESULTS AND DISCUSSION

3.1 General Records on Biodiversity of Medicinal Plants and Fungi at Ha Giang Province

Finally, based on the field surveys and previous data of medicinal resources of the province, 1565 medicinal species were listed for Ha Giang that belongs to 824 genera, 202 families and 5 divisions of 2 kingdoms as vascular plant and fungi, most of them are dicot plants (Table 1). The new surveys have additionally recorded nearly 1000 species of fungi and plants, which is a considerable addition to the medicinal resources data of the province to the previous survey result (only 665 were recorded for 4 mountain districts as mentioned above). Therefore, Ha Giang is one of the most abundant and rich source of plants in general and medicinal plant resources in particular of the country.

The richness of medicinal plant resources of Ha Giang is also represented by 10 top families, each of one has over 20 medicinal species, special over 100 species as Asteraceae family. Total species of the topten is 413, covered for nearly one fourth of the province's medicinal plant species (Table 2).

Table 1: Results of Botanical Taxonomy Surveys for Medicinal Resources in Ha Giang Province

No.	*Taxon(s)*	*Families*	*Genera*	*Species*	*Found in Habitat*	
					In the Nature	*Cultivated*
I	**Fungi kingdom**	**2**	**2**	**2**	**2**	**0**
1	Basidiomycota division	2	2	2	2	0
1.1	*Basidiomycetes class*	*1*	*1*	*1*	*1*	*0*
1.2	*Agaricomycetes class*	*1*	*1*	*1*	*1*	*0*
II	**Plantae kingdom**	**200**	**822**	**1563**	**1432**	**131**
1	Lycopodiophyta division	2	5	8	8	0
2	Pteridophyta division	15	23	33	33	0
2.1	*Equisetopsida class*	*1*	*1*	*2*	*2*	*0*
2.2	*Other fern classes*	*14*	*22*	*31*	*31*	*0*
3	Gymnospermae division	7	15	20	20	0
4	Angiospermae division	176	779	1502	1371	131
4.1	*Magnoliopsida class*	*147*	*663*	*1277*		
4.2	*Liliopsida class*	*29*	*116*	*225*		
	Total	**202**	**824**	**1565**	**1434**	**131**

Table 2. Top Ten Richeness Families of Medicinal Species Found in Ha Giang Province

No.	*Plant Families*	*No. of Species*
1.	Asteraceae	109
2.	Rubiaceae	63
3.	Orchidaceae	45
4.	Lamiaceae	39
5.	Moraceae	34
6.	Rutaceae	33
7.	Apocynaceae	25
8.	Araceae	24
9.	Solanaceae	23
10.	Acanthaceae	20
	Total	**413**

Belonging to the largest family—Asteraceae, there are many wild medicinal plants distributed with abundant resources, such as *Siegesbeckia orientalis*, *Artemisia indica*, *Ageratum conyzoides* or cultivated one with high economic value such as *Cynara cardunculus*. Rubiaceae is the second largest family which most species are common medicinal shrubs and herbs, such as: *Mussaenda* spp., *Uncaria* spp., *Hedyotis* spp. Orchidaceae is not only rich in medicinal resources but also have threatened species such as 9 threatened species: *Anoectochilus roxburghii. A. calcareous*, *A. elwesii*, *Dendrobium nobile*, *D. longicornu*, *D. chrysanthum*, *D. fimbriatum*, *Nervilia aragoana*, *N. fordii*). Lamiaceae includes many common cultivated medicinal plants such as *Ocimum tenuiflorum*, *O. basilicum*, *Elsholtzia ciliata*, *Perilla frutescens* or wild medicinal plants with abundant resources such as *Prunella vulgaris*, *Agastache* spp., *E. penduliflora*. Within the remaining families, even their number of medicinal species is not much but there are a lot of special and valued medicinal plants. For example, it is *Alisma-plantago-aquatica* (Alismataceae), *Dicksonia barometz* (Dicksoniaceae), *Stemona tuberosa* (Stemonaceae), *Plantago major* and *P. asiatica* (Plantaginaceae), *Gynostemma pentaphyllum* (Cucurbitaceae). Those species are highly valued and potential for development at Ha Giang province. Particularly, in Taxaceae family, 2 out of 3 species are threatened (*Amento taxus yunnanensis* and *Taxus wallichiana* var. *chinensis*), the remained one—*A. argotaenia* are also rare species.

The most richness genus of medicinal plant found in Ha Giang province is *Ficus* (Moraceae) with 24 species, together with *Ardisia* (Myrsinaceae, 13 species), *Polygonum* (Polygonaceae, 12 species), *Smilax* (Smilacaceae, 12 species), *Piper* (Piperaceae, 11 species) *Solanum* (Solanaceae, 10 species), and 9 species genera including *Alpinia* (Zingiberaceae), *Clematis* (Ranunculaceae), *Desmodium* (Fabaceae), *Dendrobium* (Orchidaceae), *Cinnamomum* (Lauraceae) are most abundant genera there. In another side, *Tacca* is one of the most special genus, the 3 species found are most useful and valued (*T. chantrieri*, *T. plantaginea*, *T. subflabellata*). Similarly, genera such as *Paris* (5 species), *Gynostemma* (3 species), *Acanthopanax* (2 species), *Panax* (3 species) are also reported to be extremely useful for human health.

Diversity of life forms: The life form of medicinal species found in Ha Giang are herbs (39.68%) or shrubs (24.05%). The vine or lianas were found with 14.06% while timber species were not much rare with 21.75%. This result shows that it is not much difficult to find out the medicinal plant surrounding residential areas because mostly they are herbs or shrubs hence, it is very easy to find out in the scrubs, grasslands, cultivated land, gardens and secondary/open forest.

3.2 Some New Records for the Flora of Vietnam

Based on the results of recent surveys, four medicinal plants were new record species for the flora of Vietnam. These species include *Paris xichouensis* (H. Li) Y.H. Ji, H. Li & Z.K. Zhou and *P. cronquistii* (Takht.) H. Li, found in Sung La commune, Dong Van district,[9,10] *Lonicera calcarata* Hemsley and *Trichosanthes truncata* C.B. Clarke in J.D. Hooker found in Pho Bang town, Dong Van district.[11,12] These species are medicinal plants of high value. Due to narrow distribution in Vietnam, both of them are species of conservation concern.

3.3 Records on Forest Habitat of Medicinal Plants in Ha Giang Province

3.3.1 *Distribution of Medicinal Plant Species along Elevation*

Ha Giang is located in the northern most part of Vietnam. Because of the diversity of topography and climate, Ha Giang is special and diversity of monsoon and moisture vegetation, including tropical and sub-tropical or tropical montane habitats. Some medicinal species found in Ha Giang would be found in another location but at higher elevation habitats such as *Calocedrus macrolepis*, *Taxus wallichiana* var. *chinensis*. Some species was found in Ha Giang only such as *Mahonia bealei*. Some narrowly distribution species of Hoang Lien Son Mountain such as *Panax stipuleanatus* and *P. bipinnatifidus* have also been found there.

At elevation higher than 1000 m above the sea level, it would be found a lot of valued medicinal species of montane or sub-tropical habitats such as *Acanthopanax gracilistylus*, *Tetrapanax papyriferus*, *Trevesia palmate. Hedera nepalensis*, *Mahonia nepalensis*, *M. bealei*, *Coptis chinensis*, *Thalictrum foliolosum*, *Valeriana hardwicki*, *Lilium brownii var. colchesteri*, *Gaultheria fragrantissima*, *Illicium tsaii*, *Anoectochilus roxburghii*, *A. calcareous*. and one very special finding is pure medicinal forests as conifer forests found at the limestone summits at Phieng

Luong coomune (Bac Me district), Thai An and Bat Dai Son communes (Quan Ba district). In this habitat, *Podocarpus neriifolius*, *P. pilgeri*, *Calocedrus macrolepis*, *Cupressus vietnamensis*, *Tsuga chinensis* and *T. chinensis* are common. These habitats are very typical in Ha Giang, not easy find out that another places in the country. But most of the species is growing in a very limited habitat, narrow summits, stead slopes, so it is very difficult to harvest, it would be better if those forest is maintaining for conservation, both of biodiversity and nature medicinal plant conservation purposes. At elevation between 700 m and 1000 m above the sea level, both of common tropical and sub-tropical medicinal species were found. It is also most harvesting purpose of the local people, including species as *Ampelopsis cantoniensis*, *Prunella vulgaris*, *Stemona tuberosa*, *Schefflera* spp., *Curcuma* spp., *Artemisia indica*, *Alpinia* spp., *Gynostemma* spp. At elevation under 700 m above the sea level, mostly tropical medicinal species were found as harvesting ones such as *Sigesbeckia orientalis*, *Senna tora*, *Ageratum conyzoides*, *Uncaria* spp., *Adenosma caeruleum*.

3.3.2 *Highest Potential Habitats for the Wild Medicinal Plants*

Based on the recent field surveys, characteristics of wild medicinal plant sepcies and the nature conditions of it finding distribution, we found

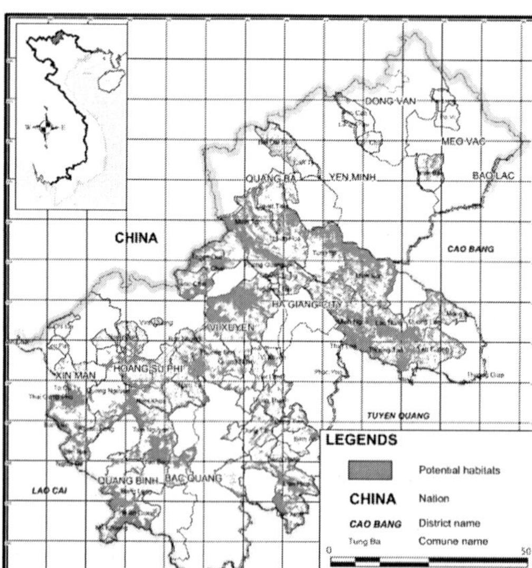

Fig. 2: Highest Potential Habitats for the Wild Medicinal Plant Resources of Ha Giang Province

that highest potential habitat for the wild medicinal plants of Ha Giang province is forest lcoated at 11 sites as: (1) Cao Bo and Thuong Son commune (Vi Xuyen district), (2) Po Ly Ngai and Ho Thau (Hoang Su Phi district), (3) Viet Quang and Duc Xuan coomunes (Bac Quang district), (4) Nam Dan, Khuon Lung, Quang Nguyen and Thu Ta communes (Xi Man district), (5) Bang Lang, Na Khuong, Tan Nam and Xuan Giang communes (Quang Binh district), (6) Yen Phu, Phieng Luong and Minh Son communes (Bac Me), (7) Bat Dai Son Mountain located in Bat Dai Son, Can Ty and Thanh Van communes (Quan Ba district), (8) Ba Tien Mountain located in Thai An commune (Quan Ba district), (9) Du Gia commune (Yen Minh), (10) MeoVac - Lung Pu communes (MeoVac) and (11) Pho La commune (Dong Van) (See Figure 2).

3.4 Records on Valued Medicinal Plants and High Potential Harvest Species in Ha Giang Province

The recently surveys also found that, in Ha Giang province, there are 97 medicinal plant species of conservation concern, belonging to 70 genera and 48 families,[13–16, 18] according to Vietnam Red Data Book, 2007, it includes 5 critical endangered species as *Coptis chinensis*, *Panax bipinnatifidus*, *Panax stipuleanatus*, *Cupressus vietnamensis* and *Cinnamomum parthenoxylon* and 37 endangered species such as *Rauvolfia verticillata*, *Podophyllum tonkinense*, *Paris chinensis*), *Nervilia fordii*, *Anoectochilus calcareus*, *Polygonatum kingianum*, *Dendrobium nobile var. alboluteum*, *Excentrodendron tonkinense*, *Aquilaria crassna*, *Mahonia bealii*, therefore, the medicinal plant resources at Ha Giang is very valued in biodiversity conservation purpose.

It was recorded that there are 40 medicinal plant species of group of species which are common e-harvesting and local trading and among them, there are 25 ones listed in the Vietnam Red Data Book (2007) or Red List of Vietnam's medicinal plant species (2006) and The Government's Decree No. 06/2019/ND-CP. So that, to prevent reducing of valued medicinal plant resources, special through the national boundary trading, it is necessary to strengthen management by the local authorities and other stakeholders.

There are 26 species or group of species have been harvesting over 10 tones per year. Special with *Ageratum conyzoides*, this species has been harvesting for 100–150 tones per year while 2 other sepcies as

Cibotiumbarometz and *Curcuma longa* also have been exploiting for 50–60 tones per year.

Most of the common exploitation in the past within 4 mountain district such as *Drynariabonii, Stephania japonica, Fallopia multiflora, Dendrobium nobile, Polygonatum kingianum* and *Lonicera japonica*[17] have been stopped harvesting list of the province, special, some of them were listed in the conservation purposes such as Fallopia *multiflora, Dendrobium nobile* and *Drynaria bonii.* All of the most valued and highest reserves species at four those district (1999–2000) also have been reduced at the moment, for example, *Callerya reticulata* reduced from 200–300 tones per year in the past to 50–60 tones currently, *Schefflera heptaphylla* reduced from 300–500 tones to 5–10 tones per year. Some species have been not reduced of harvesting mostly are herb life form and common distribution such as *Ageratum conyzoides, Ampelopsis cantoniensis, Siegesbeckia orientalis, Agrimonia pilosa, Curcuma longa* and other *Curcuma* spp.

4. CONCLUSION

Based on recent surveys conducted at 84 communes of 11 districts of Ha Giang province, together with the survey data conducted in the last century, 1565 species belonging to 824 genera, 202 families, 5 divisions of 2 kingdoms as plantea and fungi were recorded as medicinal species. The surveys also have 4 new records for the flora of Vietnam as *Paris xichouensis, P. cronquistii, Lonicera calcarata* and *Trichosanthes truncata.* 11 habitats were identified as high potential of wild medicinal plants species. At the moment, Ha Giang has 26 high potential harvesting species, 97 valued and/or threatened species are identified for the biodiversity conservation purpose. All of these results are basic for biodiversity conservation planning and also for medicinal resources management and development planning of the province.

REFERENCES

[1] Statistics Department of Ha Giang (2015). Statistics Year Book of Ha Giang province in 2014. Ha Giang, Vietnam.

[2] Nguyen, T.B. (Chief editor) (2003–2006). Checklist Plant Species of Vietnam, Vol. 2&3. Science and Technology Publishing House, Hanoi, Vietnam.

[3] Do. H.B. (Chief editors) (2004–2013). Medicinal Plants and Animals of Vietnam. Vol. 1–3. Science and Technology Publishing House, Hanoi, Vietnam.

[4] Vo, V.C. (2011–2012). Dictionary of Medicinal Plants in Vietnam. Medical Publishing House, Ho Chi Minh City, Vietnam.

[5] Institute of Medicinal Materials (2019). Data of Medicinal Plant Resources Investigation of Vietnam. Hanoi, Vietnam.

[6] Institute of Medicinal Materials (2019). Annual update checklist of Medicinal Plant Species of Vietnam. Hanoi, Vietnam.

[7] Institute of Medicinal Materials (2019). Annual update checklist Species of Harvesting and Common Use Medicinal Plant Species of Vietnam. Hanoi, Vietnam.

[8] Institute of Medicinal Materials (1975). Investigation Report on Medicinal Plant Species of Ha Giang province. Hanoi, Vietnam.

[9] Nguyen, Q.N., Pham, T.H., Phan, V.T., Hoang, V.T. and Nguyen, N.C. (2015). Paris xichouensis (H. Li) Y.H. Ji and Z.K. Zhou—A newly recorded species—in the flora of Vietnam. *Journal of Medicinal Materials,* No. 5, Vol. 20, pp. 264–267. Hanoi, Vietnam.

[10] Nguyen, Q.N., Pham, T.H., Phan, V.T., Hoang, V.T, Nguyen, X.N. (2015). Paris cronquistii (Takht.) H. Li—A newly recorded species in the flora of Vietnam. *Journal of Medicinal Materials,* No. 4, Vol. 20, pp. 203–206. Hanoi, Vietnam.

[11] Hoang V.T., Pham, T.H., Nguyen, Q.N., Nguyen, X.N. and Phan, V.T. (2013). Loniceracalcarata Hemsl. (Caprifoliaceae) – A newly recorded species-in the flora of Vietnam. *Journal of Medicinal Materials*, No. 6, Vol. 18, pp. 351–354. Hanoi, Vietnam.

[12] Phan, V.T., Pham, T.H., Nguyen, Q.N., Hoang, V.T. and Nguyen, X.N. (2015). Study on morphology characteristics and taxonomy key establishment for species of Trichosanthes L. genus in Vietnam. *6th National Conferences on Ecology and Biological Resources,* pp. 378–382. Science and Technology Publishing House, Hanoi, Vietnam.

[13] The Social Republic of Vietnam, The Government (2019). Decree No. 06/2019/ND-CP by the Prime Minister on Management of endangered, precious and rare forest plants and animals. Hanoi, Vietnam.

[14] Trieu, V.H. (editor) (2007). Non Timber Forestry of Vietnam. Agriculture Publishing House, Hanoi, Vietnam.

[15] Nguyen, T. (2006). Red List of Medicinal Plant Species of Vietnam. Journal of Medicinal Materials, No. 3. Hanoi, Vietnam.

[16] Nguye, T.B. (editor) (2007). Vietnam Red Data Book, Part II: Plants. Science and Technology Publishing House, Hanoi, Vietnam.

[17] Nguyen, B.H. and Nguyen, T. (1999). Report of project "Assessment of medicinal potential at 4 mountain districts of Ha Giang province for planning and development of Dong Van, Yen Minh, MeoVac and Quang Ba districts. Hanoi, Vietnam.

[18] Vu, A.T. and Nguyen, N.T. (2014). Survey and inventory of thereatened plant species in Ha Giang province, Vietnam. *Journal of Biodiversity,* 36(3):323–329. Hanoi, Vietnam.

Medicinal and Aromatic Plants: Status, Scope and Challenges in Nepal

Deepa Shree Rawal
Nepal Academy of Science and Technology, Kathmandu, Nepal
E-mail: rawalshree@hotmail.com; deepa.rawal@nast.gov.np

ABSTRACT: Nepal is well known for its floral and faunal diversity. It has been reported that there are about 1792 to 2331 Medicinal and Aromatic Plants (MAPs) in Nepal. In rural areas, MAPs are extensively used for subsistence, home remedies, and traditional therapies. Practice of traditional based therapies is quite popular in rural areas due to the high cost of modern medicine and absence of trained physicians. In Nepal, there are about 30 licensed domestic units producing about 400 herb-based medicines (Ayurvedic). National manufacturing unit for herbal (Ayurvedic) medicines is "Singha Durbar Vaidhyakhana" producing about 100 different traditional pharmacological and patented generic Ayurvedic products. In 1981 government owned Herbs Production and Processing Company (HPPCL) was established. HPPCL processes and produces Medicinal Extracts and Essential Oils using indigenous himalayan herbs and exotic conventional raw materials. Quality analysis of every product is carried following the scientific norms. There are various small-scale national companies that produce different types of essential oils, tea and beauty products using indigenous herbs. In recent years, few international companies are emerging in Nepal and have established their own herbal farms and factories that produce herbal drugs and various products. 'Dabur Nepal' and 'Patanjali' are examples of such international companies. According to the Nepal Herbs and Herbal Producers Association, Nepal exports an estimated 6,000 tons of herbal products annually. In 2014 the estimate was 10770 tons worth US $ 60.09 million. This shows that MAPs, can contribute in improving the socio-economic status of the Nepali people mainly living in rural areas. However, a number of problems at the level of production, harvest, marketing, processing, and value addition need to be properly addressed. Processing/manufacturing takes place in the country to a very limited extent and all the exports are in the form of raw or semi-finished forms. For many herbal drugs production companies of Nepal it is not *possible to assess the quality of the finished preparations in the existing production facility except for the physical parameters like consistency, appearance, etc. Although some structural changes have been introduced recently in this sector reformatory measure like provision for adequate physical facilities, qualified manpower, modern equipment, establishing marketing network, mobilisation of resources, implementation of research and quality assurance plan, development of proper documentation and validation system, preservation and sustainable utilisation should be promoted for the development of this sector.*

1. INTRODUCTION

Nepal is well known for its floral and faunal diversity with diverse physiographic and climatic variation (Bhattarai and Ghimire 2006). It has been reported that there are about 6,653 species of flowering plants in Nepal (Kunwar *et al.,* 2010) out of which 1792 to 2331 have medicinal and aromatic properties (Rokaya *et al.,* 2010; Baral and Kurmi 2006). Medicinal and aromatic plants (MAPs) have been identified as one of the potential high value commodities in Nepal with huge prospects for economic development (Ghimire *et al.,* 2016).

MAPs are collected wildly since ancient times by rural population of Nepal. The collected products are dried, graded and transported to the nearest trading center to be sold in the form of crude drugs. In rural areas MAPs are extensively used for subsistence, home remedies, and traditional therapies (Kunwar *et al.,* 2010). About 90–95 percent of MAPs in Nepal is collected from the wild; and cultivation of MAPs is carried out in a very small scale. There are a number of problems and challenges in the cultivation of MAPs because of which collection from the wild is preferred over cultivation, although there are problems and challenges in wild collection too (Sharma and Shrestha 2011). Indiscriminate collection of MAPs for quick monetary gain has threatened the biodiversity consequently leading to the extinction of some valuable species.

Government of Nepal has listed endangered species whose collection, use and sale have been officially prohibited that includes *Dactylorhiza hatagirea* and *Juglans regia* and *Neopicrorhiza scrophulariiflora.* Plants banned for export outside the country in unprocessed form are: *Nard-ostachys grandiflora, Rauwolfia serpentina, Cinnamomum glaucescens,*

Valeriana wallichii, Parmelia nepalensis (lichens), Abies spectabilis, Taxus baccata and rock exudates (Silajeet) (Phoboo *et al.,* 2008). Processing the plant in the form of powder, oil extract, marc (residue after oil extract), and extract of active compounds should be done for export purpose. Restricted plant species are also heavily exported in the form of herbal tea, Ayurvedic products, nutrient supplements and tonics (Sharma *et al.,* 2006; Sharma 2007). Government of Nepal has prioritized thirty four MAPs for research and management purpose (Sharma and Shrestha 2011) (Table 1).

Table 1: List of Prioritized Species

S. No.	*Species*	*Prioritized Species by Climatic Zone*		
		Terai	*Mid-hill*	*Himal*
1.	*Aconitum heterophyllum (Atis)*	Neem	Bhyakur	Yarsagumba
2.	*Aconitum spicatum (Bisjara)*	Gurjo	Ritha	Bisjara
3.	*Acorus calamus (Bojho)*	Sarpagandha	Jhyau	Jatamansi
4.	*Aegle marmelos (Bel)*	Mentha	Chiraito	Laghupatra
5.	*Asparagus racemosus (Kurilo)*	Sayapatri	Okhar	Atis
6.	*Azadirachta indica (Neem)*	Pipala	Pakhanbed	Sugandhawal
7.	*Bergenia ciliata (Pakhanbed)*	Bojho	Timur	Guchhichyau
8.	*Chammomila matricaria*	Lemongrass	Lauthsalla	Panchaule
9.	*Cinnamomum glaucescens (S.Kokila)*	Amala	Majitho	Kutki
10.	*Cinnamomum tamala (Tejpat)*	Bel	Dhasingare	Padamchal
11.	*Cordyceps sinensis (Yarsagumba)*	Kurilo	Tejpat	
12.	*Cymbopogon flexuosus (Lemongrass)*	S. kokila		
13.	*Dactylorhiza hatagirea (Panchaunle)*	Chamomile		
14.	*Dioscorea deltoidea (Bhyakur)*			

(Table contd...)

(Table 1 contd…)

S. No.	*Species*	*Prioritized Species by Climatic Zone*		
		Terai	*Mid-hill*	*Himal*
15.	*Gaultheria fragrantissima (Dhasingre)*			
16.	*Juglans regia (Okhar)*			
17.	*Mentha arvensis (Mentha)*			
18.	*Morchella conica (Gucchi chyau)*			
19.	*Nardostachys grandiflora (Jatamansi)*			
20.	*Neopicrorhiza scrophulariiflora (Kutki)*			
21.	*Parmellia species (Jhyau)*			
22.	*Phyllanthus emblica (Amala)*			
23.	*Piper longum (Pipla)*			
24.	*Podophyllum hexandrum (Laghupatra)*			
25.	*Rauvolfia serpentina (Sarpagandha)*			
26.	*Rheum australe (Padamchal)*			
27.	*Rubia majith (Majitho)*			
28.	*Sapindus mukorossi (Ritha)*			
29.	*Swertia chirayita (Chiraito)*			
30.	*Tagetes minuta (Sayapatri)*			
31.	*Taxus baccata (Lauth Salla)*			
32.	*Tinospora sinensis (Gurjo)*			
33.	*Valeriana jatamansi (Sugandhawal)*			
34.	*Zanthoxylum armatum (Timur)*			

Source: Poudel (2007).

2. TRADITIONAL USE OF MEDICINAL AND AROMATIC PLANTS

It has been reported that almost 30 percent of modern allopathic drugs are either directly or indirectly derived from plants (Marino-Bettolo, 1980). Some 25% of the prescribed drugs still contain active principles originating from higher plants and nearly two-thirds of the population in developing countries virtually depends on herbal remedy-based therapies for health care (Tiwari and Joshi, 1990; Sarkar 1987). The use of herbal medicine has been increasing even in developed countries in recent years (Khakurel *et al.*, 1998).

The traditional method of healing, or "Ayurveda," is still practiced today in Nepal. Use of traditional medicine is more prevalent in rural parts of Nepal (Kunwar *et al.*, 2013). The Ayurvedic and traditional system of medicine in Nepal are closely related to Himalayan civilization. Chinese as well as Tibetan medicine has a large influence especially in the life of the peoples living in the highest mountains (Khanal 2017). Persistence of traditional therapies is due to the high cost of modern medicine and absence of trained physicians in rural areas of Nepal (Kunwar *et al.* 2013). It is estimated that there is one physician per 30,000–100,000 people in Nepal whereas, there is one healer for every 100 people (Gillam 1989, WRI: World resource 2005). Therefore, MAPs and its medicinal use play a major role in life support systems of local community especially in rural areas of Nepal (Kunwar *et al.* 2013).

In Nepal, there are 87 licensed pharmaceutical manufacturers, out of which 45 manufacture modern medicine, 8 veterinary products and 37 manufacture herbal preparations (Nepal Pharmaceutical Country profile, 2011; Khanal 2017). There are about 400 herb-based medicines (Ayurvedic) in the form of liquids, powders, tablets, capsules, oils, pastes, pills, extracts, etc. are produced in Nepal (Drug Bulletin Nepal 1995). National manufacturing unit for herbal (Ayurvedic) medicines is "Singha Durbar Vaidhyakhana" which started producing medicines from 1950. Presently, it has been producing some 100 different traditional pharmacological and patented generic Ayurvedic products using 200 MAPs and about 50 minerals. Ayurvedic health care institutions located in different parts of the country receive herbal medicines manufactured by this unit. Therefore, the demand for medicines from this production unit keeps ever-increasing due to its wide popularity (SDVKVS 2004; Khakurel *et al.*, 1998).

3. EXPORT OF MEDICINAL AND AROMATIC PLANTS

MAPs consumption, volumes of trade and levels of demand data are not sufficient as large amount of MAPs are exported illegally from the country (Subedi 2006). It was estimated that the export of MAPs in 2006 was 33256 tons (Phoboo *et al.*, 2008) and in 2014 the estimation was 10770 tons worth US $ 60.09 million (Ghimire *et al.*, 2015). The export value of MAP products increased from USD 27.49 million in 2005 to USD 60.09 million in 2014 (mean for the last 10 years being USD 39.34 million) and this increment is primarily due to increase in price, as the trade volume follows decreasing trend over the same periods. The average annual export amount of MAPs products for the last 10 years has been calculated to be 32.62.23 thousand tons with average value of USD 55.94 million. The rise in export value of MAPs products indicates increasing demand of MAPs globally. Nepalese MAPs commodities were exported to almost 50 destinations. In terms of volume, India has been the major importer of MAPs materials all these years (Ghimire *et al.*, 2016). Average trade data of UN COMTRADE shows that in last ten years China shared 45.58% of the total value of MAPs traded from Nepal followed by India (32%), Singapore (11.26%), Hong Kong (6.52%) and Viet Nam (1.07%). This indicates that these countries mainly imported high valued MAPs such as *Codyceps sinensis* that has high price in international market.

4. FORMULATIONS FROM MEDICINAL AND AROMATIC PLANTS

In Nepal, currently there are 22 herb based marketing and producing industries and their main focus is to export oil extracts and semi processed residues (Sharma 2007). Phytochemicals are the main medicinal components that are found naturally in herbs and are extracted to make allopathic drugs. There are some scientific research activities like extraction phytochemicals from MAPs are carried out in the country (Gautam 2008, Gyawali *et al.*, 2008, 2014, Shrestha *et al.*, 2015), however, the practice of commercialization is lacking. Currently, domestic manufacturers of herbal medicines have started making phytochemicals, the raw materials used to produce allopathic drugs out of locally available herbs. However, many pharmaceutical companies are interested to process the phytochemicals for export as there is limited use of herbal products to manufacture modern medical drugs. For example the chemical that is extracted from the Himalayan Yew, popularly called Lauth Sallo (*Taxus Baccata*), is used to manufacture allopathic drugs to cure cancer and most of such products are exported in their raw state instead of in finished or semi-finished form (www. kathmandupost.ekantipur.com/news). This is due to the lack of sufficient scientific research, training, resources and infrastructural facility in the country. Nepal Pharmaceutical country profile shows that there is little scientific research and development for discovering active substance from the locally available MAPs of the country. The manufacturing capabilities of Nepal are summarized in the Table 2 below.

Table 2: Manufacturing Capabilities of Nepal

Research and Development for discovering new active substances	No
Production of pharmaceutical starting materials (APIs)	No
The production of formulations from pharmaceutical starting material	Yes
The repackaging of finished dosage forms	Yes

Source: Nepal Pharmaceutical Country Profile, 2011.

A new chapter in the history of Herbal Extracts and Essential Oils commenced with the establishment of Government owned Herbs Production and Processing Company (HPPCL) in 1981 (www.fao.org/docrep/x5336e/x5336e0j.htm). HPPCL is the first company in the country for processing and producing medicinal extracts and essential oils using indigenous Himalayan herbs and exotic conventional raw materials. The sources of raw materials used are cultivation in its own farm and collection from private farmers land and from wild sources. Quality analysis of every product is carried out in the central laboratory at Kathmandu prior to storage and shipment. Quality assurance at HPPCL is a unique sequence of scientific norms with regard to international standards and trade practices and providing guarantees for customer satisfaction.

HPPLC, therefore, is capable of exporting indigenous products in the form of essential oils, herbal drinks and some crude drugs to neighboring and third countries. At present, this company is capable of exporting indigenous products like Lichen resinoid, Sugandha Kokila oil, Anthopogan oil, Tagetes oil, and Jatamansi oil as well as exotic varieties such as Palmarosa oil, Citronella oil, Lemongrass oil, Sancho, Massage oil, Sancho herbal drink, Sheelajit etc. and some crude drugs to neighboring and third countries. (www.hppcl.com.np). Nepalese essential oils have been well-received in the regional and European markets. The conventional oils such as Palmarosa, Citronella, Lemongrass and Tagetes have a growing demand from foreign customers similar with certain newly introduced unconventional items like oil of *Rhododendron anthopogon.* Oils like Jatamansi and Xanthoxylum require greater effort for successful export. However, the future of the essential oil industry looks promising with foreign firms entering Nepal for the manufacture of soaps and detergents (www.fao.org/docrep/x5336e/x5336e0j.htm). Major aromatic plants available for commercial processing and approximate quantities processed in Nepal are provided in Table 3.

Table 3: Major Medicinal and Aromatic Plants Available for Commercial Processing and Approximate Quantities Processed in Nepal

Species	*Quantity Available (metric tons)*	*Quantity Processed (metric tons)*
Gaultheria fragrantissima (leaves)	400	200
Nardostachys jatamansi (rhizomes)	200	80
Lichens *(Parmelia nepalensis, Usnea* spp., *Ramalina* spp.)	300	60
Xanthoxylum armatum (fruit)	400	50
Rhododendron anthopogon (leaves and twigs)	80	20
Juniperus indica (berries)	30	X
Cinnamomum glaucescens (berries)	100	80

Source: www.fao.org/docrep/x5336e/x5336e0j.htm

There are various small-scale national companies that produce different types of essential oils, tea and beauty products using indigenous herbs. In recent years, few international companies are emerging in Nepal and have established their own herbal farms and factories that produce herbal drugs and various products. 'Dabur Nepal' and 'Patanjali' are examples of such international companies. International companies like Dabur Nepal and Patanjali have established their own herbal garden and manufacturing companies in Nepal.

5. PROBLEMS AND CHALLENGES

MAPs can contribute immensely to revenue collection thus subsequently, help in improving the socio-economic status of the Nepali people mainly living in rural areas. However, a number of problems at the level of production, harvest, marketing, processing, and value addition need to be properly addressed (Sharma and Shrestha 2011).

Sustainability and consistent supply is a major issue that is providing hindrance for continuous exportation. Supply of MAPs and essential oils from Nepal is not enough and sustainable. For example, demand of lemongrass is high in the international market. But Nepal's production of lemongrass is not even 10 tons a year, whereas India's production of lemongrass per year is about 15,000 tons (Sharma and Shrestha 2011). Cultivation of MAPs can provide more sustainable supply of MAPs than collection from the wild. But in the case of Nepal, there are a number of problems in cultivation of MAPs. For example, there is lack of market information, unavailability of quality seeds, longer gestation period etc. due to which cultivation of MAPs is not carried out on a large scale and farmers prefer to cultivate traditional crops as they have to wait for a longer period to realize income from its cultivation (Sharma and Shrestha 2011).

The marketing channel for crude herbs (aromatic and medicinal) is quite complex. Currently, HPPCL has bilateral contracts, renewable annually, with the village and rural processors. Thus the company, to some extent, shields the local processors from the uncertainties and fluctuations in the international markets with regard to the prices of the essential oils and extracts. In the case of raw materials (botanicals), however, local and regional price fluctuations seriously affect the income of the true village collector who is at the mercy of the middleman or village trader (http://www.fao.org/docrep/x5336e/x5336e0j.htm).

MAPs and essential oils that are used in preparing medicines, food supplements and other products for human consumption should maintain the quality and standard and should ensure that they do not pose danger to human, animal and plant life or health. In case of Nepal, Department of Plant Resources (DPR), Ministry of Forest and Soil Conservation, Government of Nepal, is the central agency authorized to issue quality certification of MAPs and essential oils.

However, DPR is not fully equipped and capable of certifying quality of products. Its role is limited to providing CITES certification, checking chemical composition to ascertain whether the product is adulterated or not (Sharma and Shrestha 2011).

Another major factor that is affecting the marketing of MAPs and its product is the certification. For the export in EU the European Spice Association (ESA), which represents 12 major national spice associations in Europe that has developed an 'ESA Contract' which indicates minimum quality standards for imported herbs and spices, such as the maximum permissible contents of extraneous matter, maximum content of ash and heavy metals, packaging and labeling requirements, etc., and methods of arbitration and enforcement procedures (Nepal Pharmaceutical Country profile, 2011). Nepal does not even have basic pest data of listed MAPs as importing countries demand specific pest data for each MAPs for exports. Hence, the exporters first send samples of products for quality inspection to the importers, mainly in third countries, and only after they receive green signals from importers do they export their products. There have been cases when samples, mainly of essential oils, sent for quality inspection to importing countries could not pass the test (Gurung 2010). Some traders in Nepalgunj have been making use of the accredited testing facilities in India, especially in Delhi, to send samples and export products abroad (Sharma and Shrestha 2011).

Major parts of MAPs are exported from Nepal in raw form. Processing/manufacturing takes place to a very limited extent since there are problems and challenges in undertaking processing/manufacturing activities. The government should facilitate the transfer of modern and relevant technology for processing. Being an LDC, Nepal should make use of the special treatment provision of Article 66.2 of the Agreement on Trade-related Aspects of Intellectual Property Rights (TRIPS) of the WTO which states that "Developed country Members shall provide incentives to enterprises and institutions in their territories for the purpose of promoting and encouraging technology transfer to least-developed country Members in order to enable them to create a sound and viable technological base" (Sharma and Shrestha 2011). Additionally, importation of technology should be complemented by developing and/or enhancing skills and knowledge of human resources in the country.

6. STRATEGIES AND SCOPE

The world market for MAPs and its products is increasing and the demand and prices of MAPs are rising each year (Phoboo *et al.,* 2008). For Nepal, MAPs is one of the major revenue generating products hence, has potential in improving the economy of the country. However effective utilization, management, conservation and scientific research is lacking in this matter. For the conservation and mass scale production of MAPs *in vitro* study techniques like micropropagation, tissue culture techniques should be promoted to fulfill the demand (Pant 2008). Likewise, scientific research activities and facilities for herbal extraction and formulation should also be prioritized. For this purpose, national priority should be given to scientific studies of MAPs. Policies should be formulated to facilitate the judicial and sustainable utilization MAPs. If harnessed effectively, this sector can make a significant contribution to the national GDP. There is an urgent need to develop agrotechnology for the domestication of wild aromatic and medicinal plants, especially those species, which are exploited heavily. Villagers need to be trained in postharvest techniques (drying, storage) to minimize wastage and unnecessary losses. The currently practiced trade pattern, where the true collector is exploited, needs to be rectified. The determination of royalties on collected herbs should be based on a more realistic approach in order to promote local processing. The ideal method would be to have the lowest royalty on plant parts that could be collected with the least impact on the plant's natural growth like fruits, with increasing royalties on plant parts that endanger the survival of plants like roots and rhizomes (www.fao.org/docrep/x5336e/x5336e0j.htm).

In Nepal, there is no specific legislation to regulate the safety, efficacy, quality, sale-distribution, promotion and utilization of herbal medicines belonging to traditional systems but quite a good amount of exercise has been done to formulate policies and guidelines on herbal medicines, especially in the line of integrating them with PHC services of the national health care system. There is an acute shortage of professional manpower on herbal medicines. There is also a great deficiency of evaluated information on their practical use. There is a need to look at the toxicity and efficacy of herbal remedies in the light of their past history, usefulness and extent of admixture with allopathic therapeutic agents and animal products (Khakurel *et al.,* 1998).

Therefore, fully equipped laboratories should be developed to ensure quality assurance and certification in the country. All research activities carried out within the country should be coordinated by a national agency, which should also function as a liaison between national and international institutes and organizations for sources of information and technology. New findings on NWFPs and medicinal plants should be shared among the concerned agencies organizations and for the rational utilization of MAPs Multi-national companies and joint-ventures with foreign firms should be promoted (www.fao.org/docrep/x5336e/x5336e0j.htm).

7. CONCLUSION

If harnessed effectively sustainable utilization of MAPs can make a significant contribution to the national GDP. Therefore, the current main concern should be the resource utilization of MAPs within the country to produce finished products. Therefore, national priority should be given to MAPs and its product enhancement, diversification and manufacture of finished products like pharmaceuticals and cosmetics. For this purpose, Multi-national companies and joint-ventures with foreign firms should be promoted. Structural and policy changes should be introduced and promoted for the development of adequate physical facilities, qualified manpower, modern equipment, establishing marketing network, mobilization of resources, implementation of research and quality assurance plan, development of proper documentation and validation system, preservation and sustainable utilization of MAPs.

REFERENCES

[1] Baral, S.R. and Kurmi, P.P. (2006). Compendium of medicinal plants in Nepal. Chabahil, Kathmandu, Nepal: Rachana Sharma publishers.

[2] Bhattari, K.R. and Ghimire, M. (2006). Commercially important medicinal and aromatic plants of Nepal and their distribution pattern and conservation measure along the elevation gradient of the Himalayas. Banko Jankari 16(1):1–13.

[3] Gyawali, R., Jnawali, D. and Kim, K.S. (2008). Phytochemical Screening of Some Species of Nepalese Medicinal Plants (Eds) Jha PK, Karmacharya SB, Chettri MK, Thapa CB and Shrestha BB, Ecological Society (ECOS), In Medicinal Plants in Nepal: An Anthology of Contemporary Research, Mass Printing Press, Kathmandu, Nepal.

[4] Gyawali, R., Dahal, B., Gautam, R., Shrestha, S., Joshi, S., Luitel, A. and Khanal, D. (2014). Phytochemical Studies on Traditional Medicinal Plants of Nepal and their formulations, *International Journal of Biology, Pharmacy, and Allied Sciences* 3(2):189–2013.

[5] Gautam, L.N.S. (2008). Extraction of Medicinal Plants Through Green Chemistry (Eds) Jha PK, Karmacharya SB, Chettri MK, Thapa CB and Shrestha BB, Ecological Society (ECOS), In Medicinal Plants in Nepal: An Anthology of Contemporary Research, Mass Printing Press, Kathmandu, Nepal.

[6] Ghimire, S.K., Awasthi, B., Rana, S.K., Rana, H.K. and Bhattarai, R. (2015). Status of exportable, rare and endangered medicinal and Aromatic Plants (MAPs) of Nepal. Report submitted to Department of Plant resources (DPR). Ministry of Forest and Soil Conservation (MoFSC), Kathmandu, Nepal.

[7] Ghimire, S.K., Awasthi, B., Rana, S.K., Rana, H.K., Bhattarai, R. and Pyakurel, D. (2016). Export of medicinal and aromatic plant materials from Nepal, *Journal of Plant Science,* 10. 24–32.

[8] Gillam, S. (1989). The traditional healer as village health worker. *Journal of Institute of Medicine,* 11:67–76.

[9] Gurung, Khilendra (2010). "Essential oils sector study in Nepal: A detailed study of Anthopogon, Juniper and Wintergreen essential oils". Kathmandu: German Technical Cooperation (GTZ) Include.

[10] Khakurel, B., Prasad, R.R., Bhattarai, D.D. and Sheak, A. (1998). In the name of the herbal medicine, *Journal of Institute of Medicine,* 20(1) Available at http://jiom.com.np/index.php/jiomjournal/article/view/13/15.

[11] Khanal, D.P. (2017). History of Pharmaceutical Development in Nepal. *Journal of Manmohan Memorial Institute of Health Sciences,* 3(1): 86–93.

[12] Kunwar, R.M., Mahat, L., Acharya, RP. and Bussmann, R.W. (2013). Medicianl plants, traditional medicine, markets and management in far-west Nepal. *Journal of Ethnobiology and Ethnomedecine,* 9:24–34.

[13] Kunwar, R.M., Shrestha, K.P. and Bussmann, R.W. (2010). Traditional herbal medicine inFar-west Nepal: a Pharmacological appraisal. *Journal of Ethnobiology and Ethnomedecine,* 6:35.

[14] Marino-Bettolo, G.B. (1980). Present aspect of the use of plants in traditional medicine. *Journal of Ethnopharmacology* (2):5–7.

[15] Nepal Pharmaceutical Country profile (2011). Ministry of Health and Population in collaboration with the World Health Organization.

[16] Pant, B. (2008). Application of Tissue Culture for Conservation of Medicinal Plants (Eds) Jha PK, Karmacharya SB, Chettri MK, Thapa CB and Shrestha BB, Ecological Society (ECOS), In Medicinal Plants in Nepal: An Anthology of Contemporary Research, Mass Printing Press, Kathmandu, Nepal.

[17] Phoboo, S., Devkota, S. and Jha, P.K. (2008). Medicinal Plants of Nepal: An Overview (Eds) Jha PK, Karmacharya SB, Chettri MK, Thapa CB

and Shrestha BB, In Medicinal Plants in Nepal: An Anthology of Contemporary Research, Ecological Society (ECOS), Mass Printing Press, Kathmandu, Nepal.

[18] Poudel, K. (2007). Trade potentiality and ecological analysis of NTFPs in Himalayan Kingdom of Nepal, http://hdl.handle.net/1928/3300.

[19] Rokaya, M.B., Munzbergova, Z., Shrestha, M.R. and Timsina, B. (2010). Ethnobotanical study of medicinal plants from Humla district of western Nepal. Journal of Ethnompharmacology 130:485–504.

[20] Sarkar, P.K.. Herbal/Ayurvedic/Indigenous Drugs (1987). *Drug Disease Doctor,* 2 (1): 4–13. Drug Action Forum, Calcutta.

[21] SDVKVS (2004). Singha Dubar Vaidyakhana Vikas Samiti, Ayrvedic Products of SDVKS, Singha Dubar, Kathmandu, Nepal.

[22] Sharma, P. and Shrestha, N. (2011). Promoting exports of medicinal and aromatic plants (MAPs) and essential oils from Nepal. South Asia Watch on Trade, Economics and Environment (SAWTEE), WTO/EIF Support Programme, GIZ, GmbH.

[23] Sharma, U.R. (2007). Medicinal and Aromatic Plants: A Growing Commercial Sector of Nepal. The Initiation. https://www.nepjol.info/index.php/INIT/article/viewFile/2673/2367

[24] Shrestha, P., Adhikari, S., Lamichhane, B. and Shrestha, B.G. (2015). Phytochemical Screening of the Medicinal Plants of Nepal, *Journal of Environmental Science, Toxicology and Food Technology (IOSR-JESTFT)* 1 (6): 11–17

[25] Subedi, B.P. (2006). Linking plant based enterprises and local communities to biodiversity conservation in Nepal Himalaya. Adroit Publishers, New Delhi, India.

[26] Tiwari, N.N. and Joshi, M.P. (1990). Medicinal plants of Nepal: I. *Journal of the Nepal Medical Association.* 28: 181–190.

[27] WRI: World resources (2005). The wealth of the poor: managing eco-systems to fight poverty. World Resource Institute, USA. Available at www.wri.org/publication

[28] http://kathmandupost.ekantipur.com/news/2014-01-20/local-herbal-companies-making-plant-chemicals.html (accessed September 2018).

[29] www.fao.org/docrep/x5336e/x5336e0j.htm (accessed September 2018).

[30] www.hppcl.com.np (accessed September 2018).

Development of Pharmaceutical Raw Materials in Nigeria: Efforts of Raw Materials Research and Development Council

Sirajo Musa

Raw Materials Research and Development Council,
Abuja, Nigeria
E-mail: sirajormrdc@yahoo.com

ABSTRACT: Total dependence on imported raw materials for the pharmaceutical industry in Nigeria poses a challenge to the development of indigenous pharmaceutical raw materials. Over 80 percent of pharmaceutical raw materials are currently being imported. For this reason, the industry needs to be protected and encouraged to source its raw materials locally. In Nigeria, policies and programmes have been developed at the national levels to support scientific research and development of pharmaceutical raw materials from locally sourced materials. Despite these policies and programmes, there is low activity of value addition to raw materials required by the pharmaceutical industry. The National Strategy for Competitiveness in Raw Materials and Products Development by RMRDC targets secondary raw materials needed by the industrial sectors including pharmaceutical industry that could be produced locally in the short, medium and long terms (RMRDC, 2016). Such domestic sourcing and utilization of pharmaceutical raw materials will reflect in declining levels of imports over time. The Raw Materials Research and Development Council (RMRDC), has over the years been at the forefront in the development of raw materials for pharmaceutical sector. This was done by undertaking studies to provide information that will assist the growth of the sector, R&D activities on pharmaceutical raw materials development, setting up catalytic plants to demonstrate feasibility of resource-based projects and the documentation of information on sources and utilization of identified raw materials.

Keywords: Pharmaceutical Raw Materials, Competitiveness, Herbal Plants, Secondary Raw Materials, Active Ingredients, Policies, Value Addition.

1. INTRODUCTION

Nigeria with a current population of over 180 million is estimated to be one of the fastest growing countries in the world (CIA, 2016). It is endowed with a variety of natural resources, especially oil and gas, solid minerals as well as agricultural resources. The country's growing population is accompanied by escalating health challenges and increased prevalence of chronic conditions such as non-communicable diseases estimated to account for 24% of total deaths (WHO, 2016). This resulted in high demand for management of health challenges including the need for medications and health commodities. Within the ECOWAS (Economic Community of West African States)—a regional trade bloc, Nigeria accounts for about 60% of health products consumed in the sub region by volume (UNIDO, 2008). This invariably led to the rise in the contribution of the public and private sector to overall health expenditure including pharmaceutical ones. In 2008, the total annual expenditure on health (THE) in Nigeria was 10.675 billion USD which was 5.8% of the GDP (Nigeria National Health Accounts, 2011). This shows the huge market potential for the pharmaceutical industry in Nigeria.

The pharmaceutical market in Nigeria in 2011 was estimated to be approximately 1.8 billion USD, with 13% annual growth rate (Pharmaceutical Manufacturers Group of Manufacturers Association of Nigeria (PMGMAN), 2016). According to Times of Africa (2017), Nigeria's pharmaceutical imports reached a value of 481 million USD in 2013 and a projected increase of 10.4% to reach $789 million in 2018. This will widen the country's pharmaceutical trade deficit from 475 million in 2013 to $778 million in 2018. The industry is large comprising different stakeholders such as manufacturers, importers, national regulators, wholesalers, retailers and others. The retail sector is extremely fragmented and dominated by small businesses and informal operators (Osifo and Ekuri Alade, 2017). According to the Pharmacists Council of Nigeria (PCN) in 2010, there were 724 drug distributors, 1,534 retail pharmacies and over 200,000 patent medicine vendors. The huge potential of the pharmaceutical industry resulted in 60% of drug manufacturing to takes place in Nigeria, underlining the huge sub regional market.

The pharmaceutical industry in Nigeria is not as gloomy as it might appear due to the ever increasing demand for drugs and medical care which will continue to remain an advantage to domestic producers as well as an opportunity for growth and development of herbal plants for drug production. Despite the huge growth potentials within the pharmaceutical industry in Nigeria, several challenges pose a threat to the growth of the industry. Major among other challenges is the sourcing of raw material for the industry.

The total dependence on imported raw materials for the pharmaceutical industry in Nigeria due to low development of indigenous technology despite the vast availability of herbal plants poses a hindrance to the development of indigenous pharmaceutical raw materials. Over 80 percent of industrial raw materials are currently being imported (Muanya, 2015). Also, the huge exchange rate expended on the importation of raw materials in the country in recent times has adversely affected the industry. Furthermore, drug manufacturers have increasingly asked for more than one supply source for a given raw material to mitigate supply continuity risk. For this reason, the industry needs to be adequately encouraged, protected and helped out of the many problems affecting it, particularly, in sourcing of raw materials locally in Nigeria.

To mitigate the challenge of sourcing of raw materials for the pharmaceutical industry, agricultural and herbal plants have become the most viable option for low cost drug production. The agricultural and herbal plants are increasingly becoming a source of raw materials for the pharmaceutical industry beyond the traditional fibre and nutrition industries, but are also now serving as raw materials source for pharmaceutical/health products. Today several Research and Development (R&D) activities are focusing on herbal plants as a valuable means to achieve total healthcare coverage of the population. This paper is limited to the effort of RMRDC in the development of pharmaceutical raw materials from herbal plants in Nigeria.

2. OVERVIEW OF PHARMACEUTICAL INDUSTRY IN NIGERIA

The pharmaceutical industry in Nigeria is a multi-product industry that is characteristically dominated by a small number of large sellers. The role of the pharmaceutical industry in a country such as Nigeria in the provision of safe, pure, qualitative and efficacious products to meet the healthcare needs of the populace cannot be over-emphasized.

Provision of essential medicines by this sector has helped to curb the infiltration of the pharmaceutical market in Nigeria with fake and substandard products to a relatively significant level. In order to provide essential drugs for a healthy system in Nigeria, the government of Nigeria in the last two decades has made more efforts in strengthening and empowering the pharmaceutical industry to meet the medicines requirement. These efforts by the government, over the years have impacted the pharmaceutical business and drug development from plants in the country.

Several factors, however contribute to the pharmaceutical business in Nigeria. The determining factor in the pharmaceutical business is the disease pattern, which Nigeria is no exception. According to UNIDO, malaria, HIV/AIDS, and tuberculosis, coupled with widespread malnutrition and poverty, represent a major burden of disease on the Nigeria population as well as heart-related diseases, which are also on the increase (UNIDO, 2011). The rise in these diseases significantly impacted the pharmaceutical business in Nigeria, which has led to over-the-counter medicines such as analgesics, antimalarials and multivitamins making up a large share of the market. In addition, antiretroviral (ARV), artemisinin combination therapy (ACT), anti-TB and antimicrobial anti-diarrhoeal agents as well as herbal medicines, which are life saving for patients in Nigeria have also impacted the market share of pharmaceutical business in Nigeria (Mariatou *et al.*, 2017).

Promotion and regulation of local production of these essential life-saving medicines could make them more accessible for people with life threatening diseases provided that the price of such medicines is affordable. Nigeria is one of the most promising and rapidly growing medicinal markets in West Africa with more than 150 medicinal formulation manufacturing facilities with an annual growth of 13% (PMGMAN, 2017). The estimated market size of pharmaceutical industry in Nigeria has grown to about 1.8 billion USD.

The Nigerian medicinal industry has come a long way from the era when the industry was only involved in the distribution of imported drugs by the representatives of the different foreign manufacturers such as Beecham, May and Baker, Pfizer, Glaxo and Morrison (Ugbam and Okoro, 2017). Despite the growth in the industry, an available performance index for the industry suggests poor performance with capacity utilization put at 40%. However, the industry is only able to satisfy 25% of the local demand for drugs while importation mainly from Asian countries account for the remaining 75% (Ugbam and Okoro, 2017). The pharmaceutical industry has a potential market value of between US$ 600 million and more than US$ 2 billion annually (UNIDO, 2011). The industry has a capacity to employ about 500,000 persons in the manufacturing and distribution chain. The vast majority of jobs are however attributed to the distribution chain.

3. LOCAL PRODUCTION OF PHARMACEUTICALS AND DRUGS FROM HERBAL PLANTS IN NIGERIA

Local production of pharmaceuticals and drugs from herbal plants has been a subject of intense discussion in international, regional and national forums since the 1970s (United Nation, 2011). A variety of interests such as economic, legal, regulatory and political economy have been responsible for varied and often contradictory, perspectives on what constitutes local production of pharmaceuticals and drug from herbal plants, and whether or not it should be fostered. The past decade has seen a stronger emphasis on issues of local production, technology transfer and access to medicines.

Drug manufacturers in Nigeria are confronted with several constraints, including low capacity utilization, under capitalization, a weak financial base, high production costs as a result of the high cost of raw materials inputs, poor infrastructure, difficulty in meeting WHO prequalification criteria, low level or obsolete technology, high interest rates and unstable demand (UNIDO, 2011). The fluctuations in demand are a reflection of prevailing low purchasing power within the population and the fact that Government purchases of medicines are irregular and payments may be delayed. Capacity utilization of local manufacturing facilities is running at about 40% and there is adequate capacity for production of certain categories of medicines locally from herbal plants to meet national demand and even to export to ECOWAS countries (Kaplan and Laing, 2005). Despite this potential, value addition to agricultural and herbal plants as raw material source for the pharmaceutical industry remains a major challenge.

To further boost local production of some drugs, manufacturers are upgrading their operations with the aim of obtaining WHO prequalification status which would enable them to take part in international tenders (UNIDO, 2011). The success of these certifications will be another contributing factor to an increase in local production of pharmaceutical products. This also has the potential to make these medicines readily available to the populace. However, the Nigerian pharmaceutical industry as it is today is still plagued by series of challenges, which has hampered its growth potentials.

The local pharmaceuticals and drug manufacturing industry are currently able to meet 25% of local demand. Particularly, pharmaceutical industries are able to meet domestic demand for some classes of medicines such as analgesics, however, the remaining 75% has to be covered with imports from Asian companies (Isola and Mesagan, 2014), as well as from traditional herbal medicine. The pharmaceutical industry in Nigeria is facing a major productivity crisis of sourcing raw material locally to cut down the huge foreign exchange expended on importation of raw materials. The total dependence on imported raw materials due to under-development of indigenous technological know-how and herbal plant as raw materials for drug production is a major obstacle to the development of a local pharmaceutical industry. Although, the local drug industry has continued to grow, the industry needs to be adequately helped out of the many problems particularly in sourcing raw materials locally.

According to PMGMAN (2017), all active ingredients (AIs) used by the pharmaceutical industry in Nigeria are imported mainly from China and India. This has forced pharmaceutical companies to make careful forward planning for the import of AIs because of lengthy delays (atleast three months) and logistics at the seaport due to clearance, customs and National Agency for Food and Drug Administration and Control formalities (NAFDAC). According to PMGMAN, pharmaceutical grade starch is currently imported primarily from China. This prompt the idea that local production of medicines in Nigeria should be encouraged particularly from the vast agricultural and herbal plants available in the country in order to provide increased access to locally sourced raw materials which in turn will help to lower production cost often incurred from importation of raw materials It is clear, however, that investments in local production of drugs from agricultural and herbal plants will be efficient only if drugs can be produced more cheaply locally than they can be imported on the open market. This has led to the promotion of locally sourced raw materials from agricultural and herbal plants for pharmaceutical production as a means to achieve national self-sufficiency by the RMRDC and National Institute for Pharmaceutical Research and Development (NIPRD).

4. RESEARCH AND DEVELOPMENT OF PHARMACEUTICAL PRODUCTS

The pharmaceutical sector has tremendous potentials and it plays a pivotal role in the economic growth and development of any given economy due to its strong link to health and consequently, labor productivity. Apart from the fact that it provides the drugs and other health products that helps to ensure a healthy and productive work-force, a vibrant pharmaceutical sector provides quality employment to citizens and contributes significantly to the GDP and in the process helps to save and also generate foreign exchange for the country.

The promotion of pharmaceutical research and development is another crucial health intervention. In a landmark innovation, the NIPRD, with the help of government has initiated and completed the research and development of a new phytomedicine (Niprisan/Nicosan) for the management of sickle cell anaemia. The product has been granted orphan drug status by both the United States Food and Drug Administration and the European Medicine Evaluation Agency. The fact that Niprisan/Nicosan is the only therapy which will be accessible to over 10 million sickle cell anaemia patients in sub-Saharan Africa, give a boost to the local pharmaceutical industry. NIPRD is now developing other phytomedicines for the management of prevailing priority diseases. In most cases, both primary and secondary packaging materials for the pharmaceutical industry are obtained locally. In addition, about 25 percent of excipients are locally sourced from agricultural plants.

According to PMGMAN (2016), there are local companies, which produce industrial grade starch as raw materials for the pharmaceutical industry. The NIPRD has carried out research and development into pharmaceutical grade starch as it is very advantageous to local drug manufacturers if starch could be sourced locally. Pharmaceutical grade starch, pre-gelatinised starch (used as pharmaceutical binder), and dextrose monohydrate (marketed as nutraceutical glucose powder which is a major ingredient in intravenous infusions) are few other products that are currently under development. Also, the search for solution has involved some pioneer efforts by the Raw Materials Research and Development Council (RMRDC) in the R&D of local raw materials for pharmaceutical production.

5. HERBAL MEDICINES RESEARCH AND DEVELOPMENT IN NIGERIA

Medicinal plants have, for many years, occupied a very important position in health care delivery in various regions of the world. This is true with Nigeria as well. Since medicinal plants are gaining more recognition and relevance in health care delivery in Nigeria, various agencies of government and non-governmental organizations are supporting the development of herbal medicine from plants (Okunlola *et al.*, 2007). In Nigeria, there appears to be an overwhelming increase in the public awareness and usage of herbal medicinal products in the treatment and/or prevention of diseases.

In recent times, drugs that feature in pharmaceutical industry derive their origin from one or more agricultural and plant products (Veeresham, 2012). Different plant parts have different uses in the treatment of human ailments nonetheless, medicinal plants in there raw and unrefined state are not appreciated by several persons while the use of such plants parts in treatment of various ailments is generally rebuffed, particularly where orthodox medicine is available and affordable. However, the escalating cost of medicine and drugs are causing more and more people to embrace locally sourced materials for drug production. The most important sought after medicinal plants are those containing active constituents, which can neither be synthesized by the pharmaco-chemical industries or at a very high cost nor be substituted by other chemical compounds. This has made developed countries, in recent times, to use traditional medicinal systems that involve the use of herbal drugs and remedies. According to the WHO, almost 65% of the world's population has incorporated the value of plants as a methodology of medicinal agents into their primary modality of health care (Pathak and Das, 2013). It is often noted that 25% of all drugs prescribed today come from plants (Osemene *et al.*, 2012). This estimate suggests that plant derived drugs make up a significant part of natural product based pharmaceuticals. Meanwhile, the method of pharmaceutical R&D utilized in the production of these herbal medicines from Asian countries has been established. However, this is not the case with herbal medicine R&D in Nigeria before. In recent times R&D in herbal medicine is gaining increasing interest from the pharmaceutical industry, institutions, private and non-governmental agencies in Nigeria.

Research and development of herbal medicines in Nigeria is, now, mainly funded by the private and public research institutes, universities and pharmaceutical manufacturing firms. R&D activities in herbal medicine in Nigeria is been enhanced through partnerships which include government-industry, research institute-industry, university-industry and any of these combination.

6. EFFORTS OF RAW MATERIALS RESEARCH AND DEVELOPMENT COUNCIL IN LOCAL RAW MATERIAL SOURCING FOR THE PHARMACEUTICAL INDUSTRY IN NIGERIA

The RMRDC is an agency of the Federal Government of Nigeria supervised by Federal Ministry of Science and Technology. The RMRDC is currently Nigeria's focal point for the development and utilization of the nation's vast industrial raw materials resources, thus facilitating the establishment of new resource-based industries, which in turn provide new job opportunities and contribute to the nation's Gross Domestic Product (GDP). The agency is vested with the mandate to promote the development and utilization of Nigeria's industrial raw materials. The items covered by the agency include raw materials and products at primary, intermediate and secondary stages, which are considered for domestic capacity enhancement towards competitiveness in production.

The vast natural resources such as agricultural and herbal plants in Nigeria play a significant role in the development of the country's economy, however, this role diminishing as the world economy becomes increasingly internationalized, knowledge-intensive and technology-driven. To change the narratives, value-addition to natural resources through the application of technology is imperative for a competitive economy and to attain sustainable development. This is because the ability of Nigeria to compete and prosper to a significant extent on value addition to natural resources.

Despite efforts made over the years to exploit the natural resources, very limited progress has been recorded in value-added manufacturing, including processing of agricultural resources, improvement of mineral resources, development of petrochemicals, and production of industrial machinery and equipment, among others. This led to the importation of a huge chunk of raw materials for the various industrial sectors in Nigeria due to national gap for domestic requirements to meet demand shortfalls. If domestic production is adequate in terms of production and quality, there will be less resort to importation of such items; hence, government's concern over importation will not arise. In addition, this level of import is not sustainable if it continues, considering the dwindling foreign exchange earnings, which could lead Nigeria into more economic crisis by 2020 (RMRDC, 2016). A graphic presentation of the raw materials and products import in order of magnitude is presented for the period; 2010–2015 is as shown in Figures 1.

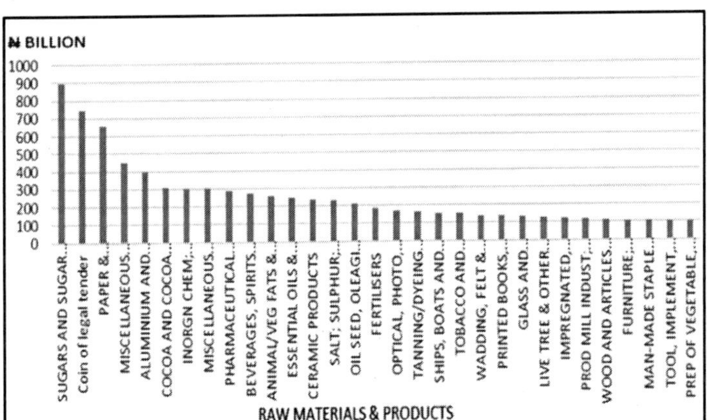

Fig. 1: Imports of Raw Materials and Products Categorised from 2010–2015

Nigeria's capacity for production of identified raw materials and products need revitalisation with appropriate stimulus targeted at commodity groups where the country has potentials and endowments. Higher potentials apply to agro-raw materials and products. The country's potentials for local production of raw materials and products particularly, from agriculture will fit into the measures of capacities of industries and businesses to meet national demand, which will in turn lead to a significant reduction in importing of items.

In living up to its mandate, RMRDC developed a national strategy for competitiveness in raw materials and products development in Nigeria. The Strategy for Nigeria's Competitiveness in Raw Materials and Products Development drafted by RMRDC will help government to focus and target appropriate raw material need by the pharmaceutical industry that could be produced locally in Nigeria in the short, medium and long terms (RMRDC, 2016). Such domestic sourcing and utilization of pharmaceutical raw materials will reflect in declining levels of imports over time. This would go a long way in attracting potential and current manufacturers into the use of local raw material inputs (Isola and Mesagan, 2016). Industrialists believe that these measures will go a long way to alleviate the problems facing the local drug industry.

However, the role and focus of RMRDC is to encourage the establishment of resource-based cottage industries in each geo-political zone, which would not only process and add value to the country's resources but also form the bedrock for industrial growth and the provision of needed raw materials by the pharmaceutical industry. Currently, we are working towards the emergence of additional resource-based industries. Our target is that at least one small-scale resource-based industry would emerge in each zone to make available adequate locally sourced material for pharmaceutical industry.

In Nigeria, policies and programmes have been developed at the national levels to support scientific R&D of raw materials to include those for the pharmaceutical industry from locally sourced materials. Despite these policies and programmes, Nigeria still has very low activity going on in the area of value addition to raw material required by the pharmaceutical industry. In other words, those raw materials for the pharmaceutical industry available in the country, lack appropriate and adequate industries that would add value to the locally sourced raw material to meet the required quality need by the industry. To mitigate this challenge of local raw material sourcing for the pharmaceutical industry in Nigeria, RMRDC is collaborating with several agencies and institutions in developing some raw materials for the pharmaceutical industry.

RMRDC has also sponsored several R&D projects aimed at promoting local raw materials sourcing for the pharmaceutical industry. Some of the R&D efforts are listed below.

1. Antiviral and immune-stimulants phytomedicines from Nigerian Plants.
2. Development of water-based thermostable Vaccine for control of new castle Disease in Rural Poultry.
3. Production of feed-based Thermostable Vaccine for livestock in Nigeria.
4. Production of cellulose from Agricultural waste and pharmaceuticals from cellulose.
5. Development and Utilization of *Moringa Oleifera* as phytochemical for water treatment.
6. Research and Development of stabilized Aloe Vera Gel and Power.
7. Anti-Malaria Evaluation of Nigeria Bitter Leaf (*Vernonia Amygdalina*).
8. Characterization, Pharmaceutical and Toxicological Evaluation of Active Hypoglycaemic (Anti-Diabetic) Agent from *Arachishypogea.*
9. Development of some Nigeria plants: Khaya Senegalese and Nauclealatifoli as Anti-Helminthics in cattle.
10. Investigation of medicinal plants used as Traditional Medicines for Diabetes and Snake Bites.
11. Production of Lovastatin from King-Oyster Mushroom and Related Species.
12. Development of phytomedicine for treatment of tuberculosis.

RMRDC in the past few years has achieved a great success in the development and utilization of the nation's vast industrial raw materials resources. Efforts are ongoing to collaborate with industries to produce some of the developed raw materials in commercial quantity. The efforts of the RMRDC are as shown in Figure 2.

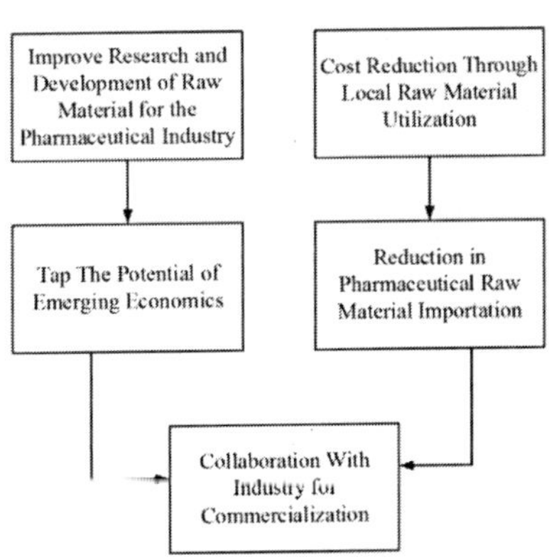

Fig. 2: Pharmaceutical Raw Materials Developmental Plan of RMRDC

7. CONCLUSION

RMRDC, over the years, has been at the forefront of the development of raw materials for pharmaceutical sector. This was achieved by:

- Undertaking studies to provide information that will assist the growth of the sector.
- R&D activities on pharmaceutical raw materials such as agricultural and herbal plants development.
- Setting up catalytic plants to demonstrate feasibility of resource-based projects and the documentation of information on sources and utilization of identified raw materials.
- RMRDC has also consistently collaborated with and acted as a link between the major stakeholders in the pharmaceutical sector, i.e. PMGMAN and Traditional Medicine Practitioners Association, with the aim of facilitating the development of local medicinal (herbs) plants.

These developments illustrate that the potentials for local production of raw materials for the pharmaceutical industry could be harnessed within the context of the Raw Materials and Product Development strategic plan to reduce levels of raw materials importation into the country. Efforts are ongoing to collaborate with the industry to produce some of the developed raw materials in commercial quantity. This is expected to boost sustainable economic development and to save lives as local resources are harnessed in the most cost-effective ways to create socially beneficial value.

ACKNOWLEDGMENT

I wish to acknowledge my Director-General and the entire management of RMRDC for nominating me to participate in this workshop.

REFERENCES

[1] CIA (2016). The World Fact Book. Central Intelligence Agency. Retrieved from www.cia.gov/library/Publication, Accessed: 10/10/2018.

[2] Isola, W.A. and Mesagan, E.P. (2016). Determinants of Pharmaceutical Industry's Performance in Nigeria, *Managing Global Transitions*, 14 (3): 267–282.

[3] Kaplan, W. and Laing, R. (2005). Local Production of Pharmaceuticals: Industrial Policy and Access to Medicines, An Overview of Key Concepts, Issues and Opportunities for Future Research, Health, Nutrition and

Population (HNP) Discussion Paper, The International Bank for Reconstruction and Development/The World Bank, Washington, January: 1–20.

[4] Mariatou, T.J., Martin, A., Alain, P., Lin, L. and Jon, B. (2017). Global Fund/FAPMA Consultative Meeting: 2017 African Pharmaceutical Manufacturers Conference, Addis Ababa, Ethiopia, 14–15 June.

[5] Muanya, C. (2015). 'Local industries can meet national drug needs'. The Guardian, 29 July.

[6] Nigeria National Health Accounts (NHA) (2011). Retrieved from http://www.who.int/nha/country/nga.pdf, Accessed: 20/10/2018.

[7] Okunlola, A., Adewoyin, B.A. and Odeku, O.A. (2007). Evaluation of Pharmaceutical and Microbial Qualities of Some Herbal Medicinal Products in South Western Nigeria, *Tropical Journal of Pharmaceutical Research*, March; 6 (1): 661–670.

[8] Osemene, K.P., Ilori, M.O. and Elujoba, A.A. (2012). Assessment of the State of Herbal MedicinesResearch and Development in Nigeria, *Tropical Journal of Pharmaceutical Research*, August, 11 (4): 645–650.

[9] Osifo, D. and Ekuri, A. (2017). Pharmaceutical Retail in Nigeria: Market Dynamics, Business Practices, Challenges and Opportunities in PPMV Practice, Africa Business Entrepreneurship Conference Paper, 21 October: 1–16. Retrieved from http://africabusiness.org/wp-content/uploads/2017/10/21_Osifo-DawoduEkuriAlade_Anadach-Submission-Africa-Business-Entrepreneurship-Conference-Paper-2.pdf, Accessed: 23/11/2018.

[10] Pathak, K. and Das, R.J. (2013). Herbal Medicine—A Rational Approach in Health Care System, *International Journal of Herbal Medicine*, 1(3): 86–89.

[11] PMGMAN (2016). Pharmaceutical Sector market Report: Nigeria Manufacturing Expo. Pharmaceutical Manufacturers Group of Manufacturers Association of Nigeria (PMGMAN). Retrieved from www.nigeriamanufacturingexpo.com, Accessed: 17/2018.

[12] PMGMAN (2017). Pharmaceutical Sector Market Report: Nigeria Manufacturing Expo 2017, Pharmaceutical Manufacturers Group of Manufacturers Association of Nigeria, 4th Annual MPAD and Nigeria Manufacturing Expo, 14–16 March, Lagos, Nigeria.

[13] RMRDC (2016). National Strategy for Competitiveness in Raw Materials and Products Development in Nigeria, July, Abuja, Nigeria.

[14] The Times of Africa (2017). Nigeria's pharmaceutical market: A gigantic ground of opportunities, April 19. Retrieved from http://thetimesofafrica.com/nigeris-pharmaceutical-market-gigantic-ground-opportunities, Accessed: 11/11/2018.

[15] Ugbam, O.C. and Okoro, E.A. (2017). A Strategic Study of the Nigerian Pharmaceutical Sector: Organizational Leadership, Market-share, and Competitive Performance, *International Journal of Business, Humanities and Technology*, Vol. 7, No. 1, March: 1–10.

[16] UNIDO (2008). Pharmaceutical Sector Profile: Nigeria-Global UNIDO Project: Strengthening the local production of essential generic drugs in least developed and developing countries. Retrieved from www.unido.org, Accessed: 15/10/2018.

[17] United Nation (2011). Local Production of Pharmaceuticals and Related Technology Transfer in Developing Countries: A Series of Case Studies by the UNCTAD Secretariat, UNCTAD/DIAE/PCB.

[18] United Nations Industrial Development Organization (UNIDO) (2011). Pharmaceutical Sector Profile: Nigeria, Global UNIDO Project: Vienna.

[19] Veeresham, C. (2012). Natural products derived from plants as a source of drugs. *Journal of Advanced Pharmaceutical Technology and Research*, 3(4): 200–201.

[20] WHO (2016). Nigeria; World Health Organization. Retrieved from www.who.int/nmh/countries, Accessed: 16/10/2018.

ABBREVIATIONS

ECOWAS - Economic Community of West African States

GDP - Gross Domestic Products

RMRDC - Raw Materials Research and Development Council

UNIDO - United Nation Industrial Development Organization

USD - United State Dollar

WHO - World Health Organization

HAI PHONG RESOLUTION

Drug Development from Herbs and Marine Medicinal Materials

Hai Phong Resolution
on
Drug Development from Herbs and Marine Medicinal Materials

EXPRESSING GRATITUDE to the Centre for Science and Technology of the Non-Aligned and Other Developing Countries (NAM S&T Centre) and Hai Phong University of Medicine and Pharmacy, Hai Phong, Viet Nam (HPMU) for organizing the International Workshop on "Drug Development from Herbs and Marine Medicinal Materials" in Hai Phong, Viet Nam from 10–12 December 2018, the participants of the workshop **expressed their appreciation** to the Government of the Socialist Republic of Viet Nam, the Ministry of Health and the Ministry of Science and Technology, Viet Nam , for supporting the workshop.

AGREEING THAT although terrestrial and marine materials have been widely used in traditional medicines, scientific research on their bio-activities is greatly undermined and emphasizing the importance of these under-exploited resources in the production of safe and efficient vaccines and drugs while maintaining sustainable socio-economic developments.

DELIBERATING ON the underlying issues and existing as well as potential opportunities and benefits for NAM and Other Developing Countries in exploring terrestrial and marine medicinal materials, they agreed that the discovery and development of natural products are slow processes, not matching the pace of high throughput screening of synthetic drugs.

AGREEING ON the potential of bioactivity of secondary metabolites and that the research in this field is multidisciplinary and brings together, but not limited to, pharmacists and allied healthcare professionals, taxonomists, biochemists, biotechnologists, bio-informaticians, organic chemists, traditional health practitioners as well as pharmaceutical industries.

WE, THE PARTICIPANTS of the international workshop, representing the governments, institutions and agencies from Bhutan, Egypt, India, Indonesia, Kenya, Malaysia, Mauritius, Myanmar, Nepal, Pakistan, South Africa, South Korea, Sri Lanka, Turkey, Viet Nam and Zimbabwe, unanimously resolve and recommend the following:

- While known bio-resources have been extensively exploited by the mankind over the ages, natural products from untapped resources, such as wild plants and marine materials, have tremendous therapeutic and pharmaceutical potential, which needs to be explored and studied by the researchers, R&D agencies and concerned industries alike.
- Efforts should be made to develop and promote sustainable development of cost-effective drugs from terrestrial and marine resources that may be directly used for healthcare management in humans and animals.
- Since the marine resources are likely to play a predominant role as resource material for drug development, efforts should be made and encouraged to study the scientific relationship between the bioactive compounds of marine resources and their functional properties.
- In order to promote research on drug development from terrestrial and marine materials, the governments of the developing countries should allocate dedicated funds so as to make available these drugs to the common man in an efficient and timely manner.
- The governments should encourage that pharmaceutical industries in developing countries focus their efforts on intensifying their local R&D activities for generating new drugs from terrestrial and marine resources as part of their commercial targets and objectives.
- It is highly desirable for the pharmaceutical industries, especially in developing countries, to allocate a certain percentage of their funds in order to promote capacity building and state- of-the-art research and encourage researchers to focus on terrestrial and marine resources.
- Researcher-industry-medical fraternity interface should be strengthened in order to support researchers, not only financially, but

also taking the product to trials, promoting the developed medicine as well as making them available to the general public.

- Clinical trials of medicines obtained from terrestrial and marine resources should be considered of high priority by the governments and pharmaceutical industries alike, so that these medicines receive authenticity and global recognition.
- Governments and pharmaceutical industries should support patenting of medicines obtained from terrestrial and marine resources for global recognition.
- Capacity building on sustainable drug development from marine resources is strongly recommended because of the fast depletion of terrestrial bio-resources due to climatic changes and increased human exploitation.
- Governments should encourage compilation and sharing of local pharmacopoeia for exchange of information on development and use of medicines from terrestrial and marine resources.

The participants from Egypt, Mauritius and South Africa expressed their willingness to host the next workshop on medicines from terrestrial and marine resources sometime in 2020, subject to institutional and official approval.

Thus, adopted this day, the 11th of December 2018, at Hai Phong, Vietnam

Author Index